Dedicated To

All Spiritual Seekers.

Look for the Light...
When you discover it,
Share that Light with others,
And vanquish the darkness!

THE

Rainbow Promise

The Christ Spirit
Emerging Within
Human Transformation

Revelation as Symbolic Psychology

Bill Evans
— Always listen to the Divine Music —

William Evans, D.Min

Contents

Forward

The Bible's book of Revelation is perplexing: How are we to understand it? Is it to be taken literally as a prophecy of events yet to come? Is it an account of events that have already occurred? Is it a chronicle of events that happened in the Roman era and thus has no significance for us today? Or do the words conceal hidden meanings, figures, and symbolism that speak of spiritual and not physical events?

Throughout history, many attempts have been made to explain the mysteries behind this book. In general, these attempts can be understood in the following four general categories:

Preterist

In the Preterist view, the events of Revelation are valid only for the original recipients of the book in the late first century and the early second century. The visions and the messages of the book were intended to help the establishment of the early Church in a hostile Roman world. Among scholars of Revelation, this view is the one most often accepted. Those who reject it argue that, if this view is accepted, then many of the events and prophecies included in Revelation were left unfulfilled, because not all of them are accounted for in the history of that early time.

Historicist

Prevalent among conservative Biblical scholars is an understanding of Revelation as a prophecy describing the course of history from the Apostle John's time to the second coming of Jesus and beyond. This opinion eliminates the problem of "unfulfilled prophecies" inherent in the Preterist view. The scholar assigns historical events during the time of John to the prophesies. Prophesies that do not have corresponding historical events are relegated to some "future event." Yet it is here that the weakness of this view is exposed: Although there have been centuries in which the prophecies may have been fulfilled, there is no agreement as to the historical events referred to by them. Instead, there is a general subjectivity, which can vary from one scholar to the next in assigning an event to each prophecy. The inconsistency between a method that proposes a concrete, objective explanation of Revelation and the actual plastic, subjective results of that method have caused many scholars to look for a different way of understanding the book of Revelation.

Futurist

By assigning the prophecies of almost the entire book of Revelation to the future instead of the past or present, the Preterist's problem of unfulfilled predictions may be resolved while, at the same time, avoiding the Historicist's problem of subjectivity. The Futurist tends to describe what the events of Revelation will be like and what meaning they will have for the people alive at that time. The weakness of this view is that it has little relevance to the people of today (except as a warning to remain faithful so that, if we are alive at that future time, we will not have to fear the terrible ordeals) and has no relevance to the people of John's time or to the people between that time and now.

Some scholars favor a combination of the Preterist/Futurist interpretation, which gives it relevance to the people of John's time. Yet its application to the people since that time remains negative. Also, there is much disagreement among the typically conservative scholars who follow this view thereby reducing its credibility.

Idealist

The Idealist view of understanding Revelation differs radically from any of the other views mentioned here. It is a symbolic or allegorical method of interpretation. By examining the meanings of the symbols found in Revelation, an understanding of the timeless forces at work in Revelation become clearer. Since no historical events are necessarily assigned to the prophecies of Revelation, this method of interpretation has equal relevance for people of all ages. Its weakness lies in its failure to accept or confront such major issues as the reality of "the events of the last times" (eschatology).

There are variations based upon these four main categories. A variation of the fourth method, the Idealist, will be used throughout this book. References will occasionally be made to historical events, but not in the context of assigning certain prophecies or predictions to those events. Instead, the intent of this book is to provide a positive approach to the message of hope contained within the pages of Revelation.

With the events which have been building since September 11, 2001, many individuals in our society have experienced an increasing level of anxiety and fear in their lives. The war against terror has presented us with a situation unknown before in American history: A struggle which seems to have no definite, final resolution. Instead, we are presented with an unending series of What ifs: What if a group of terrorists get nuclear weapons? What if biological warfare is waged? What if another world war is begun? What if the terrorists precipitate an economic crisis? What if our hard-fought for freedoms and liberties must be sacrificed? What if...? Each question asked only raises the anxiety and fear within the human consciousness until we feel the physical, mental and emotional results of constant stress and worry. Because of the heightened anxiety in the people of the world, the economy first spirals up and then down in a roller-coaster ride more frightening than any envisioned by the carnivals and amusement parks.

During such a time as this, many individuals will turn to the book of Revelation, seeking something...anything...within its pages which can shed light upon the world's events. When they open and read the words of Revelation, What will they find? A story of plagues and events that add to their anxiety? Or will they discover the message giving them hope and enabling them to deal with the level of anxiety in their lives in a positive, balance manner? By understanding the meaning behind the symbols, the story of Revelation takes on new dimensions in its prophetic message. No longer is it the scariest book of the Bible. Instead, it has a message of prophecy and hope for you, the reader, which transcends the gloom and worry of everyday life. By understanding the symbolism of Revelation, you will see "beyond the horizon" of your daily problems, and will become aware of a larger, more encompassing view of life. This new view of life will offer you hope for your personal tribulations, as well as those of humanity at large. The War on Terror will become, for you, a time of cleansing and redirection as you learn to embrace the true realities of life.

With this in mind, certain assumptions have been made about you, the reader of this book. These assumptions are as follows::

1. You are someone who is struggling to understand the world around you as well as to understand yourself and the world within you.
2. You are prayerfully attempting to grow in faith and in understanding.

3. You are willing to examine anew the Scriptural record in Revelation, opening your mind and your Spirit to any new understandings you may discover.

I do not claim that the following pages contain the definitive view of Revelation. I simply share my insights and thoughts with you, hoping that you will discover something that may help you in your faith-journey.

Introduction

Revelation Revealed

When my teenage son learned that I was writing this book, at that time a still untitled commentary on Revelation, he suggested, "Dad! I know what you can call it! 'Revelation Revealed!' " Although an intriguing title, I was acutely aware of the lack of factual information concerning Revelation. Mystery permeates everything about this book.

I remember studying the book of Revelation in the small rural church in which I first served while a ministerial student. On the first night of our Bible study, with the participants gathered around two small tables in the basement of the church, we began the adventure of digging into this last book of the New Testament. After only ten minutes of reading and discussion, one young lady stood up and, with her face flushed and eyes wide with fright, she quickly ran up the stairs saying in a trembling voice, "I can't read that! It scares me too much!"

Even though the images in Revelation can be frightening, they can also instill hope and faith within our lives, according to the attitude we take toward them. As a way of analogy, many people are frightened of the Great Unknown that we call death. Although not desiring death, others have a faith that welcome it and are not frightened by it when it does come their way. As we journey together into understanding the symbolism and meaning behind the words of Revelation, let us bring an attitude of anticipation that can sustain our present faith as Revelation is revealed to us!

Who is the Author?

Scholars are not certain who wrote the book of Revelation. There is a long tradition that John, the beloved disciple, is the author of this book. For example, the Muratorian fragment (170 A. D.) ascribes it to St. John. Even earlier (ca. 135 A. D.), Justin Martyr believed him to be the author.[1] A group known as the Alogi (ca. A D. 170) indirectly testified to the apostolic authenticity of this book when they denied that John was the author. (By denying that they believed John to be the author, they were, in effect, testifying to the tradition established at that time that John was, in fact, the author of Revelation. If such a tradition had not existed, the Alogi would not have spoken out against him being the author!). The Alogi were a group that disagreed with much of the doctrine they found in the other writings of John, mainly the Gospel of John.[2]

Yet, even with this testimony, John's authorship is not certain. As early as the third century, Dionysius of Alexandria pointed out differences of language, style, and grammar between Revelation and the Gospel of John. He also noted that tradition told of two monuments to John in Ephesus. Dionysius believed that there were two Johns: one who wrote the Gospel, and another who wrote Revelation.[3] Even though the author claims to be named John, he does not also claim to be the Apostle John. Therefore the question of authorship remains unanswered.

The date of its composition is also unknown – estimates range from before the destruction of the temple in 70 A. D. to as late as 120 A. D.

The Bare Bones

We may feel lost or bewildered upon reading Revelation. There are plagues, trumpets, seals, signs, vials, visions, woes, angels. How does it all fit together? How can any sense be made of this book?

When trying to understand some complex entity, it always helps to first view it in an outline or skeleton form. After that, muscles, tendons, organs, skin, etc., may be added layer upon layer to enhance and show detail. Let us first examine Revelation in a broad, skeletal form (as a descriptive outline):

A Skeletal Outline of Revelation

I.	Prologue	1:1 - 8
II.	Vision One: Christ Instructs the Churches	1:9 - 3:22
III.	Vision Two: The Scroll in Heaven	4:1 - 16:21
IV.	Vision Three: Babylon and the Millennium	17:1 - 20:15
V.	Vision Four: The New Jerusalem	21:1 - 22:5
VI.	Conclusion	22:6 21

Revelation begins with a Prologue containing both an introduction and a greeting. The Prologue identifies the recipients of the book and explains both its origin and reason for its existence.

From this Prologue, Revelation begins with the first vision of instructions or admonitions directed to the book's intended recipients, the seven churches in Asia. Each church receives specific instructions from Christ as to where its strengths and weaknesses lie and what they can do about each.

Then, Revelation describes the second vision of the author. This vision takes place in heaven and comprises the middle portion of the book. It is in this section that most people become confused, for the layers of plagues, trumpets, vials, scrolls, etc., peel away one after another in a seemingly endless cycle. First, there is the opening of the seven seals. The seventh seal, when opened, reveals the sounding of seven trumpets. The seventh trumpet, when sounded, reveals the three signs. The third sign, in its turn, reveals the seven plagues in a still deeper layer. If these different layers were not enough, there are interludes which intervene throughout the book. All of these layers and interludes add to the complexity of the book and make it more difficult to understand.

The fourth major section of Revelation, the third vision, describes Babylon and its destiny. With its graphic descriptions of destruction, this section strikes fear in many people.

The fourth vision is that of the New Jerusalem, the final goal of all Christians. Its description has added much to our own visions of heaven.

Finally, in the conclusion, the author is instructed to share these visions with others, so that they may benefit from them.

Throughout this book we will be using a more detailed outline, which is found in Appendix A.

Beyond The Facts

The author of Revelation, the date when it was written – even the divisions of the outline – can all be topics of debate and argument. They are tangible facts, even though the details concerning them are debatable.

For the book of Revelation to make sense, it must go beyond the tangible, physical world to encompass the unseen, nonphysical realm. The book itself speaks of such an unseen realm (1:10; 4:2, etc.), and its content is mainly about the visions that happen in this realm. Anyone reading Revelation needs first to assume the reality of an unseen, nonphysical world in which the events of the book take place. The author of Revelation often calls this nonphysical world "heaven" (4:2; 8:1, 13; etc.). If it is assumed that such a nonphysical, spiritual realm exists, and if we admit that the physical realm in which we live also exists,[4] then the next assumption we must make is that there is some kind of connection between the two. If we neglect or deny the connection, then the parts of Revelation which take place in heaven become fascinating reading but have no relevance to our lives in the physical realm. The unspoken assumption made throughout Revelation is that the events in the spiritual realm are a foretelling of the events that will occur in the physical realm. The "visions" coming from the spiritual world are the reality that the physical realm reflects. [5] To illustrate this, consider the following example:

If you are expecting company for dinner, your first thought (after cleaning the house!) concerns what you will serve. You go through the recipes you have and you choose a main dish. Then you decide what will go well with that main dish. All of this is done in your mind. You then imagine what the meal will look like, how the table is to be set, what ingredients you need, and so on. Now, the dinner may or may not proceed as you imagine it. You may overcook the meat, the baked beans may not cook at all, and the cake may fall when you remove it from the oven, or you may spill the drink all over the tablecloth. But the point to notice here is that the dinner first took place in the nonphysical realm of your mind. From there, the physical dinner came into existence. How closely the physical dinner resembles the mental dinner in your mind depends upon many factors – your skills in preparing it, the availability of the food, the promptness of the guests, etc. Yet the resemblance (or lack thereof) between the spiritual ideal dinner and the physical dinner does not have any bearing on the reality of either the spiritual or the physical. They both existed in their own manner, and there was a connection between the two.

For the book of Revelation to have meaning for you, there must be some connection between the spiritual realm of which it speaks and the physical realm in which you live everyday. It is that connection to which we now turn our attention.

Life's Journey - A Revelation

Although some scholars argue that Revelation is a prophetic writing – and the author of Revelation calls it "prophecy" (1:3) – the book of Revelation is most often called an apocalyptic writing. The term apocalypse, which is translated "Revelation" in the title of the book, refers to the belief that the present world is so overcome with evil that the only way it will change is through the direct intervention of God. [6] This is in contrast to prophetic writing, which, in essence, says that we have the power to change our evil ways if we wish to prevent the wrath of God descending upon us. Apocalyptic writing uses symbolism and imagery to explain and describe its message. This imagery is usually in black or white terms, without much gray area between the two extremes.

Apocalyptic writing is also concerned with the "end times" (or "eschatology"). It is at this point that we moderns – especially of the

Western world – become confused. Our view of history is linear. That is, we see history as starting at one time, long ago, and continuing to move forward into the future. History only travels in one direction – forward. For the ancient peoples, history was seen rather as a series of cycles or ages. Periodically, there would be the end of one age and the beginning of another.[7] In apocalyptic writing, the "end" is "... usually the end of a present age or period of persecution and the beginning of a new age in which the persecution has been removed."[8] We might also add that the end of one age and the beginning of another brings with it a new consciousness and way of looking at life and the world.

If Revelation is viewed in this sense, then we begin to understand that the main topic is not concerned with the end of the world, but it is rather concerned with the theme of relationships: (1) The relationship between good and evil (i.e., God's judgment upon evil) as well as (2) God's relationship with his people who remain faithful. This theme of relationship is explained through the imagery and symbolism of apocalypse in order to emphasize its importance. The relationship that you have with God is seen as the most important issue of your life. God has, in the person of Jesus, directly intervened into your life, and without this intervention, we would not be able to overcome the evil of our situation. Therefore, through God's actions, we are empowered to act for Him.

It is in this light which Revelation must be understood: It is a book, not necessarily of the chronological predictions of history, but rather, it is a book which describes the struggles, battles, and victories of individuals who desire to develop a closer relationship with God. Revelation is the story of your struggles – of my struggles – and, ultimately, of our victory through faith as we enter the New Jerusalem where our lives are totally dedicated to doing the will of God. This is the connection between the unseen, spiritual world of Revelation and the visible, physical world in which we live: the faith connection. Our faith defines our relationship with God and with one another.

This commentary examines Revelation as a book to help the believer develop his or her own soul. The author, if it was John of Patmos, was at least 80 years old. He had known Jesus, had been loved by Jesus, and had heard the "inner circle" instructions given by Jesus.

He had also known the teachings of the resurrected Jesus. John was a mystic and spent decades – his whole adult life – in prayer and meditation. The book of Revelation has been called the "Third book of the Cabbalah (or Qabbalah),"[9] and it contains mystical imagery (see Appendix B). The Cabbalah, ancient secret teachings of the Jewish people, is concerned with the hidden, inner life of the believer and how that inner nature can determine the action of our outer, physical life. Thus John's writings reflect this emphasis upon the inner nature of someone attempting to become like Christ. Revelation is a story of the inner journey of Jesus as he was becoming the Christ as well as a map describing, for those of us who would follow in His footsteps, exactly what to expect on our own journey.

It is also at this point that the "Parousia" or "Second Coming" of Christ connects with our lives. The importance of the Second Coming is not the end of the world, although most people do confuse these two issues. The purpose of Christ's appearance is the judgment upon our relationship with God and the subsequent actions that relationship generates within our lives. In this sense, our lives and our faith are the judgment against us or for us. The whole book of Revelation, in dealing with the daily development of our faith, is thus totally concerned with the Parousia. The "end time" is now, when we come to the end of one "era" of our lives and begin the new era as a people totally committed to God.

In The Very Beginning

In the beginning ... in the Very Beginning,
Before the advent of Man;
Before the Morning Stars sang together,
When Harmony was All,
The One expressed Itself: And Thought began ...

Although much of the interpretation of Revelation is based upon Old Testament apocalyptic writings, they fail to address the question of "Why is there a need for Revelation?" To discover the answer to this most important question, we must turn to the Biblical book of Genesis and study its story anew.

The first chapter of Genesis expresses the true story of our origins. In the following pages, I hope to unravel a story that will give substance and significance to those opening words. The interpretation for these verses come from such diverse sources as modern commentaries of scripture, ancient secret teachings, deductions from logical thought, and simply asking questions. As we will discover, the pathway by which we receive Truth is not for us to critique: The Source of all Truth is still the same!

According to some traditions, God created the universe "ex nihilo" – out of nothing. As we are not capable of imagining nothingness, it is impossible for us to imagine the universe before creation. If we can imagine it, then it must be something. Some of the Eastern religions express God in this sense: the void; the absolute potential; the calmness of emptiness. Even scientists, when describing the early moments of the "Big Bang," admit that there is a limit to how far back they can go in describing what happened, because it is not capable of being explained. And yet that is how God was before the beginning – the Mind of God consisted of pure potential: Nothing yet had been created. The Cabbalah says that the only way to understand God is to first imagine all that exists, and then eliminate everything: What remains is God. In other words, God is not capable of being described. To assist them in understanding this concept, they used the image of a circle. God, although unbounded, is like the circumference of the circle, encompassing everything, and yet there is a oneness of all that exists. Then, God, realizing Himself, withdrew into a dot within the circle. The dot represents the actualization of the potential. God is simultaneously both the circumference and the dot of the circle (see figure 1).

Genesis expresses this thought where it says of the earth that it was without form and void (1:2). At this point all was potential and had not been manifested. Then God, the first Cause, moves and says, "Let there be light." This light is then separated from the darkness. Notice that this "light" is not the sun, moon, or stars (which were created on the fourth day). This is the first indication that these opening verses of

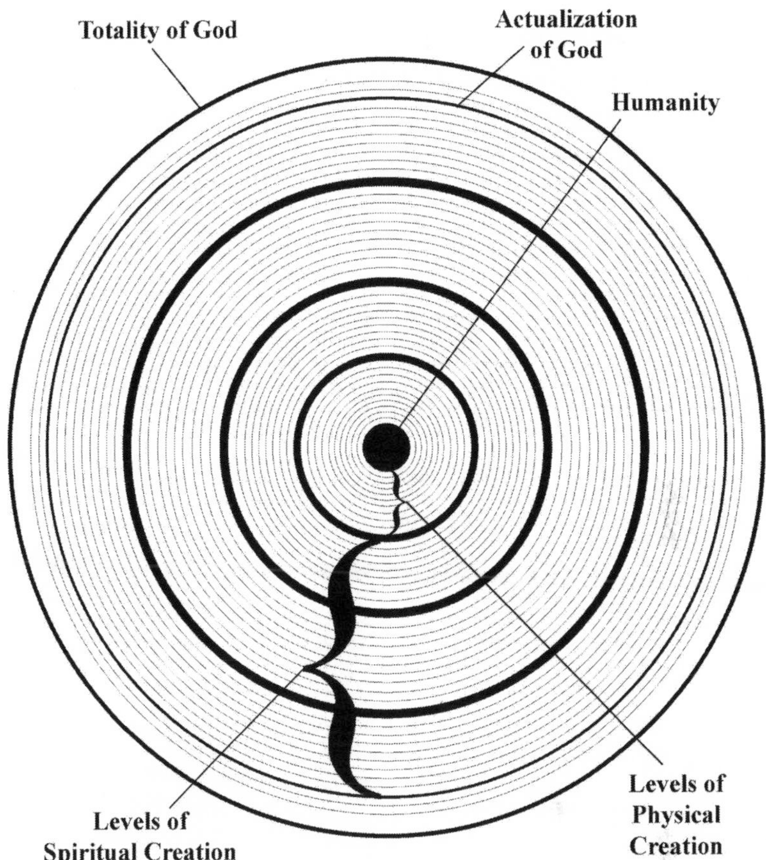

Figure 1 - The Cabbalistic View of Creation

The outermost circle symbolizes the totality of God. The next thick line represents the active, knowable God (the original "dot" mentioned in the text). The innermost dot symbolizes Humanity, which is totally contained within the essence of God, but does not partake of all of God's creation. The circles within each of the dark bands represent different parts of God's creation, which partake of more and more of His essence as the

the Bible are about more than just the physical creation. If this light is not that of the sun, the moon, or the stars, then what could it be? This light was not physical light, but rather the light of awareness, the light of consciousness – of what can be known. It was separated from the darkness (or what is subconscious, unknowable). The darkness is not evil. The distinction between the light and the dark simply signifies the difference between potential and actuality. Therefore, in the first "day," God created actuality out of the pure potential which is Himself.

Returning to the thought of the Cabbalists, the "dot" is the same as the "light" of the first day as described in the Bible. The Cabbalah then adds a series of ever smaller concentric circles within the "dot" as an explanation of the different stages of creation. Each circle is contained within the totality of God, but each circle, being smaller than those outside of it, encompasses less and less of God's totality. Finally, in the center is a smaller dot which represents humankind. Each circle represents a different phase of creation, with the extreme inner circles representing the physical creation and the outer ones representing the nonphysical or spiritual creation.

The understanding of the Cabbalists that the spiritual orders of creation came first, with the physical being the last to be manifested, is expressed in the Bible through the two stories of the creation of Man: One in the first chapter of Genesis, and the other in the second chapter. The first chapter describes the creation in the Mind of God, where humankind (adam or 'adham[10]) is created in the spiritual realm, but not the physical realm. The "idea" of humanity as companion to God was first formed in the Creator's mind. Although difficult for us 21st century, scientific, and materially oriented individuals to grasp, an "idea" in God's mind has more reality than any physical object that we can perceive with our five senses. Therefore, from the moment when God "thought" of humanity, humanity existed. It is this manner of existence that is important for our purposes, and a closer examination of the Scriptures might bring a few surprises.

First of all, as we read these first chapters of Genesis, we notice that the name for God changes as we progress further into the creation story. It begins by using the Hebrew term "Elohim" for God. One of the strongest tenants of the Hebrew faith was their monotheism: "Hear, O Israel, the Lord, thy God is One!" Yet the term "Elohim" is plural. In English translation, this term, is often rendered simply

"God." In verses 26 and 27 of Chapter 1, we read the following as God is preparing to create humankind:

> Then God said, "Let *us* make man in *our* image, after our likeness ... So God created man in his own image, in the image of God he created him; male and female he created them." (Italics added.)

Why is there so obvious a departure from the concept of the One God in these opening verses? Why does Christian theology gloss over such inconsistencies?

God is all: He/She/It encompasses everything. I use the expression "He/She/It" to refer to God not out of disrespect, but from the lack of an adequate pronoun in the English language to express the totally encompassing nature of God. God contains both masculine and female characteristics and much more. God is a plurality within a singularity; this is exactly what the diagram of concentric circles by the Cabbalists represents.

The second importance of the verse quoted above concerns the actual creation of humankind: We were created in the image of God: "He created them male and female." As first created, we were like God: spiritual beings encompassing both the masculine and feminine characteristics; spiritual beings that were separate from, but one with God; spiritual beings who, by being like God, could be true companions with Him. This is our true nature – one which we have forgotten and from which we have fallen. The glory of God was once ours! What happened to us that we lost all of this? The remaining creation story gives us the answer to this question.

A Little Later ...

In an instant, in the Bigger Bang,
I emerged within One Thought.
Many were I, though One together,
And it was His Song I sang!
Children of the One – I looked ...
and then I moved.

When everything was first created, it was "good." As humankind, the spiritual beings created in God's image, we possessed individual consciousness and were free to learn and to act on our own. Our actions corresponded with God's, and we were happy to simply observe the Mind of God. Unfortunately, our freedom of will and expression soon added new dimensions to God's creation. Since each of these "human beings" was Spirit (where Spirit "is the essence of life" [11]) and each possessed an individual mind (but, as yet, did not have any physical form), each spiritual human entity was capable of thoughts or ideas different from its neighbor. Just like the ideas of God, these ideas of God's companions were given reality simply by being "thought." And as each spiritual entity experienced its own series of thoughts, it became more unique and individualized. That portion of each entity which was its memories and record of experiences – that which made it unique – was the entity's soul.

God's desire was that we each develop our soul through our unique thoughts and experiences and then return to Him to join together in our Oneness, yet knowing ourselves to be separate from Him. The only problem was that, in order to allow us enough freedom to become creatively unique, God had to allow us the freedom to think and to do that which we were never meant to do: to become totally separated from Him in consciousness. This possibility always existed, and we, through our desire to express ourselves, have emphasized the self or "separateness" of our existence. By emphasizing the knowledge that we are separate from God, and de-emphasizing our oneness with God, we have gradually forgotten our original estate: companions with God.

The Hebrew language in those first couple of chapters of Genesis betrayed this slipping away of our consciousness of being one with God by the terms used for God. When first created, God was "Elohim," or as is most often translated in English, "God." This is the term used throughout the first chapter of Genesis when the entire universe was created in the Mind of God. Everything was in harmony with God at that time. Then, God's special creation – the spiritual humans with their separate, individual consciousnesses – began to play with creation and to have new experiences. Some of these experiences brought them into contact with the three dimensional world of the physical.

According to various readings from the well documented psychic, Edgar Cayce, these spiritual entities began to choose certain portions of themselves to manifest to others, so that their differences would be apparent, rather than their oneness. The spiritual human became "associated" with the physical creation. The spiritual consciousness, however, was not designed to work in the three-dimensional plane of experience. As a result, we began to believe that we were physical creatures and forgot our spiritual nature of being one with God.

Even the Bible, when it talks of the physical creation in Chapter two of Genesis, uses a different term for God: Yahweh-Elohim. This term is usually translated "Lord God," signifying a descent in our consciousness to being separated from God. No longer are God and His created on the same level of consciousness. Now God is viewed as outside and different: He is higher than the physical plane and thus is called "Lord God." In the story of the creation of the physical humankind, which begins at this point in Genesis, the earth does not have any vegetation, nor does the physical human being yet exist: Physical humanity and the world are yet "ideas" within God's mind. At this time, the physical adham, humanity, was formed out of the dust of the earth, and the Lord God "breathed into his nostrils the breath of life; and man became a living soul" (Genesis 2:7).

The "breath of life," the soul, now inhabits the physical body: The record of that entity's experiences – the uniqueness of that individual – now resides within the flesh. Because the soul, a multidimensional creation, is now encased in the three dimensional physical world, its consciousness of the originally spiritual human is severely limited. In fact, a new consciousness, better suited for the three dimensional existence, was created. A portion of the spiritual humanity's mind remained in awareness, but most of the consciousness was set back and became the "subconscious mind." This division of consciousness into the conscious mind and the subconscious mind is the same type of movement made by God when He separated the light from the darkness on that first day. The subconscious mind of the physical human is that which is unknown or unknowable, while the conscious mind is that which is knowable. There is nothing evil about the subconscious, although we often depict it as full of monsters and evil creatures. This depiction has many similarities to the images within Revelation, as we shall see later. It was also this subconscious mind which retained the ability to directly communicate with God. Because the conscious mind was removed one step from God, Scriptures record humanity as now calling God, "Lord God," recognizing this distance in the relationship between God and Man.

When One Becomes Two ...

Barely turning, ever so slowly,
I slip from where I stand.
Life is full: Ever exciting!
Yet sleep is what I crave!
The sleep of One ... and then of two ...
We sleep until this day.

At the time of the creation of physical humanity, when the Lord God created Adam and breathed His Spirit into the physical clay, the scriptures state that "man became a living soul" (2:7). Since the soul – that which makes each spiritual human unique – was in the image of

God and contained both masculine and feminine qualities, then Adam at this stage was both male and female – a wholeness within himself.

God, knowing both wholeness and aloneness, then decided to create a help-meet or companion for Adam (2:18). God put Adam into a "deep sleep" and removed a "rib" from his side and created woman. The Hebrew term for "rib" (tsal'ah) is better translated as "side." In other words, God took one side of the androgynous Adam – the feminine side – and separated it from him to create the complementary part of humanity: the woman. Now at this point in creation, the man was physically male, and the woman was physically female (where the Hebrew term for male means "to mark so as to be distinguished" and the Hebrew term for female means "to puncture"). This is not to say that each of them was incomplete. On the contrary, they were still complete or whole within themselves, but the awareness of one side of their wholeness was placed into the subconscious mind and the awareness of the other side was placed into the conscious mind. In addition, the physical body now manifested the conscious sexuality and not the subconscious. Yet, for the male, the feminine counterpart is still there, in his subconscious, while the masculine side of the female is in her subconscious.

This separation of human sexuality into the subconscious and conscious is symbolized by God placing man into a "deep sleep." The Hebrew at this point implies that man entered a trancelike condition characterized by being slack or languid. The ancient Eastern people would have seen in this phrase a reference to deep meditation where the consciousness is capable of being altered or shifted. It was at this level that humanity became male **or** female, depending upon which set of characteristics was to be emphasized in the conscious mind and which set would be relegated to the subconscious. It is also at this level that the physical form is determined: The driving force behind whether the union of an egg and sperm will become a male or female is the decision by the unified, nonphysical mind of the soul as to whether or not it desires to emphasize one side or the other. The process described in Genesis of the human soul becoming languid while a separation is made between the two sexual manifestations of the soul occurs each time a baby is conceived. Notice that nowhere in scripture does it ever state that God awakened man from this "deep sleep"! Thus the soul goes into this altered condition – or the deep sleep – during the process of physical conception. It is also while in this deep sleep that the Bible records "the fall" of humanity.

Me, Myself and I

In dreams we see our visions ...
In sleep we see our Truth.
Our life slithers from our grasps, '
'till One doth come, forsooth!

Before considering Chapter three of Genesis and "the fall" of humanity, it should be emphasized that at this point of physical creation, humanity has already "fallen" from the awareness of being one with God, and that the consciousness was first split into two parts: the subconscious, which retains the direct awareness of God and who we truly are as spiritual beings, and the conscious, which contains the wholeness of who we are as androgynous physical humans. But then the conscious part was split into two parts also. One part was made subconscious or unmanifested, and the other became conscious or manifested in the physical. This process tended to push the original subconscious mind even further into the background until it became the "superconscious."[12] The significance of this movement will become clear later in this section.

According to Genesis, it was the serpent that very craftily convinced the woman to eat from the Tree of the Knowledge of Good and Evil. We in the West have associated the serpent with Satan, the devil, the lord of evil and destruction. Yet the ancient peoples looked upon the serpent as a symbol of knowledge and immortality. As the symbol of knowledge, it "tempts man to the knowledge of himself."[13] This is exactly the serpent's role in the Biblical story of creation: After the woman and the man eat of the forbidden fruit, they realized that "they were naked" (Genesis 3:7). After eating the fruit, then came knowledge about their own condition. They were now physical creatures – or that is what they believed. By eating of this fruit of the

Tree of the Knowledge of Good and Evil (which, as its name implies, is concerned with polarities such as good/evil and spirit/flesh), the man and woman became aware of themselves as not only separate from God, but as different from Him: Now they thought they were flesh instead of spirit; now they experienced death which was common to all physical creatures. Not only did they become aware of their flesh bodies, but they also began to believe they were the flesh bodies instead of being the spiritual entities who had once been companions with God. The original and continual sin of humanity has been our choice to consider self more than God. We have come to believe that we are tiny creatures of dust living on a small, insignificant planet. We were so concerned with experiencing ourselves, that we forgot about our relationship to God.

Just as the serpent of self caused our downfall, it is also the symbol of our salvation. When the Hebrew people were wandering in the wilderness and began to complain about the difficulties they faced, poisonous snakes began to bite them and many of them died. Moses then made a bronze snake, placed it upon a tall pole and told the people that if anyone is bitten, he should look at the bronze serpent on the pole, and that person would live (Numbers 21:4-9). Jesus referred to this Old Testament story when He remarked, "Moses lifted up the serpent in the desert. It is the same with the Son of Man. The Son of Man must be lifted up too. Then everyone who believes in him can have eternal life" (John 3:14-15). Lifting up the self to be crucified is the way to salvation, for it is the self or selfishness that has caused the fall of humankind.

By emphasizing the self, both man and woman descended even further from the consciousness of being one with God. We had fallen so far that we actually forgot that we were supposed to be companions with God. We believed ourselves to be simply physical beings living on a physical world in a physical universe. God could not allow us to become immortal physical creatures, because then we would never remember who we were and could never return to God to be His companions; therefore, we were not allowed to eat of the "tree of life." We had left the garden of a direct relationship with God and had entered a world of our own making, where we could only survive through hard work. Even the Biblical term of God, Jehovah, or simply Lord, in Chapter 4 of Genesis, reflects this further descent away from unity and into self.

Revelation Is Needed!

When we understand the Biblical story of creation in these broad terms, we begin to see our need for salvation. It was because of this need that the Christ Spirit or Logos (Word) entered into the world in the physical form of Jesus. It was also because of this need that John received his message through his vision and then wrote the book Revelation. Because humanity's basic sin is simply self, the good news or message of Revelation is directed toward the overcoming of self while in the flesh. We, as individuals, have added the physical to what we are. Our souls, being the record of all we have experienced, are not simply spirit: Our souls include the physical as something worthy of saving – of spiritualizing and glorifying – so we may return to God and share with Him all that we are. Then we can be true companions with Him. The story of Revelation tells us what to expect as we accomplish that goal.

Chapter One

In the Spirit

Chapter one sets the stage for understanding the remaining chapters of Revelation. Nestled among the terminology are assumptions that the author, John, makes about the recipients of this book: who is reading it; what they already understand about God, Jesus, and the Holy Spirit; why this book is valuable to the reader; and what their nature is. John spent his life in exile, because he threatened the assumptions of the established faiths of his time (1:9). The outcry of those in political and religious power of the time was so great against the early Christians, because their assumptions about the purpose of life, the nature of God and humanity, etc., was radical for their time – and, I believe, still radical today.

Because John did not have an adequate language to explain the concepts behind the workings of the human soul, much of Revelation is written in the language of dreams and visions. Today, using terminology from psychology, we are able to more clearly express some of the concepts found in Revelation. As we examine what John saw in meditation, we may be surprised at the accuracy of the vision as regards the physical structure of the human body and what we know about the psychological makeup of the mind.

Chapter 1:1-3

Revelation 1:1

The Revelation of Jesus Christ, which God gave unto him, to shew unto his servants things which must shortly come to pass; and he sent and signified it by his angel unto his servant John:

Revelation 1:2

Who bare record of the word of God, and of the testimony of Jesus Christ, and of all things that he saw

Revelation 1:3

Blessed is he that readeth, and they that hear the words of this prophecy, and keep those things which are written therein: for the time is at hand.

Symbolism/Meaning

Revelation - A making known of truth that has been hidden.

his servants - Those that follow in the footsteps of Jesus, i.e., that are putting into practice what Jesus taught them.

things which must shortly come to pass - Refers to the events which must occur in the life of each of "his servants" as they struggle to be one with God and Christ

his angel - An angel is a messenger – one who does the will of God in bringing a message to an individual or group. It was this angel which allowed John to see and understand the visions which follow.

the word of God and of the testimony of Jesus Christ - If the author of Revelation is the same John who wrote the Gospel of John, then he understands Jesus to be theWord of God (John 1:14). The word of God is an active force – it denotes action in the universe, not simply written words.

prophecy - A prophecy is a call to action, not only a prediction of the future. (See Jonah for a prophesy which did not come true, because the people were active in their repentance.)

the time is at hand - the time is now. It is here if we but have ears to hear and understand. Refers to the evolving of each individual into the pathway of Christ... i.e., where we become like Christ also. With this revelation in our possession, our soul development should quickly proceed!

Commentary

In the opening verses to Revelation, John states what the book is about (1:1) and reveals how he came into possession of its knowledge (1:1, 2). In both verse 1 and verse 3, John tells us that the events depicted in the book are soon to take place. This was John's way of stressing the importance of the book for his readers. It is from these two verses that the Preterist interpretation of Revelation gains its validity.[1] Yet if the Revelation was intended to show to his servants what must shortly come to pass, the question we must ask is, "To whom does the revelation apply?" Were the visions intended to be prophecies designed to influence and convert the nonbelievers, or were the events recorded in Revelation intended for the servants of Christ (i.e., Christians)? If it is the latter, were they only for the Jewish Christians, or were they for Gentile Christians as well?

From the first three verses, it would seem that this revelation (or apocalypse) is intended for all those who were truly followers of "the Way."[2] By referring to the book as **prophecy**, John is acknowledging that his book is designed to bring about some action in the life of the one reading it. Thus we may make the assumption that John is writing to those who are ready to act upon their faith: They have accepted the validity of Jesus' Messiahship, and they are now ready to demonstrate that faith in their lives. Anyone who opens one's own soul to development and who follows up with further action is blessed (v.3).

As understood in this book, **things which must shortly come to pass** refers to the events which must soon occur in the life of each believer as he or she struggles between a selfish, sinful "self" and a desire to be more like Jesus. Part of the message of Revelation is that there will be struggles as an individual approaches the Christ like life. In fact, as mystics (such as John) understood, the human predicament involved the struggle between the realization of one's divine origins and the desire to develop a uniqueness separate from the Divine. Even

Jesus struggled with the desire to do things his own way as opposed to allowing God's will to be done through him (as evidenced in the temptation story). John, in writing these visions down, is revealing to all Christians exactly what Jesus suffered as well as warning all believers what to expect within their own lives. As each believer grows ever closer to God, the time is near when all this will take place within his or her life.

Chapter 1: 4-8

Revelation 1:4

> **John to the seven churches which are in Asia: Grace be unto you, and peace, from him which is, and which was, and which is to come; and from the seven Spirits which are before his throne;**

Revelation 1:5

> **And from Jesus Christ who is the faithful witness, and the first begotten of the dead, and the prince of the kings of the earth. Unto him that loved us, and washed us from our sins in his own blood,**

Revelation 1:6

> **And hath made us kings and priests unto God and his Father; to him be glory and dominion for ever and ever. Amen.**

Revelation 1:7

> **Behold, he cometh with clouds; and every eye shall see him, and they also which pierced him: and all kindreds of the earth shall wail because of him. Even so, Amen.**

Revelation 1:8

> **"I am the Alpha and the Omega," says the Lord God, who is and who was and who is to come, the Almighty.**

Symbolism/Meaning

seven churches - The seven spiritual centers located within the body.

from him which is, and which was, and which is to come - The Christ Spirit.

seven Spirits - Guardians of the contact between the spirit world and the physical world.

before his throne - A throne represents power.

the faithful witness - Jesus was the first and only one to not have any doubt about who he was and his relationship to God.

first begotten of the dead -Not just that Jesus died and came back to life, but that Jesus was the first to fully gain the consciousness that He and God were one. Therefore He was born of the spirit (as opposed to the physical, which is seen as death).

cometh with clouds -A reference to the vindication of what Jesus taught and said.

Alpha and the Omega -The first and last letters of the Greek alphabet.

Lord God - John's consciousness or awareness of God has been raised in meditation.

Commentary

John addresses his writing to the **seven churches** in the province of **Asia.**[3] By using the word "**churches**" (εκκλησια – those who are "called out"), it would seem that this book is directed only to those who were practicing the teachings of Christ, that is, to Christians – those who attempt to live his or her life in an imitation of Christ. As believers read this book, they were discovering what was "soon to take place" concerning themselves – not someone else. The book of Revelation is for and about the believer. As such, it is a book of hope.

It is also the contention of this commentary that Revelation was written as a story of the inner journey of Jesus as he was becoming the Christ as well as a map showing those of us who would follow in His footsteps exactly what to expect on our own journey of faith. This makes Revelation relevant for us today. We do not have to push its relevance aside by believing that it applies only to the first century Christians, nor do we create fear for the future by saying the world will end when a certain building may be built in Jerusalem.

At the time Revelation was written, there were more than seven churches in Asia.[4] Why were just these seven singled out in 1:4? An answer to this question involves the symbolism and mysticism of that age. Seven was a number that symbolized the perfection and completion of God (see Appendix B). As the Church made up the "body of Christ," the seven churches represented the seven areas of contact between the physical body of believers and the spiritual source of their belief. In mystical terms, this was analogous to the seven chakras, that is, the seven spiritual centers of the human body (see Appendix C). By addressing the "**seven churches**," the symbolism encompasses: (1) the perfection of God; (2) a source of contact between the perfect spiritual realm and the imperfect physical world; and (3) the idea that Revelation can refer to an individual as well as to a group. Since the seven churches are viewed as the seven points of contact between the spiritual realm and the physical, then **Asia** would symbolize the human body in this context. This is the first indication that Revelation is something more than just a book which proposes to talk of external, historical events. Instead, this book and its message are also intended for the inner development of individuals as they struggle toward oneness with God.

This writing of John's is also stated to be "**from him which is and which was and which is to come**." This statement refers to the Christ Spirit, not Jesus the individual. The Christ Spirit is the universal. Jesus, through his obedience, became the Christ by partaking of the Christ Spirit – that spirit of unselfish obedience to the will of God. The Christ Spirit, the Word (Logos) referred to in the Gospel of John, existed from the beginning of creation and will continue to exist throughout all eternity. Jesus took that Christ Spirit and made it flesh by living out a life of obedience to God's will. In this sense, John views the message of Revelation as coming from both the Christ Spirit that exists in the world through the Holy Spirit ("**him which is**") and the Christ Spirit that was in the form of Jesus (**and which was**). This message comes from the Christ Spirit as it will be expressed through those individuals who will embody the Christ Spirit in their own lives in the future (**and which is to come**).

In addition, this greeting comes from the **seven Spirits** before the throne. The number seven is used to represent the completeness and perfection of God. Spirits, as well as angels, are often seen as supervisors or guardians of certain activities involving the will of God. Here they can also embody the personality or characteristics of an individual or group or even an institution. They are seen as the overseers of the transfer of information between the spiritual and the physical realms through the seven spiritual centers of contact (see Appendix C).

Since these seven Spirits were **before his throne**, we know that they carry great power. A throne represents power. To stand before a throne is to be influenced by or be under the power of that throne. In this context, the power of the throne belongs to the Christ Spirit. The symbolism of the seven spirits tell us that the power of the Christ Spirit comes ultimately from the perfection of God and is disseminated through the activities of those spirits, as they are the gatekeepers between the spiritual and the physical realms.

In addition, this revelation comes from the individual soul, Jesus Christ, the **first begotten of the dead**. With this title, John continues to express the mystical, Eastern manner of viewing the world. To say that Jesus is the firstborn from the dead is to further imply that the reality that we know of as physical life is but a shadow of the higher reality of life in the spiritual realm. Jesus was the first of those to see through the illusion of our so-called reality and to be born into the consciousness of being one with God. Since he is the firstborn, it also implies that others will follow as we begin to recognize that what we call "life" is more like "death" when you compare it to the heavenly realm. Jesus being the firstborn from **the dead** implies that we are the dead, because we neither have direct consciousness of God or of who we are meant to be: companions with God.

John acknowledges that Jesus learned to become one with the forces in the earth (the flesh) that rule mankind, **the prince of the kings of the earth**, and, as Christ, to rule over these forces ("even the wind and waves obey Jesus" [Mark 4:41]).

The phrase, **cometh with clouds,** is often associated with the second coming, yet it has another meaning. To say that Jesus **cometh with clouds** is an idiomatic expression in Aramaic which means that his work and his life will be vindicated, and the truth will be shown through it. He may have been killed as a common criminal, but his truth will reign, and people will someday see Jesus for who He truly is:

He is coming "with glory."[5] This passage refers to the time when Jesus will be revealed as the Christ. In the lives of those who are struggling to become more Christ-like, they recognize Jesus as the Messiah and accept him as such. Even those who pierced him (by their denial of him and their refusal to follow him) will recognize him through the lives of his followers.

When the **Lord God** refers to Himself as the **Alpha and Omega**, he is using the first and last letter of the Greek alphabet to symbolize being all-inclusive – He is all that is, the One. This is also a reference to the Christ Spirit as manifested in the individual soul of Jesus. Jesus was the first to conquer death through his obedience, and he is "the Way" through which we shall find an end to our trap of sin. Jesus was also the first in that he was in the beginning with God (see the prologue of John's Gospel), and he is also the last in that he is the culmination of all we are meant to be.

Chapter 1:9-11

Revelation 1:9

> **I John, who also am your brother, and companion in tribulation, and in the kingdom and patience of Jesus Christ, was in the isle that is called Patmos, for the word of God, and for the testimony of Jesus Christ.**

Revelation 1:10

> **I was in the Spirit on the Lord's day, and heard behind me a great voice, as of a trumpet,**

Revelation 1:11

> **Saying, I am Alpha and Omega the first and the last: and, What thou seest, write in a book, and send it unto the seven churches which are in Asia; unto Ephesus, and unto Smyrna, and unto Pergamos, and unto Thyatira, and unto Sardis, and unto Philadelphia, and unto Laodicea**

Symbolism/Meaning

I John, who also am your brother - John is not above others. Like Jesus, John, too, is struggling to lay aside self and be a channel for God to manifest in the physical.

the tribulation - a period of hardship, struggle, and sacrifice

the kingdom - life lived with the consciousness of God ever foremost

patience of Jesus Christ - the believer's method of traveling through the tribulation to the kingdom.

Patmos - John actually was exiled to Patmos, an island in the Aegean Sea, where he wrote Revelation.

in the Spirit - a change in consciousness. **behind** The underlying source or purpose.

write ... and ... send it unto the seven churches - stresses importance of the message for the spiritual life of the reader.

Commentary

In Chapter 1, verses 9 and 10, John presents a short introduction as to who he is in relation to the reader of Revelation. First, John states that he is a brother, neither higher nor more knowledgeable than anyone who would read what he has written. This is not, on John's part, a crude attempt to be humble. It reflects the consciousness of being One with God and with others. All of humanity was created for the purpose of being spiritual companions with God (Elohim). How far we all have fallen is exemplified by finding ourselves in the physical. It is therefore imperative that we all work together to help each other rise to a consciousness of being one with God. That is the purpose of Revelation: to help those who read it, who hear it, and who keep those things which are written therein (1:3) to become conscious of being more than simply physical creatures and to raise our consciousness of God.

John stresses to the readers that he shares with them both **tribulation** and **the kingdom and patience of Jesus Christ.**. The **tribulation** of a believer's life is described in Chapters 4-20 of Revelation. The imagery of these chapters tells of the hardships one must face and the sacrifices which must be made to become Christ-like. Even Jesus was not immune to this tribulation: He had his own sacrifice to make.

When one's consciousness is raised to the point of knowing oneness with God, however, then that which others see as a sacrifice does not seem that way to the one making the sacrifice. Did Jesus see the giving up of his life as a "sacrifice" when he knew he would experience the resurrection and receive that life – and more – in return? We realize that Jesus' "knowledge" of his resurrection was a leap of faith: He had no doubt of the resurrection, but neither could its assurance be proved in any manner that would satisfy the requirements of today's scientific inquiry. Thus, what Jesus did for us was a struggle of immense proportions: He raised his consciousness or awareness of God to the point of being One with God without any physical or external assurance of what that awareness could mean. At least we, having seen Jesus as the example, have him to guide us!

When one has raised his or her consciousness of God sufficiently to be aware of God at all times, then one enters into the **kingdom**. Chapters 21 and 22 of Revelation describe this kingdom in symbolic terms as it tells of the joyous changes within an individual when the victory through Christ is totally accepted.

One reaches the **kingdom** through the process of **patience**. Since we are unique souls inhabiting physical bodies and our awareness has been divided several times into consciousness and subconsciousness, we can only become aware of whom we really are through the process of patience. Just as a baby must have the patience to first crawl and then stand and finally take a few hesitant steps, we must begin where we are. With regular prayer, meditation, service, and selflessness we begin the long road to awareness and consciousness of God and our relationship with Him. The book of Revelation describes this process in symbolic terms.

John speaks of his own patient endurance when he says he was exiled to the island of Patmos **for the word of God, and for the testimony of Jesus Christ.**. He is not attempting to gain the sympathy of his readers with this statement. On the contrary, John realizes that by his exile, he was given the opportunity to experience these visions of Revelation so that he could share them in this book. The "Word of

God" for John was embodied in Jesus (see the prologue to John's Gospel), and thus it was both the Word of God and the choice by Jesus to be a witness or testimony to that Word that gave John this opportunity. John is acknowledging his thankfulness. It is said, in legend, that John spent his years on Patmos living in a cave on the island, spending his hours in meditation and prayer – an opportunity he would not have had, otherwise!

It must have been during one (or more) of these periods of deep meditation that John experienced these visions of Revelation, for he says he was **in the Spirit**. In John's time, this phrase had several meanings:

1. It could mean that John was filled with God's Holy Spirit and was inspired by that Spirit to write Revelation.

2. It is believed that, in deep meditation, people can travel with their astral body, that is, their "spirit body" travels anywhere at the instantaneous speed of thought, while their "physical body" remains at rest.[6]
3. The vision that John received came not from the physical realm, but from the nonphysical world of the spirit. In order to see and hear in that world, John had to leave his physical body behind, probably in trance or deep meditation: His consciousness was altered.

It was commonly believed that whatever happened in the earth (the physical) had already been foreshadowed by an analogous event in heaven (the spiritual). Thus the events that John records in Revelation are a foreshadowing of what happens in the physical life of individuals on earth. The spiritual events show the underlying source or purpose of the events in the physical. This is why John heard a voice **behind** him – the voice describing what is "behind" all of the events of Jesus' revelation. The voice is loud and is described as sounding like **a trumpet** to signify the importance of what was to come. Trumpets were used in their culture to announce the coming of an important person, or the beginning of a special time (such as the time of worship, prayer, etc.).

The voice tells John that he is to record or **write** down the vision and to address it to a list of seven churches. Because so few people could read and write during John's time, written records were highly valued. To say **write** to the seven churches means: "What you will see in this vision is of great importance. Remember it and communicate it to others, for it will contain truth which will awaken the seven spiritual centers within each believer who hears it." As we shall see later in our study of Revelation, anyone who wishes to gain the consciousness of being a companion with God must allow all seven spiritual centers of the body to be opened up; the Spirit can then move freely through them, bringing to our consciousness the remembrance of who we are and what our purposes may be. Jesus told his disciples in the Gospel of John, "But the Counselor, the Holy Spirit, whom the Father will send in my name, he will teach you all things and bring to your remembrance all that I have said to you" (John 14:26). For this to happen, though, all seven spiritual centers must be opened. That is why Revelation is addressed to these **seven churches** within the physical body: to instruct and awaken them to the consciousness of the Spirit.

Chapter 1:12-20

Revelation 1:12

And I turned to see the voice that spake with me. And being turned, I saw seven golden candlesticks;

Revelation 1:13

And in the midst of the seven candlesticks one like unto the Son of man, clothed with a garment down to the foot, and girt about the paps with a golden girdle.

Revelation 1:14

His head and his hairs were white like wool, as white as snow; and his eyes were as a flame of fire;

Revelation 1:15

And his feet like unto fine brass, as if they burned in a furnace; and his voice as the sound of many waters.

Revelation 1:16

And he had in his right hand seven stars: and out of his mouth went a sharp two edged sword: and his countenance was as the sun shineth in his strength.

Revelation 1:17

And when I saw him, I fell at his feet as dead. And he laid his right hand upon me, saying unto me, Fear not; I am the first and the last:

Revelation 1:18

I am he that liveth, and was dead; and, behold, I am alive for evermore, Amen; and have the keys of hell and of death

Revelation 1:19

Write the things which thou hast seen, and the things which are, and the things which shall be hereafter;

Symbolism/Meaning

I turned to see - a focusing of understanding.

seven golden candlesticks - the light which is given off by activity of the seven spiritual centers.

Son of man - title for one aware of being a human soul in its entirety.

golden girdle - a strengthening of the soul's purity in purpose.

hairs ... white - wisdom.

eyes ... as a flame of fire - zealous for a cause.

his feet like unto fine brass - refined as in a furnace; purified.

many waters the diversity of the Spirit – as if many were combined into one.

in his right hand - in the power of.

seven stars - the angels of the seven churches (see 1:20).

two edged sword - choices, which each person must make.

sun - purity.

fell at his feet - attempt to worship.

he that liveth, and was dead, and ...am alive forevermore - the lost awareness of being both physical and spiritual has been regained for eternity.

keys of hell and of death - death does not exist for one who possesses a consciousness of God.

hereafter - after others know of their true purpose and relationship with God

Commentary

After hearing this voice, John **turned** to see. This is a turning in consciousness – an altering of his own consciousness or awareness. When this is done, he is aware of **seven golden candlesticks**. The candlesticks are symbolic of the places within the body that ancient mystics have called "chakras" (see Appendix C). These areas of the body, which are associated with the endocrine system, are said to radiate different colors, depending upon the chakra involved and the degree of spiritual the individual has achieved. These colors, which different individuals throughout the ages have claimed to see, collectively are known as the aura of an individual. When John sees the **candlesticks** in this vision, he describes them as **golden**, telling us that these chakras represent someone who is highly attuned or conscious of God. The seven golden candlesticks are the seven spiritual centers radiating their purity.

In the midst of these centers is the vision of one like **the Son of man**. Note that this image is of one like the Son of man, rather than being **the** Son of man, Jesus. "Son of man" is a title which Jesus used for himself during his ministry here on earth to refer to his connection with all of humanity. He was born of woman; he was truly physical in all respects; and he was aware of his existence as a spiritual being that God created to be His companion. Since man refers to the totality of one's existence (the physical body + the conscious mind + the subconscious mind + the superconscious mind + the life-giving Spirit), the title son of man expresses the awareness of being both physical and spiritual. Jesus was aware of who and what he was. John, in this vision, is telling the reader that each of us has the same potential as did Jesus: to become aware (conscious) of our existence in both the physical and the spiritual (or nonphysical) realms.

This awareness brings with it certain characteristics which John expresses in his description of the one like a son of man. The **golden girdle** around the breast describes the purity of the soul's purpose as it has made its will one with God's will. The **white hair** tells us that the Spirit possesses great wisdom and power and is able to do great things. His **feet** refer to that which one stands upon – the basis for what he does. Since these feet are as **fine brass, as if they burned in a furnace**, we know that the basis of this soul's wisdom and understanding has been tested and tried and found to be true. The Spirit expresses itself and accomplishes its purpose in myriad ways, for its voice sounds like **many waters**.

The Spirit is also able to control the work of the seven spiritual centers. The **seven stars**, as John tells us later in 1:20, represent the **seven angels** of the seven churches. The function of an angel is to deliver a message or protect the one in its charge. **One like the Son of man** holding the stars **in his right hand** represents the Spirit or the inner awareness, which now directs the seven spiritual centers in their work. The work of the spiritual centers is essentially to make choices: Should the energy or power of the spiritual message from God be used for selfless or selfish purposes? This is the significance of the **sharp, two-edged sword**: Choices can cut either way, but it is only with the full light (**sun shineth in his strength**) of the awareness of God that our choices can be selfless.

When John sees this vision of the soul as it is meant to be, he is overcome with awe: **he fell at his feet as though dead**. This vision is of the soul as expressed by Jesus, but it is also the potential that each of us possess. The Spirit tells John not to fear, because what this Spirit has become (fully aware of being One with God in mind and purpose, yet possessing a unique consciousness and awareness of itself) is also the goal of every soul. This is the **first and the last:**. The soul known as Jesus was the first to reach this stage of awareness. This State of Oneness is also available for every other soul. It is only within this awareness that we truly know ourselves to be alive; we will then know that physical death can not hurt us, because we are not basically physical. In fact, when we are most conscious of ourselves as physical beings, then we are "dead." True life is not identical with physical life. As this Spirit in John's vision expresses it: **I am he that...was dead; and, behold, I am alive for evermore**! It once was dead in that it saw itself as a physical creature. But now, in full awareness of being a heavenly creature and a companion with God, it is alive forever.

The Spirit next expresses a truth by saying **I have the keys of hell and of death**. Our soul either possesses the awareness of being a physical entity (**death**) or of being a spiritual entity (life). It also possesses the understanding of what we sometimes term "punishment" or "retribution" (**hell**). The Christian faith has always had difficulty with the concept of justice within one's lifetime. We have, over the years, developed the concepts of heaven, as a reward for virtue and faith, and hell, as a punishment for the lack of faith and the misuse of one's soul. We express divine retribution by quoting scripture (" 'I am the One who punishes; I will pay people back,' says the Lord" [Romans 12:19], or "A person harvests only what he plants" [Galatians 6:7]). But when we do not see justice happening in the physical world, we then say that justice will be served in the next world after death.

The idea of purgatory is another attempt we have made to express this same concept. Yet here in Revelation, we hear the Spirit stating that it holds the **keys of hell**, or to the idea of divine retribution. What does this mean? Simply that the process of becoming fully aware of ourselves as spiritual entities involves the learning aids of what we, still in the physical awareness, think of as punishment. If our consciousness was raised to a new level of awareness, then what we once thought of as a bad situation or as an unjust punishment would be seen in a new light. We would recognize a "negative" situation as an opportunity to raise our awareness further by confronting an area in our life whereby we may learn and express a spiritual truth. As scripture puts it, "We know that in everything God works for the good of those who love him" (Romans 8:28). If we are essentially and basically spiritual entities, then we must take time during the physical life to prepare for the spiritual life. Consider this thought: If a spiritual being takes on the clothing of the material world (born into the flesh) and subsequently forgets that it is spiritual, it will not spend its time learning spiritual values and habits. Later, when it sheds its fleshly cloak (when we die), it suddenly discovers it is unprepared for the spiritual life – it has not been trained to live in a nonphysical world. Its existence in the spiritual will be like a hell. Thus we each, through our actions on this earth, build our own heaven or hell, and both heaven and hell are actual experiences (albeit "spiritual" experiences) for us when we shed this earthly flesh.

In the last verse of this chapter, the Christ Spirit explains to John the symbolic significance of several images used in previous verses: The **seven stars are the angels of the seven churches**. In ancient times, the stars, being in the "heavens," were believed to be angels residing in heaven. Each person, organization, and nation was believed to have a guardian angel that expressed the personality of the individual or institution. Thus, the wise men, when they saw a certain star, came looking for the newborn child whose new guardian angel (or star) appeared in the sky. Here, the stars are the guardian angels of the seven chakras or points of contact between the spiritual and the physical. The image of the **seven candlesticks...are the seven churches** explains that the seven spiritual centers are there to bring God's light (or power) into the physical world (thus the image of a candlestick).

Chapters Two and Three

John's Progress

In Chapters 2 and 3, we discover the messages, admonitions, and reproofs given by the Christ Spirit to the seven "churches." Since adequate commentary is provided elsewhere as to the historical, economic, and political situations abiding in each city of these churches during the time when the Revelation was written, such comments will not be included in this writing except where it might illuminate a difficult passage. Here, we will examine the messages of the Christ Spirit to the angels of each church. The angels represent particular guiding forces related to their respective spiritual center. Remember that these messages may also be interpreted as directed to the Body of Christ as well as to our own body.

Since the churches were "in the world," then these two chapters are dealing with the nature of humanity as we deal with the worldly. If the churches symbolize the points of contact between the spiritual and the physical, then these chapters also are dealing with the relationship between the two as regards our emotions, thoughts, and actions as Christians in the world but not of the world.

All of this hidden knowledge was revealed to Jesus when his awareness of his true relationship with God had advanced. Jesus, in turn, revealed it to John, who is now revealing it to us (see 1:1). We are spiritual beings who have become so enmeshed in the physical that we have lost conscious contact with the spiritual. Jesus discovered how to consciously reawaken that contact. He then told John to write down the process of how to reopen contact with God. As a result, we have the book of Revelation.

Superficially, Chapters 2 and 3 do not seem to be as important as the later visions John experiences. Yet they are essential for a complete understanding of those visions. We must first understand how a spiritual God contacts the physical human being if we are to correctly interpret those contacts.

The messages to each of the churches symbolize knowledge about each spiritual center of the body and how our body reacts to the creative energy flowing through it. If we understand how and what is happening to us as our souls grow and develop, then we will not be as afraid when new experiences come our way. Through understanding, we can also make the best use of God's creative energy in service to others.

As we begin our examination of the messages from the Christ Spirit, we must recognize the relationship between each glandular center of the body and its corresponding physical/emotional action and spiritual significance. Appendix C summarizes these relationships. In addition, all the messages of the Christ Spirit to the body assume that:

1. God has given us a supply of life-force energy, or energy that keeps the body alive, known by the Hindu term kundalini.
2. God has also given us access to spiritual energy, known by the Hindu term prana, without which we could never become fully aware of ourselves as companions and co-creators with God.
3. Both kundalini and prana are aspects of God's creative, spiritual energy that we use to produce behavior and actions that reflect either God's intention for that energy or our own intentions and desires.

As the energy flows through each chakra, we choose how to use this energy to accomplish some action or thought in the physical world. For most of us, it is our ego and not our true self that decides how to use the energy. The ego, according to Carl Jung, is "the subject of our consciousness"[1] i.e., it is that part of ourselves that we often think of as "I". Our ego can work for us or against us. It works for us as it chooses pathways of physical survival – the self-preservation instinct. It works against us as it chooses to use the energy for self-preservation in ways that are designed to suppress our true self. When the ego attempts to place itself in control, or when our true self abdicates responsibility for its actions by allowing the ego to assume our identity, then we experience a loss of self-awareness. We project our ego personality outward for others to see. It is like a shell that we create around us so that our true self is not seen. The danger begins when we start to think that we are the shell instead of the self inside. If we invest a lot of our kundalini in this shell, the enhanced ego will gain a life of its own – at the expense of the life of our true self. The ego will take over control from the true self, thereby blocking or shutting down the flow of both kundalini and prana. Without this flow of energy, we not only die, but we also lose the opportunity to know God and His will for us.

For God's energy to flow freely through the chakras, several conditions must be met:

1. The chakras must first be "cleansed" by the application of prayer, meditation, and proper attitudes and thoughts, so that the kundalini may be raised to a higher level or purpose.
2. Once the chakras are cleansed, our kundalini is raised. Then prana is invited to enter and to further cleanse and spiritualize each chakra, so that the proper choices are applied to the creative energy as it flows through the system. This process is accomplished by placing the Christ Spirit at the center of one's life.

Chapters 2 and 3 of Revelation are a description of John's progress toward opening and cleansing his own spiritual centers. Each church is related to a particular chakra. The strengths and weaknesses of each church are described, and John is told what he needs to do with the kundalini in order to open the chakras to the prana. The remaining chapters of Revelation describe the total cleansing and spiritualization of both the chakras and the body, which occurs as the Christ Spirit is allowed to direct the soul's activities.

Spiritual Center #1

Revelation 2:1

Unto the angel of the church of Ephesus write; These things saith he that holdeth the seven stars in his right hand, who walketh in the midst of the seven golden candlesticks;

Revelation 2:2

I know thy works, and thy labour, and thy patience, and how thou canst not bear them which are evil: and thou hast tried them which say they are apostles, and are not, and hast found them liars:

Revelation 2:3

And hast borne, and hast patience, and for my name's sake hast laboured, and hast not fainted.

Revelation 2:4

Nevertheless I have somewhat against thee, because thou hast left thy first love.

Revelation 2:5

Remember therefore from whence thou art fallen, and repent, and do the first works; or else I will come unto thee quickly, and will remove thy candlestick out of his place, except thou repent

Revelation 2:6

"Yet this you have, you hate the works of the Nicolaitans, which I also hate.

Revelation 2:7

He that hath an ear, let him hear what the Spirit saith unto the churches; To him that overcometh will I give to eat of the tree of life, which is in the midst of the paradise of God.

Commentary

Both kundalini and prana must have a force behind it in order to pump or raise it throughout the body. This first spiritual center acts as a motor to send the energy through the remaining chakras.[2] As the energy is raised through the various chakras, we have the choice of whether or not to alter this energy before it reaches the final chakra and is transformed into a physical manifestation[3] or expression. The degree to which we change this energy determines how much we live for others or for ourselves.

In this message to the angel at Ephesus, the Christ Spirit praises good **works**: those activities that reflect the unselfish use of God's creative energy. Praise is also given for **patience** while testing for false prophets. A test of validity must, by its very nature, make a comparison. The standard for comparison is whatever the individual holds or believes to be true. Since the book of Revelation is directed toward the believer, the standard that the believers would hold would be the actions and the words of Jesus as taught by those who had known him. Having read and believed the written word in the Bible, believers today would hold the same standard. Thus the Christ Spirit praises an individual who, wishing to grow spiritually, chooses to act according to his highest moral concept of what is right. Also, if we have allowed the ego to make our decisions for us, then by holding a high ideal, the ego can be trained to strive toward that ideal. The function of the first chakra – the first spiritual center – is to pump the kundalini and the prana to the other chakras. The effect and strength of that energy manifesting in our physical bodies is determined by how high our ideal is: the higher the ideal, the higher the vibration that pumps the energy.

The reproof comes when an individual abandons this method of decision making and begins to make choices based upon selfishness. When a person no longer fulfills God's desires, but instead uses the creative energy to fulfill selfish desires, then it can truly be said that they have abandoned their **first love**. This phrase can also refer to the altering or adulteration of God's original intent for His creative energy. The **first love** refers to God's intention of how the energy is to be used. When we choose to use this energy for selfish purposes, we have abandoned the primary intentions for this energy. If we have abdicated the divine responsibility of making our own choices by allowing the ego to be our decision maker, then the ego may decide to do whatever it can to perpetuate its own existence, rather than use God's creative energy for the highest good. The ego's primary existence, when allowed to act without guidance, is to perpetuate the physical as long as possible. This is why there is a warning against the practice of immorality and lasciviousness (**hatest the deeds of the Nicolaitans**) – such practices are for the physical and only tend to lead us away from the awareness that there is more to our existence than just the physical.

If we successfully defeat the temptation to leave God and the spiritual behind while pursuing the purely physical, then the result is to eat of the tree of life. This infers that life is spiritual in origin as well as in practice. We may call our physical existence life, but we do so only because we have forgotten what true life – spiritual life – is like. In Revelation, the Christ Spirit refers to our physical existence as death while calling our spiritual existence life. This reversal of our normal usage of those words, when seriously considered and contemplated, will bring to our awareness a new outlook to all we do, say, and think.

Also, the soul must not forget its true nature – that of an eternal companion with God. In this sense, eating of the tree of life refers to the eternal quality of the soul. Only in becoming aware of our eternal nature are we able to fully experience it. If we believe we are only physical creatures, then we believe that death is inevitable, and we fear the inevitability of it. If we continue to fall away from the consciousness of being God's companions (our first love) and believe ourselves to be only physical, then we will lose any remembrance of who we are, and, in effect, close the door to any spiritual energy attempting to enter into our lives. This is the meaning behind **remove thy candlestick out of its place**. Even our spiritual muscles must be exercised or they will cease to function. If this candlestick, the first spiritual center, is removed from its place, then God's spiritual energy would never have the opportunity to be raised to a higher level of expression; we would never be able to raise our consciousness of who we are. When we close the door to this spiritual center completely, then the result is indeed, death – death of our spiritual nature. When we open the door to this spiritual center, then the result is life – eternal life!

Recap of Spiritual Center #1

1. This center serves as a motor to raise God's spiritual energy throughout the remaining chakras.
2. A choice is made at this center concerning the general use of that energy.
3. The choice is based upon one's ideal of love: What is the highest concept of love held?

Spiritual Center #2

II. Vision One: Christ Instructs the Churches 1:9-3:22
D. Letter to the Church in Smyrna...2:8-11

Revelation 2:8

And unto the angel of the church in Smyrna write; These things saith the first and the last, which was dead, and is alive;

Revelation 2:9

I know thy works, and tribulation, and poverty, (but thou art rich) and I know the blasphemy of them which say they are Jews, and are not, but are the synagogue of Satan.

Revelation 2:10

Fear none of those things which thou shalt suffer: behold, the devil shall cast some of you into prison, that ye may be tried; and ye shall have tribulation ten days: be thou faithful unto death, and I will give thee a crown of life.

Revelation 2:11

He that hath an ear, let him hear what the Spirit saith unto the churches; He that overcometh shall not be hurt of the second death.

Revelation 2:12

"And to the angel of the church in Pergamos write; These things saith he which hath the sharp sword with two edges;

Commentary

This second spiritual center puts value upon whatever we decide to do with God's creative energy. Similar to the way God performed His acts of creation and then proclaimed them to be good (Genesis 1), we tend to give a good or bad interpretation to our own use of the energy arising within us. This creative energy, if properly used by each spiritual center, does not take away from the life force which we possess. However, if we insist upon altering or changing this energy in subtle ways to create something for our own purposes, we impoverish ourselves in order to give a little of ourselves to whatever we are creating. It is in this manner that our ego places value upon our creation. If the ego is in control, then it places more or less value upon what we have done, depending upon how much of ourselves we have put into changing God's intent for the creative energy. Even in the physical, we tend to value our accomplishments more if we put a lot of energy into them. Whatever we have left alone, we tend not to value as much.

In the scriptural verses, the message given to this spiritual center praises it for its endurance of **tribulation** as well as its **poverty**. In giving our life to our creative urges (and thereby impoverishing ourselves a little), we often have to suffer the results of what we have done. If we misuse the creative energy and give in to selfish indulgences, we suffer the consequences (reap what we sow!) This is our tribulation. If we allow the creative spiritual energy to enter and be transformed without much change, then there is not much for the ego to value (**poverty**). Of course, when the energy is not changed, then God's intention for it is left intact, and, in reality, we are stronger for it (**but thou art rich**), since a portion of our life force has not been given to our creation.

The **blasphemy of them which say they are Jews and are not** refers to us when we deceive ourselves into believing that our selfish actions are the works of God. In Matthew 23, Jesus had a lot to say about such overt actions by the Pharisees and the teachers of the law: Jesus strongly reiterates that the purpose or intentions behind our actions are more important than the actions themselves. When we attempt to say that our actions are those of God, then we have deceived ourselves, but not God.

In 2:10, the Christ Spirit tells us not to fear to endure the consequences of our own actions. We may discover ourselves restricted in our actions (**cast some of you into prison**), but this restriction is nothing more than a trial to discover the sincerity of our desire to grow in spirit and to do what is right. If we remain faithful to this desire to be more Christ-like, then we will discover that the "for me only" attitude of selfishness will die (**death**), and we will gain **a crown of life**.

In 2:11, the message of Christ mentions **the second death**. Although we will learn more about this death in 21:8, we discover in the story of Genesis that the physical human being is twice removed from the immediate presence or awareness of God: once, when we developed and exploited our awareness of being separate from God in Spirit; and, secondly, when our awareness descended into the flesh so much that we forgot that our spiritual nature existed. If we are to conquer our present state of affairs, it will involve spiritualizing the physical to such a degree that we can return to God, bringing our spiritualized physical existence with us into God's presence! This is the great Good News which Jesus exemplified through his resurrection and subsequent ascension to God: The physical, now part of our experience, is capable of being purified, cleansed, and presented to God when we return as His companions. It is this process of purification which the book of Revelation describes.

Recap of Spiritual Center #2

1. At this spiritual center, value is placed upon the creative use of kundalini as well as prana.
2. When we alter the creative energy by placing selfish values upon it, we impoverish ourselves by giving of our life to what we create.
3. On the other hand, if we faithfully allow God's intention for the
   energy to be expressed, then we increase our own life.

Spiritual Center #3

Revelation 2:12

"And to the angel of the church in Pergamos write; These things saith he which hath the sharp sword with two edges;

Revelation 2:13

I know thy works, and where thou dwellest, even where Satan's seat is: and thou holdest fast my name, and hast not denied my faith, even in those days wherein Antipas was my faithful martyr, who was slain among you, where Satan dwelleth

Revelation 2:14

But I have a few things against thee, because thou hast there them that hold the doctrine of Balaam, who taught Balac to cast a stumbling block before the children of Israel, to eat things sacrificed unto idols, and to commit fornication.

Revelation 2:15

So hast thou also them that hold the doctrine of the Nicolaitans, which thing I hate.

Revelation 2:16

Repent; or else I will come unto thee quickly, and will fight against them with the sword of my mouth.

Revelation 2:17

He that hath an ear, let him hear what the Spirit saith unto the churches; To him that overcometh will I give to eat of the hidden manna, and will give him a white stone, and in the stone a new name written, which no man knoweth saving he that receiveth it.

Commentary

The third spiritual center (associated with the adrenal glands located on top of each kidney in the area of the body known as the solar plexus) deals with the emotions of fear/courage or anger/

persistence. Adrenaline, produced by the adrenal glands, provides us with the familiar flight or fight reaction often called the self preservation instinct. When applied to us in a spiritual sense, it becomes the **two-edged sword** mentioned in 2:12: We fear to lose our selfish "self" (the ego), even though through losing it, we would gain the soul. Yet it takes a leap of faith to be willing to lose what we have if we have no "proof" of gaining something better.

Spiritually, the phrase, **I know...where thou dwellest, even where Satan's seat is,** represents the condition of humanity in its fallen state. We use this third spiritual center to choose whether to use the spiritual energy for ourselves or for others. It is here that we make the choice of how to manifest that energy in the world. It is also here that temptation lies at the door. Satan, in his many pseudonyms, is called "the tempter," and when we are tempted, that temptation is seen as a stumbling block over which many of us stumble. Satan sets up his office of operations in this third spiritual center, as it is the most vulnerable to temptation. It is the giving in to the physical temptations that cause us to be for self rather than for others. In fact, when they are not released, certain emotions connected with the self, such as anger, are concentrated in this solar plexus region of the body. This spiritual center produces the positive emotion of courage to stand up for one's actions when we are steadfast in our Christ-like actions.

Yet, we all experience those times when something, which we can not explain, forces us to act in ways contrary to Christ's desires for us. For example, we can be so persistent in some beliefs that we begin to worship the belief rather than God. We may begin with a simple belief or guiding principle of life which is good. As time passes, and we hold on to that belief, we may exhibit behavior that, though holding to the letter of the law, has lost the spirit of the law. It is at this point that we have created idols out of our beliefs. And, since we created the beliefs in the first place, we would then be worshipping our own creations instead of God.[4]

By being so persistent in worshipping our own beliefs that we become stubbornly attached to them, we place stumbling blocks in our own spiritual pathways. Even when these beliefs originate from some highly respected teacher or leader, we must be careful not to treat these beliefs as if they are God. We may use them, but we should not worship them as idols.

Again, in 2:15, the message to this spiritual center warns against perverting or adulterating the spiritual energy by using the fear of losing our selfish ego as a "reason" for lashing out at others. The Nicolaitans were those who advocated sexual perversion and immorality as a way of life. A Nicolaitan, therefore, would be one who perverts the spiritual energy for selfish reasons.

At this point, notice how the battle lines are being drawn: The selfish self is opposed to the self-less self. This is the message and story of Revelation – the inner struggle which goes on within every person who truly strives to be more Christ- like.

In 2:16, Christ promises that if we do not purge ourselves of the adulterous tendencies to pervert the energy of this third spiritual center, then he will come and fight against these tendencies himself with the **sword of my mouth.** By this, he tells us that His word as spoken through others or through our own awareness will point out our blasphemous actions. Therefore, either we discover our own sins, or else the rest of the world will discover them for us.

It is in this third spiritual center that we must accept responsibility for what we have created. When we make this acceptance, we begin to understand the power of this creative energy. This understanding is food for our souls. It is **hidden manna**. When we understand that our every action is either selfish (therefore destructive) or selfless (therefore constructive), then we begin to more carefully choose our actions and even our thoughts. We view life in a new way – a way that is not of our own making, but rather, is given to us through the spirit of being for others: this is the Christ Spirit.

After experiencing this acceptance of responsibility for our every thought and action for a certain amount of time, we will discover a cleansed life. It will be as if we have a new, clean foundation for living each day (a **white stone**), and we will be known to others as a changed person: we will have a **new name** written by Christ as he works through us. This new name can only be known by ourselves, because only we know what has gone on within us as we struggled to overcome the selfish self.

Recap of Spiritual Center #3

1. This spiritual center is crucial in our ability to grow in awareness of God through our application of our highest ideals.
2. The manner in which the creative energy will be expressed in the physical is chosen through the exercise of this third spiritual center.
3. Our actions at this level determine whether we are of service to others, or are a hindrance to them as we seek to serve only ourselves.

Spiritual Center #4

II. Vision One: Christ Instructs the Churches	1:9-3:22
F. Letter to the Church in Thyatira	2:18-29

Revelation 2:18

And unto the angel of the church in Thyatira write; These things saith the Son of God, who hath his eyes like unto a flame of fire, and his feet are like fine brass;

Revelation 2:19

I know thy works, and charity, and service, and faith, and thy patience, and thy works; and the last to be more than the first.

Revelation 2:20

Notwithstanding I have a few things against thee, because thou sufferest that woman Jezebel, which calleth herself a prophetess, to teach and to seduce my servants to commit fornication, and to eat things sacrificed unto idols.

Revelation 2:21

And I gave her space to repent of her fornication; and she repented not.

Revelation 2:22

Behold, I will cast her into a bed, and them that commit adultery with her into great tribulation, except they repent of their deeds.

Revelation 2:23

And I will kill her children with death; and all the churches shall know that I am he which searcheth the reins and hearts: and I will give unto every one of you according to your works.

Revelation 2:24

But unto you I say, and unto the rest in Thyatira, as many as have not this doctrine, and which have not known the depths of Satan, as they speak; I will put upon you none other burden.

Revelation 2:25

But that which ye have already hold fast till I come.

Revelation 2:26

And he that overcometh, and keepeth my works unto the end, to him will I give power over the nations:

Revelation 2:27

And he shall rule them with a rod of iron; as the vessels of a potter shall they be broken to shivers: even as I received of my Father.

Revelation 2:28

And I will give him the morning star.

Revelation 2:29

He that hath an ear, let him hear what the Spirit saith unto the churches.

Commentary

In 2:18, it is the "**Son of God**" who speaks as opposed to one like the "**Son of Man**" in 1:13. Of course, Jesus, who called himself the Son of man, is also the Son of God, but the two titles represent different aspects of himself. Since this fourth spiritual center is in the position of balancing the lower three centers against the upper three centers, it is appropriate that the role of the Christ Spirit shifts its emphasis at this point. The first three centers dealt with our actions, emotions, and experiences in regard to the world. The upper three centers are more concerned with our "potential for awareness of our divine nature"[5] Thus the new emphasis becomes one of a zeal for refining the divine relationship between God and ourselves [**eyes like unto a flame of fire** (zeal), and ... **feet are like fine brass** (refined metal)].

Verse 19 is interesting, because it relates the progression of one who has progressed to the fourth spiritual center. Love was needed in the first center, faith in the second, while the third spiritual center emphasized service. Here, in the fourth center, patient endurance is needed. The soul growth and development is noted by the Christ Spirit as he tells John that his latter works exceed the first. If there is to be growth, the application of one's ideals must take precedence. As the Bible often notes, it is not enough to mouth pious platitudes without actions to support what you say. Thus the Christ Spirit praises the individual who has progressed this far.

Such spiritual advancement is not without its dangers, as 2:20-23 point out to us. In 2:20, Christ tells us that we still tolerate the activities of "Jezebel" (see I and II Kings for a description of this referent's actions) who seduces **my servants** to commit acts of selfishness.

Who are **my servants**? Since we understand the speaker to be the Son of God at this point, then **my servants** would be all those urges, actions, and desires that would carry out the will of God. The servants of Christ are those who follow Him; since His will is to do the will of the Father, then those who follow Christ are those who do the will of God. Also, as we are examining the progressive spiritual development of an individual as the various spiritual centers are being cleansed, the use of **servants** does not refer to individuals, but rather to our created ideas and thoughts that give rise to our actions. **Jezebel** is that part of us which would redirect the pure spiritual energy into actions which serve only our "self" rather than others. Thus Jezebel represents the self-directing force within us, sometimes known as the **ego**. The Christ Spirit is saying, therefore, that, even though this fourth spiritual center can instill heavenly qualities to our thoughts and actions, we still possess an ego which feeds on the selfish idol-worship of ideas and beliefs (2:12-14, above).

This selfish ego does not truly understand the power of the creative energy given to us by God. It has not accepted the responsibility of its own actions as actions which affect others: it does not think about the results of its actions. Its own, immediate self-gratification is all that concerns the ego. Thus, in 2:21, we learn that the ego, even when given the opportunity to reconsider (rethink or repent) its actions, does not avail itself of that opportunity. For, to even begin to consider the implications of its actions upon others would be the beginning of the end for the ego.

The ego, since it will not change, must suffer the consequences of its actions. "You made your bed, now lie in it," is the modern equivalent of 2:22. Since the ego perverts the creative, spiritual energy into selfish uses, we (those who **... commit fornication** with her) must also suffer the consequences (**tribulation**) of this selfish action upon ourselves. Only those uses of the creative energy in an unselfish manner will escape the destructive karma.[6]

If the ego is allowed free rein and is not stopped in its seduction of the creative energy for selfish purposes, the destructive karma would end up destroying us. For this reason, the Christ Spirit states that he will take away the life from our creations, thus effectively killing them (2:23). This is part of God's mercy upon us: Without His mercy, we would know only death from the karmic forces. With God's mercy, we are allowed the opportunity to begin anew, this time to use the creative, spiritual energy for others and not for our own selfish purposes. When this happens, then all the spiritual centers know about the change (**all the churches shall know ...**) and understand that the Christ Spirit is aware of all the choices we make, no matter whether they are loving choices or selfish choices.

Yet, even God's mercy will not change the condition or situation into which our internal actions have placed us. We will receive exactly what we have created. Our creations (our thoughts, our words, our actions) will no longer have a life of their own, but we must still accept responsibility for all that we have thought, said, or done: **I will give unto every one of you according to your works.** This is similar to what happens at the moment of conversion for a new Christian: the new Christian's life has been inwardly changed, even though the external (worldly) conditions may still be the same. Thus a new believer is given the opportunity to be in control of how the creative energy is used. The ego loses control. The new believer can begin a life of service for others, instead of allowing the ego to control all thoughts, words, and actions for selfish reasons.

In 2:24 and 2:25, the Christ Spirit admonishes those ideas and beliefs (as well as thoughts, words, and actions) that are not selfish and have not been seduced by Jezebel's selfish intents to remain the way they are, and they will receive no other burden. They are to stay that way until the Christ Spirit returns in the later cleansing.

To those who do remain faithful, always being for others, the promise is that they shall have power over their selfish inclinations and be able to break them as a potter would break the imperfect vessels he produces that are not suited for others to use. Thus the true spiritual uses of our creative power will be more powerful than the selfish urges and inclinations. This is one way of stating that the Christ Spirit is greater than the ego of self. The phrase, **even as I received of my Father**, refers to Jesus receiving the power of the Christ Spirit from God. It also implies that, in our reaching this stage in spiritual growth, we, too, will become like Jesus, receiving power from God to use for others. In fact, when we reach this stage, it will be the dawn of a new day for us (**give him the morning star**), as we realize not only the extent of the power we have, but also the freedom we have to be of service to both God and humanity. No longer will we have to listen to the dictates of our ego. We will be free to choose how to serve others, and the power we have to do so will come from God.

Recap of Spiritual Center #4

1. This fourth spiritual center serves as a balance between the lower three chakras ("Earth") and the upper three chakras ("Heaven").
2. The ego, or the independently acting creation of our selves, will feed upon our application of God's creative, spiritual energy, if we allow it.

3. The spiritual power and energy which comes from God is stronger than the ego, and can help us conquer the ego.

Spiritual Center #5

Revelation 3:1

And unto the angel of the church in Sardis write; These things saith he that hath the seven Spirits of God, and the seven stars; I know thy works, that thou hast a name that thou livest, and art dead.

Revelation 3:2

Be watchful, and strengthen the things which remain, that are ready to die: for I have not found thy works perfect before God.

Revelation 3:3

Remember therefore how thou hast received and heard, and hold fast, and repent. If therefore thou shalt not watch, I will come on thee as a thief, and thou shalt not know what hour I will come upon thee.

Revelation 3:4

Thou hast a few names even in Sardis which have not defiled their garments; and they shall walk with me in white: for they are worthy.

Revelation 3:5

He that overcometh, the same shall be clothed in white raiment; and I will not blot out his name out of the book of life, but I will confess his name before my Father, and before his angels

Revelation 3:6

He that hath an ear, let him hear what the Spirit saith unto the churches.

Commentary

With this spiritual center, we enter the realm of the Spirit within us. The fourth spiritual center was the seat of the ego or self within us and dealt with "our experiences related to love in the earth."[7] This fifth spiritual center "... relates to the Spirit and may reflect the spirit of obedience ... or the spirit of rebellion."[8]

Here we are dealing with the will – our ability to choose right or wrong. Free will is one of the greatest gifts we have from God, but it is also one of the most dangerous. By exercising our free will, we can choose to do what is wrong – even to deny or defy God. That is what the ego does each time it directs creative energy into selfish thoughts or actions. By choosing our will instead of God's, we are creating a world without God. In fact, we are attempting to become gods ourselves as we create our own little worlds.

It is for this reason that, in 3:1, Christ says to us that we have a **name** of being alive (i.e., of being a god) but, in truth, we **art dead,** because our creations do not have a life of their own. When we try to create our own world (i.e., attempt to be in charge and in control of all that we do and say), we bestow upon it value because we give it part of our life. Without us, it would not exist. In fact, we live our lives through our own creations. Thus, although it seems that we are alive, we are dead, for we have actually given away our life to whatever it is that we place value upon in this world (e.g., wealth, power, family, job, prestige, etc.).

In 3:2, the Christ Spirit tells John to **be watchful**. This is a reference to the Genesis story of our fall into the physical consciousness and our loss of awareness as being spiritual beings and companions with God. Since this fifth spiritual center deals with the spiritual realm of our existence, we are admonished to regain this awareness of our nature before we completely lose this connection with God.

We are then admonished to **strengthen the things which remain.** By this, we are told to allow free reign to whatever creative energy we still have. We are not to adulterate it by letting our ego use it for selfish purposes. Creative energy, received from God, is already infused with the spirit of being for others. The reason God gives it to us is so that we may strengthen what is already there as we choose our thoughts, words, and actions to be for others instead of for ourselves.

In this manner we are raised to a higher awareness or consciousness of God's presence within us.

In effect, this means we must return God's gift of free will back to Him. When we willingly give up the ego's desire to change everything from being for others to being for one's self, then we have made the greatest step toward being Christ-like. To make this step is not easy and involves a long, difficult, internal struggle with the ego, which does not want to relinquish control. The story of Revelation concerns that struggle and describes the "tribulations" and difficulties it causes.

At the level of the fifth spiritual center, Christ tells us to remember that we have you **received** of God's creative energy and to **hold fast** to God's original intent for that energy while we **repent** (re-think) our own actions toward it. If we do not awaken to this greater consciousness and begin to use the energy in selfless ways, Christ reminds us that the karma of our actions will return to us in unexpected ways. Like a thief at night, our actions shall return to us, and we may not always understand why such seemingly "unfair" circumstances happen to us. This explains those times in our lives when we want to shout, "Why me, Lord?" when we do not remember nor understand that our own selfish use of God's gifts has brought our own sins back to us in an unexpected manner.

Even while warning us of the consequences (3:4), Christ tells us that we still have **a few names even in Sardis which have not defiled their garments**. In other words, some of our choices have truly been unselfish choices for others. These choices have left undefiled the original purpose of God's creative energy, and therefore their color is **white** (symbolic of purity).

In the same manner, when we learn to use our will to choose God and not self, then we, too, will know and live a pure life, undefiled by the taint of selfishness (**shall walk with me in white**). We will be alive because what we create (i.e., what we say and do, along with our intentions and purposes) will possess the force of life from God, and our creations will not drain the spiritual life from us (**... I will not blot out his name out of the book of life ...**). Instead, our life energy will increase as Christ confesses our name before God and the angels.

Thus we will become more aware of our true relationship with God just as John was being instructed in his relationship.

One lesson we learn at this spiritual center is how to give thanks to God in the midst of trouble. By acknowledging that our trouble could be a form of karma, whereby we are receiving, in kind, what we have mostly unconsciously dished out to others, then we should thank God for giving us the opportunity to grow from our mistakes. The first time we say "Thank you, Lord" in the middle of our problems, we may wonder why we are saying it. Yet the more often we do give thanks, and mean it, the sooner we begin to realize (or gain insights) as to why we have troubles. We can then, like King David in the Old Testament, learn to never repeat our sins.[9]

Recap of Spiritual Center #5

1. By placing value in the external, physical life we create, we drain ourselves of our true, spiritual life.
2. By opening this fifth spiritual center, we begin to awaken to an awareness of our true nature – spiritual beings and companions of God.
3. When we become aware of our true nature, then we will gain spiritual strength.

Spiritual Center #6

II. Vision One: Christ Instructs the Churches	1:9-3:22
H. Letter to the Church in Philadelphia	3:7-13

Revelation 3:7

And to the angel of the church in Philadelphia write; These things saith he that is holy, he that is true, he that hath the key of David, he that openeth, and no man shutteth; and shutteth, and no man openeth;

Revelation 3:8

I know thy works: behold, I have set before thee an open door, and no man can shut it: for thou hast a little strength, and hast kept my word, and hast not denied my name.

Revelation 3:9

Behold, I will make them of the synagogue of Satan, which say they are Jews, and are not, but do lie; behold, I will make them to come and worship before thy feet, and to know that I have loved thee.

Revelation 3:10

Because thou hast kept the word of my patience, I also will keep thee from the hour of temptation, which shall come upon all the world, to try them that dwell upon the earth.

Revelation 3:11

Behold, I come quickly: hold that fast which thou hast, that no man take thy crown.

Revelation 3:12

Him that overcometh will I make a pillar in the temple of my God, and he shall go no more out: and I will write upon him the name of my God, and the name of the city of my God, which is new Jerusalem, which cometh down out of heaven from my God: and I will write upon him my new name.

Revelation 3:13

He that hath an ear, let him hear what the Spirit saith unto the churches.

Commentary

The sixth spiritual center, symbolized by the Church at Philadelphia and the pineal gland in the body, is "most often referred to in mystical literature as being the higher mind or the Christ center."[10] There is a belief that this center has a direct connection to the second spiritual center through what is mystically called "the silver cord" and that the second spiritual center, along with this silver cord, is the seat of the soul.[11] In medical fact, the pineal gland does secrete a hormone, melatonin, which inhibits the production of testosterone, a hormone produced by the internal cells of the Leyden gland, which is associated with the second chakra.

What all this means in spiritual terms is that, as we progress in our spiritual development to this sixth level, we attempt to use the power of this level to either open or close the door to the creative energy entering at the second chakra. In this manner, that creative energy given to us by God and arising within us is affected by the Christ center (3:7-8).

The Christ Spirit also is the one who has **the key of David**. The story of David in the Old Testament is an intriguing story filled with excitement and action. Even though David commits numerous sins, is ambitious, and loves his women, he is described by God as being a man after His own heart (Acts 13:22). The reason for such an endearing description is centered on David's almost constant conscious awareness of God's presence with him. In the Psalms and stories of David, he is always singing praise to God as he acknowledges God's goodness and blessings. Even when David occasionally drifts away from God, commits some terrible sin, and then experiences the result of his actions (karma), it brings David back into a relationship with God, rather than separating them even further. The key to David's closeness was the conscious awareness of being a companion to God. When the Christ Spirit says he has **the key of David**, he is emphasizing the role this spiritual center plays in the growth of our souls. For at this level of spiritual growth, we begin allowing the mind of Christ to guide and direct our very thoughts and actions. Yet, before accomplishing this, there will be an internal rebellion by the ego as it resists the influence of the Christ Spirit. To arrive at this level in spiritual development is a struggle that seems overwhelming at times. When we first reach this level, we occasionally allow the Christ Spirit to guide us, yet we also give in to the ego and selfishness. We only allow the Christ Spirit to have a small amount of power in our lives at first (**thou hast a little strength**), but that small amount is enough to expose the false excuses and justifications of the ego (3:9) as it attempts to exert its power and influence over us.

When we acknowledge the lies and deceptions of our own ego, then we realize – in a painful manner – that we have created the selfishness and greed within us through the misuse of God's creative energy. We are responsible for who and what we are through our decisions and the exercise of our own will. It is the acceptance of responsibility for our condition that allows us to return control to our spiritual self. When our selfish actions return to us in karmic conditions, instead of those conditions overwhelming us and placing burdens upon us, we accept them for what they are: opportunities for the soul to grow stronger in its awareness of God. This awareness and acceptance of responsibilities allows us to face the consequences of our actions and not be hurt by those consequences. Christ also gives us strength to endure the temptations which come our way. (**I will keep thee from the hour of temptation ... to try them that dwell upon the earth.**) Notice that this does not mean we will never be tempted. It simply means that, in those times of temptation, we will discover the inner strength, coming from this sixth spiritual center – the Christ center – to face temptation without giving in.

In addition, at this level of soul growth, the power and strength of Christ comes to us quickly ("I am coming soon" [3:11]), since we have broken down many of the barriers that we have erected over the years to isolate ourselves from God. By holding fast to our ability to accept responsibility for our choices and by allowing the Christ Spirit to direct us in our further uses of God's creative energy, no one can take away the **crown** of patience which we have achieved. In patience we begin to develop new responses to external, as well as internal, stimuli. Our behavior changes, and we become stronger, more stable individuals. The promise by Christ is that he will make those who conquer **a pillar in the temple of my God**. We must remember that scripture says our bodies are the temples of God. We worship God within ourselves. Therefore to be a **pillar in the temple of God** is to possess a strong, stable internal response to external physical circumstances – a person who is calm in the midst of problems. Such people as this can truly be described as having the Christ dwelling within them. (**... I will write on him the name of my God ... and my new name.**). In addition, Christ tells us in this message that these persons will also have written upon them the name of the New Jerusalem – the city of God. This New Jerusalem is the new consciousness or understanding we achieve when we realize that we are already dwelling within God's kingdom.

This will only come about when we listen to that voice of God within us from the sixth spiritual level. By allowing this level to express the Christ Spirit within us and influence the lower levels, then we will begin to hear **what the Spirit saith unto the churches.**

Recap of Spiritual Center #6

1. The sixth spiritual center opens us to the "mind of Christ."
2. Soul growth increases rapidly with the opening of this spiritual
   center.
3. The awareness of being in God's presence is the result of living at
   this spiritual level.

Spiritual Center #7

II. Vision One: Christ Instructs the Churches	1:9-3:22
I. Letter to the Church in Laodicea	3:14-22

Revelation 3:14

And unto the angel of the church of the Laodiceans write; These things saith the Amen, the faithful and true witness, the beginning of the creation of God;

Revelation 3:15

I know thy works, that thou art neither cold nor hot: I would thou wert cold or hot.

Revelation 3:16

So then because thou art lukewarm, and neither cold nor hot, I will spue thee out of my mouth.

Revelation 3:17

Because thou sayest, I am rich, and increased with goods, and have

need of nothing; and knowest not that thou art wretched, and miserable, and poor, and blind, and naked:

Revelation 3:18

I counsel thee to buy of me gold tried in the fire, that thou mayest be rich; and white raiment, that thou mayest be clothed, and that the shame of thy nakedness do not appear; and anoint thine eyes with eyesalve, that thou mayest see.

Revelation 3:19

As many as I love, I rebuke and chasten: be zealous therefore, and repent.

Revelation 3:20

Behold, I stand at the door, and knock: if any man hear my voice, and open the door, I will come in to him, and will sup with him, and he with me.

Revelation 3:21

To him that overcometh will I grant to sit with me in my throne, even as I also overcame, and am set down with my Father in his throne.

Revelation 3:22

He that hath an ear, let him hear what the Spirit saith unto the churches.

Commentary

This final or seventh spiritual center is associated with the "Master Gland" of the body, the pituitary. This gland, in conjunction with the hypothalamus, receives orders from both the conscious and unconscious mind and then "directs" the body's responses by secreting and storing various hormones in response to those orders. The spiritual significance of the seventh spiritual center is that it receives the spiritual creative energy, which has traveled through the other six spiritual centers (which have been influenced by that creative, spiritual energy) and then directs the physical body to respond in kind to this spiritual energy. John is told that this chakra does not influence nor change the creative energy: It simply directs the body in its actions. The seventh chakra is the master link between the spiritual and the physical.

In this message from Christ, He states that this center is **neither cold nor hot**. This is a reference to the center's lack of zeal in giving direction to all of the spiritual energy, whether for selfish or unselfish reasons. It is possible and desirable that this center direct the body to respond for others: The problem is that it does not – John is **lukewarm**. That is why there is no praise for this spiritual center. If it were truly directed completely by the Master, it would be on fire with the desire to influence the body into action for others and not for self.

This center feels **rich**, because it directs the physical body in its responses. Although a busy place, from a spiritual point of view, it is **wretched, and miserable, and poor, blind and naked,** as it does not emphasize the spiritual, unselfish uses of God's creative energy.

The counsel of Christ is to buy of me gold refined in the fire. If we were to choose our thoughts and actions from the refined spiritual values which we have received from Christ, then we would indeed be rich with the gold of life. These spiritual values have already been refined in the trials by fire of daily life. By choosing the unselfish life, we shall not be ashamed of all we do (shame of thy nakedness). We shall be changed from the blind people who we once were, when we could not see of what our relationship with God consisted, to individuals who can see and consciously understand both our divine nature and our physical manifestations and the consequences of our actions. As we attempt to choose spiritual values and behavior, we will discover that it is not easy: The ego will struggle against us, even as we attempt to come closer to God. These tribulations and difficulties are simply what we must experience if we are to grow. God allows these troubles because He loves us and wants us to become conquerors. In order to reach this goal we must be persistent to the point of being zealous.

Christ promises that to the conqueror He will come in to him, and will sup with him, and he with me. He will daily assist us, giving us the strength and spiritual nourishment we need. In 3:21, Christ offers a great promise to the one that overcomes all problems: The one who conquers, will be allowed to sit with me in my throne. This promise is to be one with Christ and with God. We must sit with Christ on his throne – i.e., be totally in accord with the goals, actions, and spirit of Christ himself!

Recap of Spiritual Center #7

1. This seventh spiritual center is responsible for actually producing the physical result from the creative energy we have been given.
2. When we live our lives at this level, we will actively be accomplishing God's will.
3. The opening of this center – the combining of one's faith with action – is the goal of all true believers.

Summary

Chapters 2 and 3 of Revelation give us an overview of the spiritual progress of John in particular, and us in general, as we strive to become Christ-like. Each spiritual center has its own purpose in developing our expression of God's creative energy. The ultimate goal is to develop an inner nature and awareness of God's presence as well as expressing the external actions of being for others. It is this spirit of being for others that we call the Christ Spirit. The journey to become one with this spirit is difficult, complete with dangerous battles between who we think we are (the ego) and who we really are (God's created self). The ego has convinced us that it is really us: We identify with its decisions and actions. We have forgotten our true spiritual nature: we are companions with God.

The story of Revelation is given that we might "wake up" and remember who we are. It also lets us know that we do not have to struggle alone. Jesus has traveled this path before us, and he is there to guide us as we take the path least trod.

Chapter Four

The One On the Throne

In the first three chapters of Revelation, John describes the purposes and complex interactions of the seven spiritual centers found within the human body. He shows how God's creative spiritual energy is enhanced or altered by the choices we make at each spiritual center. The manner in which we physically manifest this spiritual energy will depend upon what we hold as ideals (i.e., spiritual concepts/ examples/qualities to which we aspire) and to what degree we are conscious of our spiritual nature.

Chapter 4 in Revelation continues the description. By backing away from the detail of Chapters 1 through 3 and attempting to get a "feel" of these three chapters as compared to the remainder of the book, we begin to notice that all John has described in the first three chapters is easier to understand from both a purely physical and a spiritual position. What John described is acceptable and believable. Most people can gain some insight from those three chapters without too much confusion; they learn that they are physical beings in possession of a soul. Beginning with Chapter 4, however, comprehension of the text falls rapidly. Why is this? What is special about Chapters 4 through 22 that make them difficult to understand?

To answer this question, we must remember that John was in a state of meditation when he experienced the visions recorded in Revelation (**in the spirit**, 1:10). One of the goals of meditation is to cleanse and "open" the seven chakras and allow the energy (kundalini) to flow unhindered through each chakra. Much time and energy is spent in learning how to accomplish this. Because of this time spent learning to become aware of the kundalini as it flows through each chakra, students of meditation become quite familiar with the physical "experiences" associated with the opening of the individual chakras. These "experiences" can range from feelings of movement and heat, to the generation of audible psychic "sounds."[1]

John, being a mystic, and having spent much time in meditation, was quite familiar with the conditions and awareness one encounters as each chakra opens. It is this familiarity that enables John to describe his experiences and visions in Chapters 1 through 3. In Chapter 1, as John enters into meditation and greets the seven chakras (1:4), he brings the Christ Spirit with him into the meditative state. Chapter two is a description of the initial phase of John's meditation: the preparation one always makes when entering into the presence of God. Beginning in verse 10 of Chapter One, John experiences the first vision: a "status report" of his progress toward acquiring a constant consciousness of God's presence. This status report pertains to how well his chakras were doing. Because John was familiar with the way his chakras worked, this psychic report on his progress was expressed in familiar images. Notice that each spiritual center was given a grade: there was both praise and/or constructive criticism directed toward them. Each chakra, except the seventh, received praise for the progress achieved. This seventh, and final chakra was the lukewarm spiritual center that was not filled with zeal to physically manifest the God-given energy. In other words, John was told that he needed to act upon what he already knew to be right. Thus John was told repeatedly to **write what you see** (1:11, 1:19)! This command would help him to open his seventh chakra and to share with others this process of becoming constantly aware of God in one's consciousness – the process which Jesus uncovered throughout his life and now reveals to John.

In Chapter 4 and following, John is given a much greater detailed vision of what happens to one who is successful in soul growth and whose chakras are completely cleansed, allowing God's will to be done in and through the physical ("Thy Will be done on earth as it is in Heaven"). Because John had not yet experienced this completeness, he was not as familiar with it as he was with the condition or status of his own soul growth. These visions were given to John through a series of symbols, much in the same way that we receive messages in dreams. The images and symbols which flow through John's visions during the remaining chapters of Revelation are often tenuous and difficult to grasp and understand, especially when reading it for the first time.

In the overall vision, the author of Revelation experiences a non-judgmental, mystical interpretation of our inner actions as all the chakras are opened. From Chapters 2 and 3 we received some critical advice from the Christ Spirit as to the true purpose of the seven spiritual centers. The purpose of these seven centers is to transform the creative spiritual energy into physical actions for others. In other terms, God's Word is made flesh through the proper use of these centers.

Yet, because of interference from the ego and the selfishness it represents, we have become internally fragmented with our 'self' split into myriad personalities. The ego wants to use God's energy to maintain its own, selfish existence. As we will discover in this chapter, there are characteristics, commonly called the "personality," which we project outward into the world. This personality can be as multifaceted as we choose. At different times, we may emphasize one or more characteristics over another. In addition, the "true self" or our "inner self" lies deep within us, hidden by the characteristics of our outwardly projecting personality.

This chapter presents an intriguing vision of who we are and how we operate from within.

Chapter 4:1-3

Scripture

Revelation 4:1

After this I looked, and, behold, a door was opened in heaven: and the first voice which I heard was as it were of a trumpet talking with

me; which said, Come up hither, and I will shew thee things which must be hereafter.

Revelation 4:2

And immediately I was in the spirit: and, behold, a throne was set in heaven, and one sat on the throne.

Revelation 4:3

And he that sat was to look upon like a jasper and a sardine stone: and there was a rainbow round about the throne, in sight like unto an emerald.

Symbolism/Meaning

a door was opened in heaven - A doorway to consciousness – a new insight, vision or awareness.

after this - i.e., after the new awareness.

in the spirit - heaven is a spiritual place ... i.e., it is nonphysical.

throne - a center of power or command as well as a symbol of authority.

one sat on the throne! - refers to the one to whom we have given authority to make judgments in our lives – usually our consciousness, but can refer to the Christ Spirit.

jasper and sardine stone - stone in the breastplate of judgment (see Exodus 28:17-20). This implies that the one sitting on the throne has taken the position of being judge.

rainbow ... emerald - green (emerald) is the color of the Christ consciousness. It also symbolizes growth, healing, etc. In addition, the rainbow was a reminder of God's promise to Noah that He would never again destroy every living creature (Gen. 8:21 and 9:11). Thus we must not interpret the visions of disaster that follow in Revelation as though God had forgotten his promise to Noah.

Commentary

Verse 1 in Chapter 4 recognizes the next step in awareness which John is taking in his journey and revelation: **a door was opened in heaven** picks up the images found in 3:20 where the Christ Spirit urges John to open the door of consciousness and to become fully aware of our relationship with God and our spiritual heritage. John, in 4:1, is recording what happened when the door was opened, and he entered a new awareness. This first verse is an invitation (or imperative) to grow in spiritual awareness so that we can view our lives from God's viewpoint. What happens to us in our lives takes on new meaning when we die to this world and live to the spirit. To understand why certain events happen, we must see them from God's understanding. This spiritual awareness we are being asked to enter is called "heaven," but it is not the heaven of perfection we normally assume whenever we use that word today. Remember, the ancient people believed in many different layers or levels of heaven, each one different from the ones below or above it.

This heaven John is about to enter is a new awareness – a step further away from the physical and closer to God. It is this awareness and the experiences it presents that constitute the Revelation which John is about to be shown (**...which must be hereafter**). Since John is writing this down, this is a revelation not only for him, but also for each of us as we travel this path.

The first thing we become aware of in this new state of awareness is the center of our own consciousness (throne) and the one who controls our life (**one sat upon the throne**). Since the throne is a symbol of power, the one seated **on the throne** has power. Notice that the two **stones**, being those found in the Old Testament breastplate of judgment (Exodus 28:17-20), symbolize the ability to judge. The one who sits upon the throne is therefore the one who has power to judge. We usually think of this one as being the Christ, yet this is not always the case. Instead, the one seated on the throne may be the combination of our urges, thoughts, beliefs, and habits that we have given the power to rule over us. This part of ourselves that we have allowed to rule our lives and make judgments can choose either for good or for ill.

If this last chakra were to be opened without our having first put the Christ Spirit upon the throne through our adherences to certain ideals, then we would be opening this chakra to our own detriment. If our own, selfish urges were those that sat in power and judgment, the decision they would make would not be for the service of others, but rather for the enhancement of the created self – the ego.

The **rainbow**, which is predominately green, symbolizes the capability of this stage of consciousness to heal. In Genesis, the rainbow is a symbol of God's promise not to again destroy the earth by water. In this connection, it is a sign of healing with the green color adding to this symbolism. When all spiritual centers are fully open, they will bring healing because we will again be one with God. This stage of consciousness deals with our conscious judgments made in the earth. Normally, when we think of where we are located, we identify ourselves with the brain or our thought processes – i.e., our minds. Yet, our minds and our brains are **not** the same, even though most of us make this mistaken equivalence. We make this mistake because we have abdicated the throne of our own lives, allowing the consciousness to be controlled by the ego or various desires and wants within our lives. This vision which John experiences is a spiritual representation of the processes within our own inner selves.

Chapter 4:4-8

Scripture

Revelation 4:4

And round about the throne were four and twenty seats: and upon the seats I saw four and twenty elders sitting, clothed in white raiment; and they had on their heads crowns of gold.

Revelation 4:5

And out of the throne proceeded lightnings and thunderings and voices: and there were seven lamps of fire burning before the throne, which are the seven Spirits of God.

Revelation 4:6

And before the throne there was a sea of glass like unto crystal: and in the midst of the throne, and round about the throne, were four beasts full of eyes before and behind.

Revelation 4:7

And the first beast was like a lion, and the second beast like a calf,

and the third beast had a face as a man, and the fourth beast was like a flying eagle.

Revelation 4:8

And the four beasts had each of them six wings about him; and they were full of eyes within: and they rest not day and night, saying, Holy, holy, holy, Lord God Almighty, which was, and is, and is to come.

Symbolism/Meaning

Four and twenty seats, ... elders 24 refers to the "whole Man" (i.e., 7 (spiritual) + 5 (man) x 2 (the two natures of man) = 24). They are seated in power, symbolizing the power which is both potential and real within each of us.

white raiment - radiating purity.

crowns of gold - the value of their power and judgment.

lightnings and thunderings and voices - from the seat of consciousness comes a myriad of choices, decisions, insights, dreams, voices, etc.

sea of glass - This sea is within our consciousness. When God creates a new heaven and a new earth, there will **not** be a sea in the new heaven (see Rev. 21:1).

four beasts - since there are four of them, they deal with the earthly (or beastly) forces. They are also a combination of the creatures seen by Ezekiel (Ezekiel 1:4-28) and by Isaiah (Isaiah 6:1-4).

lion - king of the jungle ... ruler ... courage ... justice. (This same imagery is used for the lion in The Wizard of Oz.).

calf - propagation ... the creative or sexual urges, even to the propagation or creation of ideas, thoughts, habits, prejudices.

man - thoughtful ... possessor of a soul ... flesh ... capable of reason.

eagle - feeds on flesh, and traditionally can soar higher than any other bird. Related to the inner (and higher) realms of consciousness.

six wings - wings symbolize "making something happen" – getting it to fly. There are six wings to symbolize the physical, mental and spiritual aspects of life, and the two directions we can take (either for good or for evil).

eyes within - the many aspects of ourselves (I's), filling us with our many personalities both during our waking hours and in our dreams (all day and night).

Holy, holy, holy - they serve God by serving us.

Commentary

There are 24 cranial nerves of the head[2] which bring messages of the outside world to our brain. In 4:4 the 24 elders relate in some way to the manner in which we sense or perceive the world. While it is commonly believed that we possess only five physical senses which allow us access between the physical and the mental realms, we must also recognize that the seven spiritual centers are pathways between the physical world and the nonphysical or spiritual world. This provides us with 12 (i.e. 5 + 7) ways of sensing or influencing the physical. In addition, the brain has two halves, each of which possesses a unique mode of perception. (The right brain perception deals with creativity, artistic skill, etc., while the left-brain perception deals with logic, numbers, etc.) These two halves of the brain each receive messages from all 12 avenues of sensation, thus accounting for the 24 different pathways for our awareness of the physical and spiritual world to reach our consciousness. It is the job of the one seated upon the throne to take all these 24 pathways of sensation and make judgments or decision based upon what it receives.

When decisions issue from this center of self, they may be expressed as flashes of insight (**lightnings**), the rumble of judgments (**thunderings**), or the voice of conscience (**voices**). Even as the decisions are made, the seven spiritual centers (**seven lamps of fire ... seven Spirits of God**) are standing by ready to receive our decisions and act upon them. These centers of contact between God and ourselves are always ready to accomplish God's will; nevertheless, it is our decision which determines whether or not they will do our will or God's will. When we pray, in the Lord's Prayer, "Thy will be done on earth as it is in heaven," we are asking, in effect, for the strength to make the correct decisions for others that will allow God's purpose for

His creative energy to be manifest in our physical actions and behavior. These seven spiritual centers will accomplish that very thing if we allow them the freedom to act as God intended. When our decisions are selfish, then we force these seven spiritual centers to pervert God's will.

The **sea of glass** mentioned in 4:6 is not mentioned again until Chapter 13. The sea is the womb from which life emerges. Water has always been a symbol of life in Biblical thought. In Genesis 1:2 God hovers over the waters out of which He created the universe. The Christian concept of baptism is one of new life coming out of the waters of this sacrament. In Chapter 13 of Revelation, the sea gives birth to the beast. (More will be said about this in the commentary on that chapter.) Here, the sea is before the throne to tell us that as decisions are made and judgments are passed by the one seated on the throne, those actions result in creation and life. We are co-creators with God. The sea is **like crystal** implies that it is calm and undisturbed. John is told that all outside disturbances and inner emotions must be calmed if one is to progress to the next stage of awareness.

The four creatures mentioned in these verses are used to symbolize the worldly desires, which each of us possess, and the highest expression that we, as humans, can reach. The church has often used these four creatures to represent the four Gospels. The **eyes,** both in front of and behind these creatures, symbolize their existence, influence, and significance both in our conscious mind (**before**) and in our subconscious mind (**behind**). These beastly influences can see what we do both in consciousness and unconsciousness. Since these creatures can represent both positive (constructive) as well as negative (destructive) influences in our lives, it would be beneficial to examine the significance of each creature as it relates to us in our spiritual growth:

1. The **lion** symbolizes, at its best, courage in the face of danger. At its worse, it symbolizes those influences which would rule over us and destroy us with their anger. Because of its association with courage and

anger, this creature influences us most through the third spiritual center. Also, just as the lion is called the king of the beasts, the influence at this center or level has a tendency to rule over us. When we are under stress, either due to overwork, unexpressed anger at others, grieving the loss of a loved one, or other issues, we often feel the results of this stress in the region of the stomach and intestines. This area of the body is called the solar plexus region and is also the area of the body associated with the third spiritual center.

2. The **calf** symbolizes our attitude of propagation or self-preservation, whether we think in terms of the physical (the sexual urges), in terms of the mental (the propagation of an idea or thought), or in terms of the spiritual (an act of creativity which lifts others up). Thus the influence of this creature is mainly upon the first and second spiritual centers where God's creative energy is first born within us and encounters the influence from the self.

3. The third creature, **man**, is a difficult concept to grasp at first. The other creatures are easily understood as animal or beastly influences.A creature with the face of a Man causes us to stop and think. The lion and the ox influence who we are and what we do, yet it is the power of making decisions – the power of the will – that puts those influences into actions. Without the ability to choose and make conscious decisions based upon both conscious and subconscious knowledge and influence, we would not be wholly human. Thus the creature with the face of a man symbolizes that which we have become – i.e., the person whom we have designed and built through the making and

carrying out of all our decisions. This creaturely influence is most evident in the fourth spiritual center, wherein resides the ego (see previous chapter). The influence of this creature, when combined only with that of the lion and the calf, can center our thoughts and actions totally upon the world and the satisfaction of our own desires. If we are to rise above our physical desires, it is necessary for there to be one more creature of influence.

4. This final creature of influence, the **eagle**, being a bird of prey that in legend traveled higher than any other bird, represents both an influence to prey upon the flesh and to fly high in the lofty realms of spirit. Thus the beastly influence of this symbol, associated with the upper three spiritual centers, can lead us into the evil of preying upon others, or can be that which keeps us in touch with God's spirit.

The combination of these four creatures represents the "self" which we create and project outward for all to see. The "eyes" of each creature could also represent the many characteristics of self that we create through our decisions. Notice that the true self is separate from these images of our self that we create. The true self becomes hidden from the outward, projected self whom everyone sees. We even come to consciously believe and think of our projected self as our true self – even to the point of fearing to let it be known who we "truly are." We fear rejection by others if we allow our true self to be exposed. Therefore, our projected image, shaped by the influences of the four creatures, takes the place of our true self, which remains hidden deep within us.

Chapter 4:9-11

Scripture

Revelation 4:9

And when those beasts give glory and honour and thanks to him that sat on the throne, who liveth for ever and ever,

Revelation 4:10

The four and twenty elders fall down before him that sat on the throne, and worship him that liveth for ever and ever, and cast their crowns before the throne, saying,

Revelation 4:11

Thou art worthy, O Lord, to receive glory and honour and power: for thou hast created all things, and for thy pleasure they are and were created.

Symbolism/Meaning

And when ...- the point here is that **when** the earthly forces recognize their creator, **then** they praise the One who lives forever. And when the creatures surrender to the higher power, so do the twenty-four elders. The choices will not be made by the ego, but will be made by the God within us.

Commentary

Each of the creatures that represent our projected self has six "wings." Since the beastly influences are directed toward the three manifestations of human nature (the physical, mental, and spiritual), and since the influences can be used for either our selfish will or for God's will, there are six ways of expressing each of these influences. The wings are a symbol of transportation: Angels had wings so that they could travel from the spiritual realms to earth. These creatures serve in the same capacity as angels: that is, they are the messengers that carry the decisions of the one on the throne (our seat of consciousness) to the various parts of the body, mind, or spirit.

These influences are ever present (**they rest not day and night**) in our lives. They also sing the praises of God, even as they carry out our selfish desires! The creaturely influences within us recognize their true purpose and whom they should be obeying, even though we may not. They realize when we have chosen to serve self rather than God, and, as they lend their creaturely characteristics to what we have chosen, the guilt accompanies them. These creatures are the messengers of guilt as well as our conscious decisions.

In the last three verses, the emphasis is upon the when. Since the creaturely influences always sing praises to God and always recognize Him, then when they give glory to the one who sits upon the throne, they are recognizing God at the conscious center of our lives. This represents a shift from earlier times when the one sitting upon the throne was not God or Christ, but rather our own, self-constructed "center of self" (the "ego"). This new situation occurs when we allow God the central position in our conscious lives, so that He controls our lives. Because it is the four creatures which are praising God, we must conclude that the worldly, earthly characteristics of our human nature must be in accord with God's will in order to enter this new level of awareness.

When we allow the Christ Spirit to sit upon the throne, and the living creatures recognize it in that position, then the 24 elders or the 24 ways of sensing both the physical and spiritual worlds – also recognize that the Christ Spirit is the one in control, making the decisions. Realizing that the ego no longer will make decisions about the use of creative energy, they then give up their power (**cast their crowns before the throne**) in deference to the true self. God is the One who truly "creates." What we call "creating" is simply manipulation of God's creative energy. When the ego is no longer in control, then the true self can emerge as if from the dead and translate the will of God into physical action.

John was given this vision of the true center of the self, even though John had not yet reached this stage in his own life. The vision that follows was information about the process experienced by Jesus and yet to be experienced by John and others.

Chapter Five

Who Is Worthy?

III. Vision Two: The Scroll in Heaven .... 4:1 - 16:21
A. Introduction and Setting .... 4:1 - 5:14
1. Prelude: Being in the Spirit in Heaven. 4:1-2a
2. Description of Heaven .... 4:2b - 11
3. Vision Background: The Scroll and the Lamb .... 5:1 - 5:14

The book of Revelation describes what must happen within our selves as we progress to the stage of being fully aware of God's presence. In a sense, this book is about knowing ourselves. When we choose to be totally obedient to God's will and, through meditation and prayer, become aware of God's constant presence in our lives (i.e., when we have the mind of Christ), then a change occurs within our consciousness that affects body, mind, and soul. This change is not one of degree – simply being a "better" person. Rather, it is a change of kind: We are transformed into a new type of human being. As we exist now, with our true divine self locked away in a physical consciousness and a created ego or personality masquerading as our "self," we are masters of self-deception. The ego has usurped power from the true self (also called the higher self or inner self) and has deceived us into believing that it (the ego) is the true self. We project our ego's personality traits outward in an attempt to deceive others into accepting it as our true self. In addition, we have deceived ourselves (with the ego's help) into believing that our "true self" is weak and ineffectual and should not be allowed to express itself.

This deception continues as long as the ego sits on the throne from where it effectively screens our experiences and sensations and decides what gets sent to the true self. The true self is not a static, unchanging portion of who we are. Rather, it is a developing, growing self, always being built by reflection upon our experiences. Yet it is the one upon the throne who determines what our true self will experience and, ultimately, what it will become. Therefore it is essential for soul growth that the one upon the throne be of our highest ideal.

If the Christ Spirit is given the throne, then the transformation of consciousness begins. Chapter 5 describes this process of transformation. In this chapter, the true self accepts total responsibility for what it has become. On account of this, it is able to fully cleanse and open all the chakras; the creative energy – both kundalini and prana – can be totally directed for others.

The vision of Revelation is the story of what happened to Jesus and what will happen to us when we allow the Christ Spirit – the spirit of being for others – to sit upon the throne of our lives.

Chapter 5:1-5

Scripture

Revelation 5:1

I saw in the right hand of him that sat on the throne a book written within and on the backside, sealed with seven seals.

Revelation 5:2

And I saw a strong angel proclaiming with a loud voice, Who is worthy to open the book, and to loose the seals thereof?

Revelation 5:3

And no man in heaven, nor in earth, neither under the earth, was able to open the book, neither to look thereon.

Revelation 5:4

And I wept much, because no man was found worthy to open and to read the book, neither to look thereon.

Revelation 5:5

And one of the elders saith unto me, Weep not: behold, the Lion of the tribe of Juda, the Root of David, hath prevailed to open the book, and to loose the seven seals thereof.

Symbolism/Meaning

book - a record of the soul's experience.

written within and on the backside - part of the record is in the conscious (within) and part is within the subconscious (backside).

seven seals - the seven points of contact between the physical and nonphysical keep the records from being remembered or known by us. . It should be noted that God will not take the initiative to break the seals and carry out His Will for humankind. Instead, He waits for us to achieve our destiny by ourselves. It would take a human being who willingly put him or herself at the disposal of God's will to achieve that destiny.

angel - guardian between the conscious and unconscious.

Who is worthy...? - who is worthy of reaching the awareness that we are divine beings and companions to God?

Lion - symbolizes the courage of Jesus to face all of man's sins and accept the outcome for them.

tribe of Juda, the root of David - again, symbolic of Jesus, tracing his genealogy back to King David and the tribe of Judah.

Commentary

Again, in 5:1, we confront the one who was **seated on the throne**. In most people, the one on the throne is the ego, which usually decides to direct the God-given energy toward self preservation and enhancement. In the circumstances described in this vision, the one seated on the throne is the Christ Spirit. It is the powerful Christ Spirit who holds a scroll, (a written record of our soul's experience) within his right hand. The information contained in the scroll relates to both our conscious awareness (**within**) and our subconscious (**on the backside**). The problem is that the subconscious information is locked away (sealed), and we are unable to access it until the proper conditions are met.

When we experience something, the conscious mind filters the experience, allowing us to "remember" only selected portions of it –

those portions that we are able to understand and value at the present time. The rest of that experience is placed in our memory storehouse to be opened and reexamined at a later time when we are capable of understanding the significance of that experience. This storehouse of memories is a complete record of who we are – not only our conscious self, but also the subconscious self. It is a record of the soul's experience that will be exposed to us when we can comprehend each experience in its true light of either karma or God's grace.

There are **seven seals** which keep us from knowing about these experiences. These seals correspond to the seven spiritual centers: the chakras. Until now, portions of the seven chakras have been sealed or closed to certain purposes or functions in the life of a spiritually developing person. Without having all the chakras fully open and functioning as originally intended, our awareness of who we are is limited, because we do not see our lives from the viewpoint of God. Each spiritual center must be totally opened to the Christ Spirit before all our memories can be seen in their true light. As long as we remain selfish, we will not be able to withstand the truth of our experiences. When we allow the Christ Spirit to lead us and to have control of our lives, then the centers will open the memories, so that they may be examined and understood.

Verses 2 through 4 of Chapter 5 express the situation of humankind. We insist upon keeping our ego or selfishness at the center of our lives. Because of this, we are unable to truly know ourselves and to understand why events have unfolded in our lives the way they have. God gave us free will to choose between right and wrong, between life and death. When we choose the self, we choose death. Even God is unable to force us to make the correct choice. Thus John weeps because **no one was found worthy** to truly understand who and why they are. In fact, no one is even able to see that this record of the soul's experiences even exists (**And no man ... was able to open the book, neither to look thereon**)!

In 5:5, we learn of the persistent courage (**Lion**) of Jesus to sacrifice his ego for the will of God. Jesus was the first to examine all his memories and to understand why life is the way it is. Jesus was the first to totally view his experience on earth from God's viewpoint. He was the first to open all seven seals, so that the seven spiritual centers could perform at their full potential and accomplish everything "for others." The image of the **Lion** also refers to allowing the Christ Spirit to rule over him (see 4:7). Because Jesus, the man, had the courage (**Lion**) to accept responsibility for humanity's fall from that rule, he was able to break the seals that kept him from knowing himself and God. As we see in the next section, it is the true self who steps forward to break the seals. Since the act of breaking the seals involves attuning one's true self to the will of God, it is only natural that it be the one who receives the scroll. John is given this vision of what happens when a person reaches that level of attunement.

Chapter 5:6-10

Scripture

Revelation 5:6

> **And I beheld, and, lo, in the midst of the throne and of the four beasts, and in the midst of the elders, stood a Lamb as it had been slain, having seven horns and seven eyes, which are the seven Spirits of God sent forth into all the earth.**

Revelation 5:7

> **And he came and took the book out of the right hand of him that sat upon the throne.**

Revelation 5:8

> **And when he had taken the book, the four beasts and four and twenty elders fell down before the Lamb, having every one of them harps, and golden vials full of odours, which are the prayers of saints.**

Revelation 5:9

> **And they sung a new song, saying, Thou art worthy to take the book, and to open the seals thereof: for thou wast slain, and hast redeemed us to God by thy blood out of every kindred, and tongue, and people, and nation;**

Revelation 5:10

And hast made us unto our God kings and priests: and we shall reign on the earth.

Symbolism/Meaning

a new song - the purpose of the creatures is now to serve God and not the ego.

This is a celebration because the Son has claimed his Sonship. Everyone (or every aspect of humankind) joins in the celebration (see the explanation of the numbers).

Commentary

Since the Lamb is not on the throne, but rather is standing in the midst of the throne and of the four beasts, it cannot be the Christ Spirit, as is often believed. Instead, it represents the true inner self that has accepted the Christ Spirit as its own and can totally identify with that awareness. The true self is seen as a sacrificial animal because it has been pushed into the background by the developing ego and only at this point is able to be restored to its proper place. It is as if the spiritual inner self has been dead and is only now being resurrected. This is why the Lamb stands even though it has been slain.

The **seven horns** represent the power of the seven spiritual centers as they operate throughout the human body (**sent forth into all the earth**). The **seven eyes** symbolize the ability of the inner self to see and understand its true purpose for existence.

Verses seven through ten describe the body's response when the true self allows the Christ Spirit to be in control. By taking **the book out of the right hand** of the one upon the throne, the true self is showing that it is accepting responsibility for all the body's experiences. Thus the inner self becomes worthy to examine those experiences and to learn their true significance. Since it took the scroll from the right hand, it means power was transferred from the Christ Spirit to the true self. The acceptance of responsibility for his own experiences and actions is the way in which Jesus became the

Christ. Hebrews 5:8 states that, even though Jesus was the Son of God, "he learned obedience through what he suffered," and he took upon himself the responsibility for the "sins of the world." The obedience of Jesus – even the experience of suffering – was the key to his becoming the Christ. It is this acceptance of responsibility for ourselves and obedience to the original intent of God's energy for us that allows us to become sons and daughters of God.

This is the path each of us must take: acceptance for our lives and the situation in which we find ourselves. It seems to make sense to our egos to blame external circumstances, people, or events for our problems, because we do not understand or view life from the perspective of God. If we could see events as God sees them, we would understand the reason behind certain circumstances and would not be so quick with our blame. We would begin to realize that we must take responsibility for our situation, and that only we can do something about it!

Again, in 5:8, we see that when the true self takes the scroll, then all the avenues of sensing both the physical and the nonphysical world bow down to the one who can make the correct decisions. Now they will operate in harmony (**harps**) with God and the prayers received by and sent out from the self will have great influence.

The actions, purposes, and directions of the true self change when the Christ Spirit becomes a part of our experience. Thus the **24 elders** and the **four beasts** sing a **new song.** No longer will they be forced to carry out actions contrary to the will of God. No longer will their influence be used in a selfish manner. They now serve God!

Chapter 5:11-14

Scripture

Revelation 5:11

And I beheld, and I heard the voice of many angels round about the throne and the beasts and the elders: and the number of them was ten thousand times ten thousand, and thousands of thousands;

Revelation 5:12

Saying with a loud voice, Worthy is the Lamb that was slain to receive power, and riches, and wisdom, and strength, and honour, and glory, and blessing.

Revelation 5:13

And every creature which is in heaven, and on the earth, and under the earth, and such as are in the sea, and all that are in them, heard I saying, Blessing, and honour, and glory, and power, be unto him that sitteth upon the throne, and unto the Lamb for ever and ever

Revelation 5:14

And the four beasts said, Amen. And the four and twenty elders fell down and worshipped him that liveth for ever and ever.

Commentary

These four verses continue the theme of a celebration. The **voice of many angels** can be thought of as the voices of the memories in the following manner: An angel is a messenger, bearing a message of helpful influence from God. Memories also are messengers, bearing the information of our experiences. When we are open to understanding the importance of our experiences – to seeing our life as God sees us – then our memories bring us God's message. With that message comes spiritual understanding of who we are and why we are. Our purpose in life is understood and, because of that understanding, we and all that is within us worship God for His love.

Chapter Six

Memories and Earthquakes

In Chapter 6 we begin to see what happens when the chakras are cleansed and opened. As the seals are broken, the number seven continues to reappear: There are seven seals, with the last seal containing the sounding of seven trumpets. Within the last trumpet there are three major "signs," the last of which contains seven angels bringing plagues. The importance of these is in the reoccurring "seven": seven seals, seven trumpets, and seven plagues. We are used to living in a linear consciousness: Events begin, continue for a time, and then come to an end. Ancient peoples, on the other hand, lived in a cyclical awareness: Each day repeatedly begins with the sun rising, moving overhead, and then setting. The seasons move in succession until they, too, begin again. This cyclical nature does not mean that everything is exactly the same (for each day or season is different from the preceding one), but that there is repetitiveness to them. This cyclic nature of our experience is more like a spiral than a circle:

> Visualize a spring resting on its base, coiling upward. Taking a godlike view, looking down on the spring from the sky, it looks like a single circle. Looking at it from the ground, it appears like a series of sloping lines, each separate and distinct, advancing into the sky.

> From the godlike view, moving around the spiral is just an endless trip around the circle, each time coming back to the starting point in a rather Sisyphean effort. However, from the ground, the movement seems to pass gently upward, disappear for a moment, then appear at a higher level, ready to begin another upward journey.[1]

Revelation progresses in this spiral manner, describing the journey in consciousness as we continue to open the seven chakras and evaluate our experiences in light of our new awareness. To see ourselves as something more than simply physical creatures led by our worldly desires and lusts involves a struggle to let go of cherished beliefs and self conceptions which hinder our growth. We must accept new visions of reality – realities that are so strange as to first be incomprehensible to us. This struggle with these new realities is the story of Revelation: The symbols attempt to express the incomprehensible.

As we accept creative spiritual energy from God, we must learn, from our obedience, to allow God's purpose (which He placed within the energy from the start) to be expressed through our use of this energy. We do this through a process of becoming aware of what influences are passed on to the energy by each chakra and by learning how to raise the "vibrational" quality of the energy to match that of each particular chakra. Chapter six gives us insight into this process. By allowing God's will, inherent in this energy, to bring about its own purpose, and by not infusing this energy with our own ego or selfishness, we will be able to be more like Jesus and be able to do what he did – and more besides! The story of Revelation is both the story of how Jesus accomplished this return to God as well as how we can do the same. By understanding Revelation in this manner, we may gain insight into whom we are in relation to Jesus and how we may grow to be more like him.

Chapter 6:1-2

Scripture

Revelation 6:1

And I saw when the Lamb opened one of the seals, and I heard, as it were the noise of thunder, one of the four beasts saying, Come and see.

Revelation 6:2

And I saw, and behold a white horse: and he that sat on him had a bow; and a crown was given unto him: and he went forth conquering, and to conquer

Symbolism/Meaning

opened one of the seals - awakening the consciousness to the process of how the spiritual centers operate

noise of thunder - symbolic for authority.

Come and see - an invitation to become aware of something new.

white horse - white signifies purity and the horse signifies power. Thus this is pure, creative power or energy.

bow - symbol of God's covenant with humanity.

crown - a symbol of ruling power.

Commentary

When our inner self or soul (**Lamb**) chooses to be one with the Christ Spirit and accepts its right to attune the physical body to the high spiritual levels of the chakras, it first must deal with the four lower chakras, representing the influences of the physical world. John acknowledges the strength of these physical desires when he compares the speaking voice to a **noise of thunder**. The noise comes from one of the four living creatures (lion, calf, man, eagle), and it issues a command (**Come and see**) to the newly opened chakra. It is commanding that which has been hidden by the ego to emerge, to be seen, and to be evaluated by the inner self. What emerges from these chakras are all the experiences of the soul – experiences which the ego could not allow to be recognized, because they would have contradicted the ego's selfishness and desire for self preservation. Now that the ego no longer rules from the throne within us, the images of our experiences may be seen and evaluated.

Much has been written about the first four seals, known collectively as the "Four Horsemen of the Apocalypse." Symbolism plays a major role in our understanding of these four lower chakras. These images of the various colored horses and their riders have been understood in terms of the human emotions (hatred, greed, ambition, and power), the stages of mankind's life ("the Child, the Youth, the Adult, and Death"[2]), and the most feared circumstances of humanity (Pestilence, War, Famine, and Death). In this study of Revelation, the images are also viewed symbolically, yet from a different perspective: that of evaluating all our experience from the viewpoint of God.

The first **horse** (powerful energy) is of the color **white** to represent the purity of the energy as it comes from God. The rider of the horse – the one who controls the energy at this chakra level – carries both a **bow** and a **crown.** It has often been assumed that the bow represents a weapon (for it does state that "he went out conquering"), yet the bow may also be understood in terms of its shape, not its use, because the rider did not carry any arrows or projectiles of any kind to use with the bow. When we look at the symbolism of the shape of the bow, we remember the covenant between God and humanity following the great flood (Genesis 9:8 - 17) in which the shape of the bow (or rainbow) is the significant factor. In addition, this covenant states that "never again shall all flesh be cut off by waters of a flood, and never again shall there be a flood to destroy all the earth" (Genesis 9:11). We normally think of this covenant in terms of the second phrase of that scriptural verse that refers to a physical flood destroying the physical earth. We talk of this promise that a flood will never again destroy the earth, and, whenever we mention the flood, it is always in reference to this part of the promise. But there was also another section to that promise: "never again shall all flesh be cut off by waters of a flood." What do these words mean? All flesh shall never again be cut off from what?

When this part of the covenant is taken spiritually and placed in the context of Revelation, we can see the answer to these questions: God is stating that just as water is vital to our life, if we have too much water, we would drown; in the same manner it is also true that God's spiritual energy, while vital to our existence, can cause our spirit to drown beneath the ego's strength if we are given too much of this pure, creative energy and use it in a powerful, ego-enhancing manner. (As God notes in Genesis 8:21: "The imagination of man's heart is evil from his youth.") Is it not possible that the early members of humanity – those spoken about in the opening chapters of Genesis – were different from us in that they had access to almost unlimited amounts of God's creative energy – His spiritual substance? If so, this may help us to understand some of the differences between the people of the opening chapters of Genesis and the people of today. One consequence of having more of God's energy would be a longer physical life span, for God's energy is life itself. The heroes of ancient myths and legends (even of Genesis 6:1-4) may be stories of these individuals and what they could accomplish with abundant supplies of God's energy. In Genesis 6:3, God is recorded as saying "My Spirit shall not abide in Man forever, for he is flesh, but his days shall be a hundred and twenty years." God's decision to limit the amount of spiritual energy that we receive (or else allow what we receive to dissipate over time instead of always remaining strong and vital) and the manner in which we receive it was spiritually represented by the physical flood. The true significance of the covenant that God made with all humanity following the flood was that we would never again be allowed to drown ourselves in our selfish use of God's creative energy!

To return to Revelation, the bow carried by the rider of the white horse in 6:2 represents this covenant between God and humanity – that He supplies us with creative energy in small, manageable, portions. The **crown** given to the rider symbolizes the crowning glory of humanity: God's gift of our free will to make choices. Once the creative energy has entered through this spiritual center, then we have the power either to change it or to allow it to pass through all spiritual centers unchanged. In this instance, the crown was given to the rider, symbolizing that God's purpose for the energy is given the freedom to accomplish its goal without the ego's interference.

The rider goes forth conquering **and to conquer** is a way of recognizing that there is that struggle within us between our own desires and those of God. It is at the level of creativity that we struggle between accomplishing our own will, or allowing God's will to be expressed through us.

Chapter 6:3-4

Scripture

Revelation 6:3

And when he had opened the second seal, I heard the second beast say, Come and see.

Revelation 6:4

And there went out another horse that was red: and power was given to him that sat thereon to take peace from the earth, and that they should kill one another: and there was given unto him a great sword.

Symbolism/Meaning

another horse that was red - red usually signifies anger, fighting, or justice.

to take peace from the earth, ... kill one another - the activity of destroying.

Commentary

The **second living creature** repeats the command to **Come and see**, and the second **horse** and rider appear. This time, it is a **red** horse. Often the color red symbolizes anger or fighting. Before accepting certain symbolic explanations of certain colors to be absolute, we might find it useful to notice the words given by Edgar Cayce in one of his readings concerning the book of Revelation:

> ... let each in your study of these [colors], as in relation to the centers themselves consider the effect of the color

> upon thine own body as ye attempt to apply same by either concentration, dedication or meditating upon these. For as has been given, color is but vibration. Vibration is movement. Movement is activity of a positive and negative force. Is the activity of self as in relationship to these then positive? [3]

Since the opening of the seals is accomplished only when the Christ Spirit is in control of our lives, the color used in these images must signify some positive attribute. One suggestion has been that red also signifies justice. If the horse represents our suppressed or hidden experiences which are coming back to us under the evaluative power of the Christ Spirit, we must recognize that such experiences bring with them karmic influences. In our new state of awareness, we can see that present conditions and experiences are opportunities to express an attitude of being for others rather than for self. Thus the events present in our lives at any one time are designed to help us grow in spiritual awareness as we take our spiritual energy and transform it into physical manifestation of God. Justice, as symbolized by the color red, is the use of this spiritual energy force (the **horse**) as God intended it to be used.

The rider or the controlling influence of this chakra, was permitted **to take peace from the earth.** The **peace** which resides in the earth is a pseudo-peace: We have given value to those ideas, concepts, and principles that have made it easy for the ego to exist. In reality, much of what we value is based upon lies which our ego propagates simply to remain at the center of our lives. The lies have been constructed by the ego's careful screening of our memories, only allowing that which would support the ego's position to pass its guard. When this spiritual center is opened to allow the whole memory of experiences to pass from unconscious to conscious, it will remove the ego's pseudo-peace. When that peace is removed, there is warring between our long-held principles and the inconsistencies which the truth (in the form of our memories) has brought to light. The **great sword** of truth must "kill" the wrong ideas of the ego.

Chapter 6:5-6

Scripture

Revelation 6:5

And when he had opened the third seal, I heard the third beast say, Come and see. And I beheld, and lo a black horse; and he that sat on him had a pair of balances in his hand.

Revelation 6:6

And I heard a voice in the midst of the four beasts say, A measure of wheat for a penny, and three measures of barley for a penny; and see thou hurt not the oil and the wine.

Symbolism/Meaning

third beast - the one with the face of a man.

black horse - black signifies the unknown.

balances - to weigh something.

wheat - the bread of life offered to us.

barley - the intoxicant of being selfish (for yourself) or selfless (for others)

the oil and the wine - the end results of that which is grown (oil comes from the olives, wine from the grapes).

Commentary

When our karmic memories are presented to this spiritual center, we are confronted with those areas of our lives which deal with temptations and choices. The **black** color represents the unknown which we face whenever we must make a decision. As we attempt to "weigh" the pros and cons of our choices, there is always a sense of the unknown facing us: "What will happen if ...." The very act of making a choice is a way of shedding light upon whatever we have chosen, while leaving the other alternative(s) in the darkness.

In this context, the controlling influence of this chakra carries a pair of **balances**, and thus it is our memories that weigh and judge the choices we made for each of them. Did we allow them the opportunity to express their God-given energy for others? Or did we use them to satisfy our own desires?

In this particular vision, John also hears a voice coming from the midst of the four living creatures. This voice is a voice of warning: When we must make a decision, be sure to consider the cost. The Greek used in this section refers to a measure of wheat and three measures of barley (**choinix** or Χοινιξ). Whatever amount a measure may refer to, the important point to notice here is that just as wheat represents the, as yet, unformed flour from which life sustaining bread is made, the creative energy at this level is, as yet, unformed by our choices. We must decide whether to allow this energy to become the life-giving bread of God or to be formed into the pastries that fatten but offer no spiritual nourishment.

Our choice – our measure of what we will do with the creative energy given to us – will cost us in terms of our spiritual growth. By making the choice for others, we are making an investment in life. When we choose for self, we will have to pay for it both now as well as later.

The **three** measures of barley refer to the "weights placed upon the life force as it is tested by time, space, and patience – each as measures of understanding."[4] Once we make a choice of what to do with the creative energy, then it is tested as to whether or not our choice is compatible with God's purpose inherent within that energy. Will God's purpose be accomplished through the time and space of the physical world? Have we attempted to rush God's purpose (or our own purpose) and therefore have not had the patience to allow God to work through us?

This voice which speaks to John warns him that judgments are made of all of our choices. The most severe warning is that we do not attempt to change the God-given purpose for the creative energy he gives us. **See thou hurt not the oil and the wine** tells us not to pervert or adulterate the reason for the energy: the "spirit" behind it. Both oil and wine are the final results or "purpose" for which olives and grapes are grown. Why grow grapes and then try to make bread out of them? The inherent (or God given) purpose of a grape is to be changed into wine. The inherent purpose of God's creative energy which He gives to us is to be changed into some action which will benefit others. This is the importance of the warning to not harm the oil and the wine.

Chapter 6:7-8

Scripture

Revelation 6:7

And when he had opened the fourth seal, I heard the voice of the fourth beast say, Come and see.

Revelation 6:8

And I looked, and behold a pale horse: and his name that sat on him was Death, and Hell followed with him. And power was given unto them over the fourth part of the earth, to kill with sword, and with hunger, and with death, and with the beasts of the earth.

Symbolism/Meaning

fourth beast - the eagle.

pale horse - i.e., no color of its own.

name...was death - the ego, or that part of ourselves which is "for ourselves" (selfish) only, must die if we are to serve God. We must die to self and live for Christ.

Hell followed him - when we are selfish, then we are creating our own place in hell.

to kill with sword, ... hunger ... death ... beasts of the earth. - selfishness has the power to 'kill' in the same way that Adam and Eve ate of "...the tree of the knowledge of good and evil... for in the day that thou eatest thereof, thou shall surely die."

Commentary

To understand the symbolism and significance of this fourth spiritual center as all memories are opened to it, we need to again refer to Appendix C and the chart of the spiritual centers. The fourth spiritual center is a pivotal center, in that through this center we can be either for others or for self. Since God's energy passing through this fourth spiritual center is either allowed to accomplish God's will or to accomplish our will depending upon which of the other spiritual centers are an active influence, there is no color associated with this center. The horse has no color of its own – its color would depend upon the choices we make for others or for self. Thus our memories show us that our choices are of the utmost importance. We have a great power in our ability to choose good or evil, right or wrong, life or death. Moses, in his final discourse to the Hebrew people, emphasizes the importance of choosing life (Deuteronomy 30: 19-20):

> I call heaven and earth to witness against you this day, that I have set before you life and death, blessing and curse; therefore choose life, that you and your descendants may live, loving the LORD your God, obeying his voice, and cleaving to him.

When the Christ Spirit sits on the throne, the choices which were made by the ego must be evaluated, and, if necessary, new choices must be made as the old ones die. This is why the rider of this fourth horse is **death**. This is a symbolic way of saying that our ego's creations do not have a life of their own. We had given the ego power, and it, in turn, gave our life to our thoughts and actions. These types of selfish choices and actions must die when the Christ Spirit rules.

Because we had made such choices and created certain karmic conditions within our memories, we still must face the consequences of our actions. The saying **and Hell followed with him** is a symbolic way of saying that by our ego's choices, we had created our own karmic hell: We suffered the consequences of our choices. Now that all memories are open, we will understand why we face certain trials and tribulations. By seeing and understanding the relationships between our choices and the consequent results of those choices, many of our selfish desires lose their attraction for us. In effect, they are **dead**. Understanding the consequences of our actions kills our desire to act in certain ways! In this case, a **fourth** of the bodily (earthly) desires and actions are destroyed by the power of our new awareness (**sword**) and by simply not feeding our life to our past creations (**hunger**). The symbols of **hunger** and **beasts** stress the importance of understanding that selfish actions have a tendency to prey upon each other until they destroy themselves in the process – or they would destroy us if the Christ Spirit did not rule!

Chapter 6:9-11

Scripture

Revelation 6:9

> **And when he had opened the fifth seal, I saw under the altar the souls of them that were slain for the word of God, and for the testimony which they held:**

Revelation 6:10

> **And they cried with a loud voice, saying, How long, O Lord, holy and true, dost thou not judge and avenge our blood on them that dwell on the earth?**

Revelation 6:11

> **And white robes were given unto every one of them; and it was said unto them, that they should rest yet for a little season, until their fellow servants also and their brethren, that should be killed as they were, should be fulfilled.**

Symbolism/Meaning

altar - a place of sacrifice. Since the making of choices is being discussed in this section, the altar is therefore symbolic of a person's will.

under the altar the souls - these represent those selfless choices which we sacrificed in order to be selfish.

rest yet for a little season... - not until all lessons of the spirit are learned can the selfless forces and actions be given a just reward.

Commentary

The fifth spiritual center is primarily concerned with our will: the actual facility of choosing. When the previously unconscious memories are brought to light in this spiritual center, mention is made of an **altar**. Symbolically an altar implies a sacrifice. In this instance, the memories represent the desires and purposes of God (found in the creative energy He gives to us) that we sacrificed in order to accomplish our own will. The **souls of those who had been slain** refer to the very essences of the purposes God had intended for His creative energy. Since God's purpose contains the very life substance itself, these purposes are still alive, even though we have "slain" them by stripping them from their energy and imposed our own will upon that energy. By the power of free will, we have given our life to our desires and have forced the energy into a new mold as formed by us. We have sacrificed God's purposes for our own and have attempted to suppress God's intention for his creative energy.

But God's Word – His intentions – never return to Him unfulfilled. That is why they cry out for justice from their position beneath the altar of our will. They must fulfill their purpose, God's will, and in so doing, they reveal our will for what it is: selfish sinfulness.

The purposes of God within us then receive a **white robe**, a symbol of their purity, and they are asked to wait until they are joined by other purposes, which are to be sacrificed in the same manner. This request involves the exercise of patience on our part to wait for God to accomplish His purposes in His time rather than our own. It might also imply that God's purposes will not be totally fulfilled until all people have chosen to sacrifice their egos and allow God to rule their lives. As the next verse points out, it may take an earthquake before this will happen!

Chapter 6:12-17

Scripture

Revelation 6:12

And I beheld when he had opened the sixth seal, and, lo, there was a great earthquake; and the sun became black as sackcloth of hair, and the moon became as blood;

Revelation 6:13

And the stars of heaven fell unto the earth, even as a fig tree casteth her untimely figs, when she is shaken of a mighty wind.

Revelation 6:14

And the heaven departed as a scroll when it is rolled together; and every mountain and island were moved out of their places.

Revelation 6:15

And the kings of the earth, and the great men, and the rich men, and the chief captains, and the mighty men, and every bondman, and every free man, hid themselves in the dens and in the rocks of the mountains;

Revelation 6:16

And said to the mountains and rocks,

Fall on us, and hide us from the face of him that sitteth on the throne, and from the wrath of the Lamb:

Revelation 6:17

For the great day of his wrath is come; and who shall be able to stand?

Symbolism/Meaning

earthquake - a great disturbance.

sun became black - an uncertainty as to the central point of our lives ...

moon became as blood - The displacement of the ego.

heaven a- high state of consciousness within ourselves.

stars of heaven fell - the falling of major ideas and principles in our lives.

heaven departed as a scroll ...- since heaven symbolizes our consciousness, then this verse simply states that all we knew or believed before our 'earthquake' is, so to speak, rolled up and away and we must rebuild a new life upon the foundation which is left.

every mountain and island were moved - old concepts were uprooted and changed by a mighty wind, and the wind is a new spirit in which we now must live.

kings of the earth, and the great men...etc. - these symbolize the concepts, worldly desires, and all governing influences to which we give great power in our lives.

dens in the rocks of the mountains - our old ideas seek safety among the cracks of our consciousness or our thoughts where they believe they will be safe.

wrath - our ego and selfishness may look upon this as God's wrath, and it might disturb us greatly to find all that we once believed being shaken up and destroyed, but it is for a cleansing and a chance to grow in spirit and is thus good.

Commentary

By the time the sixth spiritual center confronts the release of all unconscious memories, it causes an upheaval which shakes up the whole life of the individual. This is the significance of the **earthquake** in verse 12: It is a shaking up of one's life so that the very foundations upon which life stood now falls apart. What could cause such a radical change? Remember, this description in Revelation concerns what we will experience when we allow the Christ Spirit to rule in the center of our lives. To accomplish this end, we must displace the ego from its position of prominence in our life. When this is done, we will be shocked at how much of our life was based upon the ego's deception. We will discover that many of our strongly held beliefs and concepts were rooted in the lies and deceptions of the ego. When the ego falls, these beliefs, concepts, and ideals must also fall. Our life will be turned upside down!

Also, when the ego, the previous "center" of our life, is gone, it will be darkened (**the sun became black**) and all aspects of personality (represented by the **moon** which reflects the light of the sun) that depended upon their strength from the ego will find their life's blood being drained away, because there is no source to sustain them (**The moon became as blood**).

The **stars** of verse 13 refer to the principles of guidance that we have followed in our life. Even though some principles are "good" principles, if they have been supported by a selfish ego, then they, too, will fall. For example, a principle of patriotism is often seen as a valid and valuable guide in many of our activities. Yet many people tend to equate the feeling of patriotism to that of loyalty to the governmental leaders. When governmental leaders are shown to be selfish and to have no real respect or concern for the citizens of that country, then any sense of patriotism based upon loyalty to those leaders would fall with those leaders. Each of us holds ideals or principles that, although once valid and useful, over time have become our idols, our objects of worship. These idols must fall when the Christ Spirit sits on the throne in the center of our lives. Even those principles and ideals that are not fully developed must fall as fruit falls before its season.

In this process of shaking up one's life, the old way of viewing reality would disappear (**the heaven departed**) and one would discover a new foundation for life which calls for new and different responses to the world around us. This is the significance of **every mountain and island were moved out of their places.**

In verse 15, the symbolism of the various types of people refers to the various principles, concepts, ideals, and ideas to which we have given power in our lives. Just as we abdicated our throne of decision-making power and allowed the ego to settle there, we have also constructed various personalities and habits of response and have pretended that these are our "true self." When the memories present themselves, in their entirety, to this spiritual center, and life is turned upside down and shaken, all of the old, false concepts and responses attempt to find a place of safety. They even request to be hidden by those principles and beliefs that remain standing, so that they will not be destroyed by the Christ Spirit, which now sits upon the throne.

The final statement and question of this chapter refer to the judgment and karma of one's actions and beliefs as all memories and choices must face the Christ Spirit.

Chapter Seven

What's In A Name?

We come now to an interlude. Six seals have been opened by the inner self led by the Christ Spirit. The seventh seal will not be opened until Chapter Eight. Between these two events, John is given a vision of the process of what happens to an individual who reaches this stage of soul development.

Since the chakras are the points of contact between the spirit and the physical, when the chakras are fully opened, then the quality and strength of the creative energy passing through them will be greater than that which passed through them during the ego's reign upon the throne. This improved quality and quantity of spiritual energy would then have an increased influence upon the physical. The individual would not only have pure thoughts and act wholly "for others," but there would also be bodily changes within the individual. The cells of the body would be affected by this greater influx of kundalini. As noted in the previous chapter, when God's Spirit within the physical was strong (as recorded in the early chapters of Genesis), the length of life was also long. The difference between those individuals and the one whom Revelation describes is that the developing ego was upon the throne in most of the early humans, while the Christ Spirit resides upon the throne in the Revelation vision.

God's decision, as exemplified by the flood in the physical, was to limit the amount of His life-giving Spirit until we choose to put the Christ Spirit at the center of our lives. Only then will God supply us endlessly with His Spirit (The supply of His Spirit is always infinite, but our access to it depends upon our choosing to put on the mind of Christ.). The effect of this life-giving Spirit upon the physical body is described in this chapter.

Chapter 7:1-3

Scripture

Revelation 7:1

And after these things I saw four angels standing on the four corners of the earth, holding the four winds of the earth, that the wind should not blow on the earth, nor on the sea, nor on any tree.

Revelation 7:2

And I saw another angel ascending from the east, having the seal of the living God: and he cried with a loud voice to the four angels, to whom it was given to hurt the earth and the sea,

Revelation 7:3

Saying, Hurt not the earth, neither the sea, nor the trees, till we have sealed the servants of our God in their foreheads."

Symbolism/Meaning

four - symbol of the earth or the physical.

angels - since there are four of them, they are the guardians of the worldly

attributes.

four winds - external, physical influences which affect Humanity.

four corners of the earth - the edges of bodily influence.

holding the four winds... wind should not blow - the angels keep the destructive physical influences from harming the body.

earth - physical attributes.

sea - life forces.

tree - growth processes.

ascending from the east- the arising or dawning of a new consciousness.

seal of the living God - God's approval.
sealed to protect or to make perfect...- to spiritualize.
foreheads - consciousness or memory.

Commentary

In verse one, John sees the controlling or guiding intelligences of the physical forces(**four angels**) preventing (**holding**) the external physical forces from influencing or harming anything that is going on within the body at this time. Some have seen the four angels as representing those in control of the "... four essences that go to make up the (a) physical body; (b) the emotional nature and all fluids; (c) the mentality; (d) the soul forces."[1] The importance of this verse is that everything that goes into the makeup of a human being – from the physical to the emotional, to the mental and the spiritual – everything is now free from external disturbance so that the inner process of growth at this stage may occur unhindered. The blowing **wind** represents any of those external influences which have been stopped by the four angels. By not allowing external influences to disturb the **earth** (the inner physical body or hereditary characteristics), or the **sea** (life forces), or **any tree** (growth processes), the individual is given a chance to develop as God intended.

In verses 2 and 3, John becomes aware of another **angel** who has the authority and power of the God who gives life (**seal of the living God**). This angel commands the other four angels to not let in any outside influence (**Hurt not**) until certain parts of the body are made perfect (**sealed**) in God's sight. The idea of sealing them on their **foreheads** refers back to Deuteronomy 6:1-9 where Moses instructed the Hebrew people to impress upon their whole being that "The Lord our God is one Lord; and you shall love the Lord your God with all your heart and with all your soul, and with all your might." This great commandment, also singled out by Jesus, was to be written on small pieces of parchment and placed in a small pouch which was then placed on the forehead between the eyes and tied there with leather thongs. This external action was symbolic of developing the sixth and seventh chakra to the level where this command brought one a new awareness of God. In the context of Revelation, it symbolizes the spiritualization of these parts of the body whose consciousness is already aware of God.

For many years, it was assumed by the Western world that consciousness resided within the brain. In this past century that assumption has been challenged by those who recognize consciousness as being independent of the brain or even the mind. The ethereal consciousness, they argue, does not equate with the physical brain, nor is there any part of the brain which can be said to be the "seat" of consciousness. For them, part of consciousness may be found even at the cellular level. This understanding of consciousness seems to be implied in this chapter of Revelation where the bodily cells (**servants of our God**), whose consciousness has arisen to the point of being aware of God's presence, are marked (**sealed**) or "spiritualized" in their consciousness (**foreheads**).

Chapter 7:4-8

Scripture

Revelation 7:4

And I heard the number of them which were sealed: and there were sealed an hundred and forty and four thousand of all the tribes of the children of Israel.

Revelation 7:5

Of the tribe of Juda were sealed twelve thousand. Of the tribe of Reuben were sealed twelve thousand. Of the tribe of Gad were sealed twelve thousand.

Revelation 7:6

Of the tribe of Aser were sealed twelve thousand. Of the tribe of Nepthalim were sealed twelve thousand. Of the tribe of Manasses were sealed twelve thousand.

Revelation 7:7

Of the tribe of Simeon were sealed twelve thousand. Of the tribe of Levi were sealed twelve thousand. Of the tribe of Issachar were sealed twelve thousand.

Revelation 7:8

Of the tribe of Zabulon were sealed twelve thousand. Of the tribe of Joseph were sealed twelve thousand. Of the tribe of Benjamin were sealed twelve thousand.

Symbolism/Meaning

a hundred and forty-four thousand - a number signifying completion, wholeness.

Israel - those who seek or strive with God.

Juda - Praise.

Reuben - Behold, A Son.

Gad - good fortune or a crowd.

Asher - straightforward, on the level, happiness.

Nepthalim - wrestled with God.

Manasses - Who causes to forget.

Simeon - God has heard.

Levi - to join or to unite.

Issachar - He will bring a reward, given me my hire.

Zabulon - Dwelling, habitation.

Joseph - He will give, He will increase

Benjamin - Son of the right hand.

Commentary

The number **a hundred and forty-four thousand** is a number which represents both fullness and perfection. Since it is applied to the physical body, it represents those parts or cells of the human body which, through their willingness to accept the Christ Spirit, have been spiritualized or brought to a consciousness of fully loving God (the first Commandment) and of being for others (the second Commandment).

The significance of those sealed being **of all the tribes of the children of Israel** may lie in the meaning of each name. First, the meaning of the word "Israel" is "one who strives with God" – it involves a struggle or a seeking to know God.[2] Thus the **children of Israel** collectively are all of those who are seekers of the consciousness of being companions with God.

Each of the twelve tribes has significance in their names also. When the names are put together in the order presented, a message may seem to appear:

> Praise God! Behold, a Son [brings] good fortune to all! [We] straightforwardly wrestle with [the] God who causes [us] to forget, [and] the God who hears. [The God who] unites, will give [us] our reward: [We shall] dwell [with Him and] He will give the son of His right hand!

Notice that one of the original sons of Jacob/Israel, Dan, is not included in this list. Instead, one of the sons of Joseph (a grandson to Jacob/Israel), Manasseh, is listed in Dan's place. One conjecture of why this was done involves the meaning of "Dan": "God has judged me." When humanity, in its fallen state, was judged, the result was death. Here, with this new consciousness of humanity's original estate restored, there is no place for death.[3]

The number of tribes (**twelve**) from which the spiritualized cells come also has significance: Since twelve represents perfection or completeness in regard to ruling (see appendix B), the twelve tribes would allude to twelve divisions of the body that rule over its (the body's) functions. Although John is not told exactly what these twelve functional divisions may be, one conception of such a division of the body's functions may be found in Appendix E. What is important to the student of Revelation is the assurance that the whole physical body is affected by the sealing of the 144,000.

Chapter 7:9-17

Scripture

Revelation 7:9

After this I beheld, and, lo, a great multitude, which no man could number, of all nations, and kindreds, and people, and tongues, stood before the throne, and before the Lamb, clothed with white robes, and palms in their hands;

Revelation 7:10

And cried with a loud voice, saying, Salvation to our God which sitteth upon the throne, and unto the Lamb.

Revelation 7:11

And all the angels stood round about the throne, and about the elders and the four beasts, and fell before the throne on their faces, and worshipped God,

Revelation 7:12

Saying, Amen: Blessing, and glory, and wisdom, and thanksgiving, and honour, and power, and might, be unto our God for ever and ever. Amen.

Revelation 7:13

And one of the elders answered, saying unto me, What are these which are arrayed in white robes? and whence came they?

Revelation 7:14

And I said unto him, Sir, thou knowest. And he said to me, These are they which came out of great tribulation, and have washed their robes, and made them white in the blood of the Lamb.

Revelation 7:15

Therefore are they before the throne of God, and serve him day and night in his temple: and he that sitteth on the throne shall dwell among them.

Revelation 7:16

shall hunger no more, neither thirst any more; neither shall the sun light on them, nor any heat

Revelation 7:17

> **For the Lamb which is in the midst of the throne shall feed them, and shall lead them unto living fountains of waters: and God shall wipe away all tears from their eyes.**

Symbolism/Meaning

a great multitude - the remaining physical/ bodily cells.

white robes - purified or spiritualized.

palms - symbols of praise.

one of the elders - the ability to sense the worlds (physical and spiritual) around us. Since all the memories are being released, there is an abundance of new sensations.

great tribulation - acceptance of our own creations and their karmic consequences.

wipe away all tears from their eyes - we will be able to clearly see the consequences of our actions.

Commentary

The 144,000 sealed or spiritualized cells of the body will serve as the catalyst for the whole body **(great multitude)** to begin the process of acknowledging the Christ Spirit on the throne. Verses 11 and 12, by encompassing all which has been spoken of up to this point (**angels ... elders ... four beasts**), emphasize that the whole of the lower centers (the chakras which have to do with the physical, emotional, and spiritual aspects of the body) recognize the truth of their new consciousness.

Remembering that the elders represent pathways by which we sense the physical and spiritual worlds, this new influx of information prompts one of the elders to ask the question **What are these ...?**. John, although in the spirit, has not yet reached the stage where the lower centers acknowledge the Christ Spirit and dedicate themselves to its service. Therefore, John returns the question to the one who asked it. The elder is able to answer that the multitude consists of those parts of the physical body which have been cleansed of their karmic memories (**washed their robes**) through the process of experiencing and facing all that we have created while the ego was in control (**great tribulation**).

As a result of facing up to our own creations and being cleansed, the lower centers are able to dedicate themselves to the process of allowing God's energy to be used for His purposes, rather than for those of the ego (7:15). In this process, physical desires are eliminated (v. 16) because God's energy will supply all that is needed (7:17).

Chapter Eight

The First Four Trumpets

With Chapter 8 we begin to experience the first spiral of sevens: the opening of the seventh seal leads to the sounding of the seven trumpets. Since the ancient peoples looked at reality as being cyclic in nature, we must emphasize that the seventh (or final) stage in any cycle is qualitatively different from the previous six, since it both introduces something new as well as repeats the old. In Revelation, the sounding of the seven trumpets is a restatement of what happens as all seven chakras are opened under the Christ Spirit. But it views the occurrence from a different point of view – that of the spiritual as it looks at the pain associated with the physical during a time of internal struggle between the spirit and the flesh.

The events described in the second cycle of seven do not necessarily happen in sequence after the first cycle. This is a process, and many events are happening simultaneously. It is difficult for us with a linearly based consciousness to grasp this cyclic mentality. We attempt to stretch and straighten out the spiral and to impose linearity upon that which is not linear. Even in my attempts to write this book, each time as I approached this chapter, I would get stuck: How did this return to the "sevens" fit in? One night I remarked to my wife, "I sure hope I can get through this Chapter 8. I've got some ideas and insights about Chapters 9 and 10, but I can't seem to get beyond Chapter 7!" To this, my wife, in a matter-of-fact way, replied, "Who says you have to write Chapter 8 first? Why not go ahead and finish chapter nine and then come back to eight?" Even though I was intellectually entertaining the cyclic concept, I was unable to remove myself from the linear mode of behavior. It took a remark from an outside source, my wife, before I was able to let the spiral return to its intended shape.

In addition, like the first verse of Chapter 8 (**And when he had opened the seventh seal, there was silence in heaven about the space of half an hour.**), I realized that there must be a time of reflection – of a cessation of struggle – before advancing further up the spiral. So, in the spirit of the message itself, I set my writing aside and became involved in the process of living what I had learned. In this process of integration, I realized that the writing of this book had reached a new beginning also. While continuing to examine Revelation as before, with emphasis upon its symbolism and how that reflects one's growth in consciousness, a new element must emerge to be a part of this commentary: the personal element. If Revelation is concerned with the personal struggles of each individual seeker as he or she develops greater soul awareness, then the symbolism of Revelation must relate to the everyday experience of you, the reader. I cannot write your story, for I am not you. Yet, I can share more of my personal story with you, in hope that you can see some of yourself in my story, and, therefore, come to understand yourself and how Revelation is a story for and about you!

Chapter 8:1-5

Scripture

Revelation 8:1

And when he had opened the seventh seal, there was silence in heaven about the space of half an hour.

Revelation 8:2

And I saw the seven angels which stood before God; and to them were given seven trumpets.

Revelation 8:3

And another angel came and stood at the altar, having a golden censer; and there was given unto him much incense, that he should offer it with the prayers of all saints upon the golden altar which was before the throne.

Revelation 8:4

And the smoke of the incense, which came with the prayers of the saints, ascended up before God out of the angel's hand.

Revelation 8:5

And the angel took the censer, and filled it with fire of the altar, and cast it into the earth: and there were voices, and thunderings, and lightnings, and an earthquake.

Symbolism/Meaning

silence - refers to a time of meditation – a state of consciousness, a time of "centering down" (prayer or meditation) before the sounding of the trumpets.

angels - the symbol of guidance within our lives.

trumpets - symbols of vibration - messages to the body - resonating with the spiritual source.

another angel - (not identified) - represents the good which we do.

golden censer - the pure container of who we are – the true self.

incense - symbolizes what we have done in our lives.

smoke - the purpose behind our actions are presented to God.

fire - that which purifies.

Cast it unto the earth - given back to the earthly forces to be re-formed into selfless actions

voices, and thunderings and lightnings, and an earthquake - when we become a new person in Christ, we still must change our old habits, concepts and attitudes. Often this is difficult and it pains us to change.

Commentary

As the seventh seal is opened, there is **silence.** What does this silence signify? To the ancient eastern mind-set, silence would mean a time of preparation, of quieting the mind and emotions in order to descend further into a new or different consciousness. In today's modern world, silence often means the absence of irritating noise, but the presence of soothing or comforting noise.[1] Here, it points to the preparation time prior to the deeper consciousness of one's journey back to God.

After this time is finished, John's vision returned again to the seven angels (the seven spiritual centers). The angels are given **seven trumpets**. A **trumpet** is an instrument that makes sound through the activity of vibration. It was used for music, but also to herald an announcement or a call to praise, prayer, or worship. In this context the sounding of the trumpets will herald the announcements of the struggles within the self.

Yet, before the struggles begin, an eighth angel appears, carrying the spiritual record of the individual's life (**golden censer**) and mixes much **incense** with the **prayers of all the saints upon the golden altar which was before the throne**. The unselfish actions, thoughts, and intentions of an individual are on the same level of purity as the already spiritualized aspects of the individual, and they are as pleasing to God as the prayers of the saints. Some of the energy which God gives to an individual has already been allowed to express God's intention of being for others. We know this to be true when we say that there is good within every person. We are all a mixture of the pure and the selfish: the amount of selfishness varies from one moment to another within any individual, as well as varies from one individual to another. That which is pleasing to God is presented to Him as the smoke rises with the prayers of the saints. That which is not pleasing to God – the selfish action of the ego – stays in the censer to be recycled. **Fire of the altar** is placed within the self now undergoing cleansing. **Fire** is a purifying agent which will burn away the selfishness. Since the fire comes from the **altar**, this fire is sometimes described as the Holy Fire of God – that which gives great pain as it purifies for what is coming. (Even John the Baptist spoke of being baptized with fire.) It is important to note that all the good which the individual soul had accomplished now becomes a force (**angel**) within the physical individual to act as leaven for the remaining physical forces. This means that the individual who, through meditation and attunement, is able to raise the kundalini through the seven chakras and to open all memories and experiences to evaluation, also prepares the chakras to act as the agents of total bodily purification. Since the seven chakras are associated with various endocrine glands within the body, it is through the actions of these glands that we experience purification. Their release of hormones brings about bodily disturbances and changes which the remainder of Revelation speaks about.[2]

For this purpose, the actions and purposes of our lives which have not been pure, are thrown back to the **earth** (body), causing us to hear the sound of judgment (**thunderings**) through the action of the conscience (**voices**), as well as experience new insights (**lightnings**) while the previous, selfish foundation of our life is completely disrupted (**earthquake**). To illustrate the use of this symbolism in my own life, one of the most far reaching disturbances I ever experienced involved my memory of a certain event within my past. At a class reunion, I was reliving a long past memorable event with some of the other participants in that event when I was politely, but firmly corrected by the others as to the "actual" course of events. I "remembered" the event as happening in a certain manner, even to the extent of being absolutely sure it happened that way. Yet, according to the other participants, I was incorrect! What disturbed me was the realization that I could be absolutely sure and yet still be wrong. My self-esteem was greatly lowered for a time as I lost my self-assurance. To me, this was more devastating than any physical earthquake. Yet the insight this presented to me concerning the deceptive memory selection of the ego has proved to be worth much more than the feeling of devastation and loss I experienced. Because of this incident, I was then able to recognize that such a mechanism as the ego exists within my self and to allow my true self to exert itself as I started to examine this phenomenon in more detail.

Chapter 8:6-13

Scripture

Revelation 8:6

And the seven angels which had the seven trumpets prepared themselves to sound.

Revelation 8:7

The first angel sounded, and there followed hail and fire mingled with blood, and they were cast upon the earth: and the third part of trees was burnt up, and all green grass was burnt up.

Revelation 8:8

And the second angel sounded, and as it were a great mountain burning with fire was cast into the sea: and the third part of the sea became blood;

Revelation 8:9

And the third part of the creatures which were in the sea, and had life, died; and the third part of the ships were destroyed.

Revelation 8:10

And the third angel sounded, and there fell a great star from heaven, burning as it were a lamp, and it fell upon the third part of the rivers, and upon the fountains of waters.

Revelation 8:11

And the name of the star is called Wormwood: and the third part of the waters became wormwood; and many men died of the waters, because they were made bitter.

Revelation 8:12

> **And the fourth angel sounded, and the third part of the sun was smitten, and the third part of the moon, and the third part of the stars; so as the third part of them was darkened, and the day shone not for a third part of it, and the night likewise.**

Revelation 8:13

> **And I beheld, and heard an angel flying through the midst of heaven, saying with a loud voice, Woe, woe, woe, to the inhabiters of the earth by reason of the other voices of the trumpet of the three angels, which are yet to sound!**

Symbolism/Meaning

Prepared themselves to sound - the acceptance, by the angels, of their duties of influencing us through their contact between the spiritual and physical.

hail - the crystallization of our intents, desires and purposes.

fire - the purifying force. 'all must be tried as by fire.'

mingled with blood - blood symbolizes the life force

third part of the trees was burnt up - the developed and "grown up" ideas and creations of the ego.

all green grass was burnt up - surface thoughts, appearances, concepts.

great mountain - symbolizes forces in our lives that we have to "climb" or get over.

cast into the sea - the conflicting purposes are cast into the 'sea' of unconsciousness.

creatures which were in the sea...died - all that which was given life by the ego.

ships - emotions.

great star - guiding principles

rivers and ... fountains of water - pathways of the life principle.

wormwood - bitterness.

sun - ego.

moon - personality.

stars -the guiding influences, i.e., our beliefs and ideas.

This last verse (vs. 13) symbolizes the importance of what is to come in the next chapter. The **angel** – or messenger from God – heard within the consciousness (**midst of heaven**) exclaiming that when the last three trumpets are sounded, it will cause great disturbances to our earthly, inner nature.

Commentary

The endocrine system now prepares the whole body for spiritualization. The blowing of the **trumpets** is symbolic of this purification process which is accomplished, in part, through the release of hormones and chemicals into the body. The acceptance by the chakras of their part in the purification process is shown in verse six where the angels who had the trumpets prepared to blow them.

The **first angel**, representing the first chakra at the gonad level, begins the purification process. As he "sounds his **trumpet**" (releases hormones within the body), we are presented with images which infer great destruction: **hail and fire, mingled with blood, and they were cast upon the earth**. The intent of this image is not to infer destruction, but to describe the means of purification. **Hail** is simply solid (crystallized) water, and water is symbolic of the Spirit. **Fire**, as noted early, is an agent of purification, and **blood** symbolizes life. Since these three come from the spiritual realm and fall **upon the earth**, they tell us that the new, crystallized, spiritual purposes of the self directed by the Christ Spirit will infuse the body with new life. In addition, since this chakra acts as a motor to raise the spiritual energy through the other chakras, this is seen as a new source of power for this chakra – a spiritual source rather than having to rely upon the force of the kundalini within the body itself.

As this spiritual energy is diffused into the body, it has certain effects: **a third part of trees ... and all green grass was burnt up**. These symbolize the destruction of those aspects of the self that the ego had created. The **trees** represent the fruit of the ego's labor, while the **green grass** symbolizes the surface thoughts or concerns of the ego. When this first chakra is cleansed, priorities will begin to change as we become conscious of our spiritual nature. This change of priorities will not come easily, since it is as if by fire that the old desires will be burned out of us. It may involve a change of occupation, friends, and/or living styles. People closest to you may not understand why you are changing – and you may not be fully aware of the reason yourself. The desires of the ego are not the same as the desires of the self whose center is the Christ Spirit, and until you are fully aware of who sits upon the throne of your life, the struggle between the two will be great!

When the **second angel** sounds his trumpet, the struggle continues as worldly thoughts, concepts, and ideas which were hindering development (**as it were a great mountain** ... that is, difficult to climb over) are thrown back into the **sea** to be reformed. Again, these are the struggles between the old physical desire of the ego and the newly instituted spiritual desires of the higher self. As a result of this struggle, part of the unconscious or unformed bodily energies (**sea**) are turned back into that which can bring life to the body (**a third part of the sea became blood**). This increase in potential vitality for the body was accompanied by the destruction of selfish thoughts and ideas (**creatures**) that the ego had endowed with our life, as well as the destruction of the emotions (**ships**) that ride the waves of our unconscious.

This struggle within one's self is easily recognized by those individuals who have made conscious decisions to reorganize their life priorities. Objects or goals that once were desirable, no longer hold any appeal. As we lose interest in these previously desired outcomes (whether a physical object, or a temporary pleasure, or a certain status in life), our emotional attachment to them also grows less. In so doing, we discover that we have renewed energy to redirect toward our new goals and desires.

In verses 10 and 11, as the third trumpet is blown, spiritual principles (**a great star**) burn (**urning as it were a lamp**) away the pathways (**rivers**) used by the ego to distribute our life to its creations. Since our life force was used to create the physical desires, thoughts, and emotions, it will be very bitter (**Wormwood**) to see them destroyed. It will be as if a part of us is being destroyed! In a sense, this will be true: The physical must be relinquished before it can be spiritualized. It is the desire to cling to the physical that makes this process so terrifying and difficult.

As these chakras are cleansed and fully opened, there are definite physical changes within the individual. Even a small change of the body's habits will bring about some physical change (as any former smoker will attest to!). Since the chakras are associated with the endocrine glands, the dumping of their chemicals and hormones into the bloodstream would possibly cause abrupt and seemingly harmful conditions within the body. Yet, just as I, when cleaning a room in my house, must first "mess it up in order to clean it up," so too must the body be "messed up" in order to be thoroughly cleansed.

In this cleansing process, the **fourth angel** sounds his **trumpet**, and one-third of the **sun**, the **moon**, and the **stars** are darkened. The **sun** and the **moon** correspond to the ego and its reflections. The personality – that which we project outwardly for others to see – is a reflection of the ego. Since the personality is based upon our selfish desires as well as upon our beliefs and guiding principles (**stars**), one third of these will be destroyed. According to Edgar Cayce, at this stage of cleansing, when so many of the pathways of our life force as well as various aspects of our "old self" are destroyed (since they were used by the ego for its purposes), there is a possibility for a partial loss of consciousness within the individual (**the day shone not for a third part of it**). This loss of consciousness even extends to a loss of the unconscious mind (**and the night likewise**).

This physical effect may come about when we have placed too much emphasis upon the physical and the comforts of life, and therefore a part of us (the ego) fights to preserve its comfort level. The struggle as the ego attempts to hold on to what it had will intensify in the following chapter of Revelation. At this point, however, the battle is for the physical body and its "preservation." The ego wishes to preserve it for the eventual goal of growing old and dying, while the Christ Spirit wishes to preserve the body by spiritualizing it through death and presenting it to God.

The ego, in its struggles, is warned (in verse 13) not to hold on to the physical desires and influences of the lower four chakras. There are still three chakras to be cleansed: the upper three chakras which are connected with the higher principles of life. If a person is clinging to the physical desires when the higher chakras are being cleansed, then the problems will be multiplied!

Synopsis

The first four chakras, referred to as the lower chakras (lower, not in the sense of a lesser importance or status, but lower in terms of physical placement in the body), are concerned with our ideas, temperaments, and created concepts dealing with the physical. As these chakras are cleansed, we discover much of our own beliefs, habits, and ideas that must be done away with if we are to reach the goal of becoming Christ-like in all respects. Because the ego has placed value upon all that it has done in addition to all that it has created, it becomes difficult for the ego to let go of its creations. The internal struggles, between the true self trying to become more Christ-like and the selfish ego, cause various physical manifestations (e.g., intense surges of emotions, loss of consciousness, etc.) as we seek to know God.

In scripture, some of the physical manifestations of an internal struggle are expressed in the description of Jesus as he prayed in the garden of Gethsemane: "And being in agony, he prayed more earnestly; and his sweat became like great drops of blood falling down upon the ground" (Luke 22:44). The bursting of the capillaries in the forehead is a rare but recognized result of extreme and intense stress. As Jesus was struggling in the final battle between the ego and the higher self, between the ego's desire for physical continuity and the Christ Spirit's desire for spiritualization of the physical (through death and subsequent resurrection of the spiritualized physical), the internal struggle was great, indeed.

Revelation, in describing the internal process of Jesus' struggle to become the Christ, is also describing our struggle. Yet we have the advantage over Jesus in that we know it can be done. Jesus blazed the trail for us and opened the door, yet we must still make the effort to go through that door. To have a breakthrough in consciousness as to our true nature, and then to change our whole life based upon that new awareness of ourselves, is our goal as well as our struggle. Revelation, in Chapter 8, has described part of that struggle, and there is much more to come!

Chapter Nine

Woe! Woe!

In Chapter 9 the description of the physical experiences inherent in the process of spiritualization continues in its graphic, symbolic manner. Remembering that God says, "The words I say ... will not return to me empty,"[1] we recognize, that in the process of spiritualization and cleansing, the spiritual energy we have received (God's Word) and subsequently adulterated by molding it to fit our own wills must be recycled through the mill of our lives. This is simply what we call karma, the facing of our own inadequacies until a change is made. That change involves allowing God's intentions for the spiritual energy to be expressed within our own physical lives.

At this point, our ego, that part of us which we have created and given power to be a substitute for our true Self (in a way, the ego can be looked upon as a "self-created self"), comes into conflict with the spiritualization process, because it is the ego's creations which have used the adulterated spiritual energy.

In order to recycle God's energy, the creations of the ego must first be destroyed by the purifying fire, and then the spiritual energy may be released for reprocessing. In Chapter 8 we read of this recycling process as it applied to the first four chakras, while in Chapter 9 we turn to the upper chakras and discover what happens to the areas of the emotions and the mind.[2]

This inner struggle between the ego and the spirit may also be characterized as a struggle between the spirit and the flesh. Being human, we are the only creatures on the earth which possess both a spiritual awareness as well as a physical awareness. We are both spirit and flesh. The physical cannot contain all the spirit, and neither can the eternal spirit embrace the temporal physical. We must struggle with these incompatible extremes until something new emerges. The spiritualization of the physical is the result of this struggle as evidenced by the resurrection and "spiritual body"[3] of Jesus. This is also our goal, and the book of Revelation describes some of the steps toward that goal.

Chapter 9:1-6

Scripture

Revelation 9:1

> **And the fifth angel sounded, and I saw a star fall from heaven unto the earth: and to him was given the key of the bottomless pit.**

Revelation 9:2

> **And he opened the bottomless pit; and there arose a smoke out of the pit, as the smoke of a great furnace; and the sun and the air were darkened by reason of the smoke of the pit.**

Revelation 9:3

> **And there came out of the smoke locusts upon the earth: and unto them was given power, as the scorpions of the earth have power.**

Revelation 9:4

> **And it was commanded them that they should not hurt the grass of the earth, neither any green thing, neither any tree; but only those men which have not the seal of God in their foreheads.**

Revelation 9:5

> **And to them it was given that they should not kill them, but that they should be tormented five months: and their torment was as the torment of a scorpion, when he striketh a man.**

Revelation 9:6

> **And in those days shall men seek death, and shall not find it; and shall desire to die, and death shall flee from them.**

Symbolism/Meaning

star - an angel, force or influence.

heaven - a state of awareness, consciousness.

key - that which opens or unlocks.

bottomless pit - our earthly, physical nature.

smoke - being of the passions, or desires of the lower self.

furnace - where purification takes place (reforming of ideas or energy).

sun - the ego.

air - what is breathed to sustain life, therefore the ego's life .

locusts - that which consumes.

scorpions - that which can sting or hurt.

seal of God - Christ Spirit.

tormented - to influence in an undesired manner.

five months - a time which refers to the things of the physical which are touched by God.

Commentary

In verse one, the fifth chakra (**fifth angel**), concerned with the will (see Appendix C), is being cleansed/opened. At this time, a life-guiding principle (**star**) enters into the physical realm (**earth**). This principle (equated with an **angel**) concerns our awareness, since it comes from **heaven**. With these characteristics, some have understood this to represent the will itself.[4] At this point, the Christ-centered self allows (**opened**) the body to feel the release of pent-up, repressed bodily lusts and desires (**bottomless pit**) as they are being destroyed and eliminated through the **furnace** of purification. Just like a reformed drug addict who must first suffer through withdrawal symptoms, the initial result of this karmic cleansing is painful. Anything which is new and growing through the process of spiritualization (**the grass of the earth...any green thing ... any tree**) is not harmed. Only the parts of the body that have not yet received cleansing (**which have not the seal of God**) are touched in this cleansing, spiritualization process. **Locusts** are used to symbolize the all consuming nature of this karmic influence, as it is painful but does not kill us. The image of **five months** is used to represent God's grace behind this painful situation (see Appendix B concerning numerology).

There are many times in our own lives when we are overwhelmed with grief or pressures, and we may wonder why so many seemingly "bad things" are happening to us. This process of spiritualization will be similar to such experiences, yet it will be tempered with the awareness of "carrying our cross," knowing that the pain is for our good rather than our detriment. As the only things that will be harmed will be our selfish desires and tendencies, it is to be a purging rather than a complete destruction of the old self. Of course, our old beliefs, desires, and selfishness will not wish to be purged, and they will fight to keep what life they have. This is the struggle which will intensify in later chapters as the ego itself enters the battle.

Chapter 9:7-12

Scripture

Revelation 9:7

> **And the shapes of the locusts were like unto horses prepared unto battle; and on their heads were as it were crowns like gold, and their faces were as the faces of men.**

Revelation 9:8

> **And they had hair as the hair of women, and their teeth were as the teeth of lions.**

Revelation 9:9

> **And they had breastplates, as it were breastplates of iron; and the sound of their wings was as the sound of chariots of many horses running to battle.**

Revelation 9:10

> **And they had tails like unto scorpions, and there were stings in their tails: and their power was to hurt men five months.**

Revelation 9:11

And they had a king over them, which is the angel of the bottomless pit, whose name in the Hebrew tongue is Abaddon, but in the Greek tongue hath his name Apollyon.

Revelation 9:12

One woe is past; and, behold, there come two woes more hereafter.

Symbolism/Meaning

horses prepared unto battle - symbolizes the struggle for power.

crowns like gold - the pseudo mastery or power of our desires.

faces of men - the true nature of our ideas ... i.e., they come not from God, but from ourselves, so they are in our image.

hair of women - an outward manifestation of inner thoughts.

teeth of lions - words which destroy.

breastplates of iron - a symbol of protection.

stings in their tails...their power - their power lay in the after effects.

King ... Abaddon ... Apollyon - means "destroyer"... the selfish side of the will (e.g., lust).

Commentary

Lust is one of the deadly sins. These verses give a more detailed description of the selfish, lustful desires (locusts) controlled by the ego's self-will, and they graphically describe why lust deserves such a reputation.

Lust is not simply a desire: It is a craving – an all consuming power (**horses**) which will do battle against anything which gets in its way. Since it attempts to control and to have mastery over the individual's thoughts and actions, John's vision pictures it as wearing what looks like a **crowns like gold**. It is not real gold, but it has the appearance of gold. This shows that the control which lust exercises over an individual is not the will of the inner self, but rather is the pseudo will of the ego. Lust is the deep desire for something that does not belong to us. In fact, the word in the New Testament that is often translated as lust (επιθυμεω) means "desire." Since the ego is of the physical world, it desires objects and experiences of that world. The face of the **locusts**, being those of **faces of men**, reveals the true nature of lust: It is an ego-created desire and is therefore created in the image of the physical and not the spiritual. Just as many people use fashion and hair styles to pretend they are something different from their true nature, lust attempts to pretend it is not based upon selfishness, even though its words (**teeth of lions**) give it away as it destroys the self. We may attempt to wrestle control from lust; nevertheless, in the long run, we do not succeed. The persistence of lust is shown in John's vision by the **breastplates of iron** that cover the **locusts**. These scales of iron protect the ego's lusts from outside attacks.

Verse 10 reiterates verses three and five as it explains that the power of lust is in what remains behind (**tails**) after lust achieves its objective. The **sting** of lust is in the guilt and shame which tears down an individual's self-worth. As the higher self allows karmic conditions to emerge during the process of spiritualization, the guilt and shame surfaces but is tempered by the presence of God's grace, which is symbolized by the number five (**five months**). Five is one half of ten, the number of completion in numerology. Therefore, this number symbolizes that the experience of guilt and shame, the karmic results of lust, is allotted just enough time to purge us of lust's attractiveness. The nature of lust is described in verse 11 by giving its **king** the name of **Abaddon** or **Apollyon,** which means "destroyer." Lust destroys the individual's selfworth.

From these verses, we learn that the process of cleansing the chakras will bring forward any latent desires (lusts) which have lain hidden in the deep **bottomless pit** of our physical desires. Although we will experience pain from this cleansing, the pain will not completely destroy us, because of the nature of the cleansing. The spiritual energy that we adulterated by imbuing physical objects with lustful desires is recycled for purposes useful to the higher self when our lusts are purged and physical objects are imbued with spiritual desires.

The final verse in this section informs us that the **first woe,** the painful experience of purging and spiritualization, is now complete, but there are still two more experiences to come.

Chapter 9:13-21

Scripture

Revelation 9:13

And the sixth angel sounded, and I heard a voice from the four horns of the golden altar which is before God,

Revelation 9:14

Saying to the sixth angel which had the trumpet, Loose the four angels which are bound in the great river Euphrates.

Revelation 9:15

And the four angels were loosed, which were prepared for an hour, and a day, and a month, and a year, for to slay the third part of men.

Revelation 9:16

the number of the army of the horsemen were two hundred thousand thousand: and I heard the number of them.

Revelation 9:17

And thus I saw the horses in the vision, and them that sat on them, having breastplates of fire, and of jacinth, and brimstone: and the heads of the horses were as the heads of lions; and out of their mouths issued fire and smoke and brimstone.

Revelation 9:18

By these three was the third part of men killed, by the fire, and by the smoke, and by the brimstone, which issued out of their mouths.

Revelation 9:19

For their power is in their mouth, and in their tails: for their tails were like unto serpents, and had heads, and with them they do hurt.

Revelation 9:20

And the rest of the men which were not killed by these plagues yet repented not of the works of their hands, that they should not

worship devils, and idols of gold, and silver, and brass, and stone, and of wood: which neither can see, nor hear, nor walk:

Revelation 9:21

Neither repented they of their murders, nor of their sorceries, nor of their fornication, nor of their thefts.

Symbolism/Meaning

four horns- the four corners of the altar curve upward like ram's horns.

golden altar - gold usually refers to the spiritual, while the altar is the place where sacrifice of self must be made.

river Euphrates - symbolic of a new beginning. Tradition has the Garden of Eden (our beginnings) located near the Euphrates and Tigress Rivers.

four angels - the controlling forces of the emotional, physical, mental, and spiritual.

prepared for an hour, and a day, and a month, and a year - i.e., for this moment of cleansing.

slay the third part of men - to destroy our selfish desires.

two hundred thousand thousand - the strength of force (see commentary).

horses - message bringers, the vehicle by which messages come to us.

them that sat on them - the messages themselves.

breastplates of fire, and of jacinth, and brimstone - all elements of fire ... the messages are for the purpose of purifying.

the heads of lions - forceful or powerful intelligences or thought

fire...smoke and brimstone, which issued out of their mouths - out of the expressions (mouths) of the message bringers (horses) come justice (fire) and transforming change (smoke and brimstone).

power ... is in their mouths, and in their tails.- intentions (mouths) and results (tails).

Commentary

Beginning with verse 13, the sixth angel blows his trumpet. This is the cleansing of the sixth chakra which deals with the maturity of spirit (Appendix C). At this time, the sixth angel is directed by a voice coming from the **four horns of the golden altar which is before God**. An **altar** is a place of sacrifice. It is a **golden** altar to represent its spiritual nature. Even though horns are also a symbol of power and strength, the horns of an altar are the four upturned corners of the altar itself. The number four relates to humankind, so the horns of the altar symbolize the four major divisions of the human being (physical, emotional, mental, and spiritual) and their relationship to each other in the presence of God. The **voice** coming from these four horns symbolizes a commanding voice of great power representing the aspects of the self which have already experienced the sacrifice of the ego's selfishness. This **voice** (that which is already under the command of the Christ Spirit) commands the sixth angel to **loose the four angels which are bound at the great river Euphrates**. Mention of the Euphrates River is always found in references to mankind's beginnings (e.g., Gen. 1:14) Here it represents a boundary point for a new beginning within the spiritualized individual.

The **four angels**, which have been bound by this river of new beginnings, are released. These angels, each symbolizing one aspect (physical, emotional, mental, or spiritual) of the cleansed human being, have waited (**were prepared ...**) for this moment to begin their job: destroying a portion of the selfish tendencies of our life (**... to slay the third part of men**). They are powerful forces as noted by the number of troops: A zero behind a number (e.g., 10) strengthens the number significantly. The more zeros, the stronger the number. Thus, **10,000** is an extremely strong number one. Also, to square such a number implies a strengthening of meaning. And if this were not enough, multiplying by two gives it double strength (**two hundred thousand thousand**).[5]

All of these images combine to demonstrate the power behind these perfected aspects of the self **(the four angels)** that we each have deep within us. When the ego first began to develop, it had to bind these four angels if it (the ego) was to mold the God- given spiritual energy into selfish creations. Now that the true self has surrendered to the Christ Spirit, these angels once again are free to destroy and recycle a portion **(a third)** of the ego's creations.

In verse 17, as John describes this vision in more detail, we learn that these are messages from the higher realms of consciousness (symbolized by the **horses** and their riders), which emphasizes the importance of this purification process. The description of the **breastplates** refers to how the heart of this matter **(breastplates)** resonates with justice and purification (**fire, jacinth and sulphur**).[5] The mental concept (**heads**) behind this process is that control (**heads of lions**) over the lower aspects of the physical self has now passed to the higher chakras and that these chakras now give voice to (**mouth**) the purification process for the advancement of the individual.

Remember, from the commentary on this sixth chakra in Chapters 2 and 3, that there is a direct link between the second and the sixth chakras. When this sixth chakra is open, it has control over the spiritual energy entering at the second spiritual center. The creations of the ego, which must be reformulated into a selfless expression of God's energy, will meet with the purifying processes (**plagues**) of so that their true purposes may be expressed. As John tells us in verse 19, the purifying force of these messages from the higher realms is found in both the intention of God's Word (**mouth**) as well as the results (**tails**) of His Word. In fact, the results (**tails**) of our purified actions provide the bite that harms the ego's creations. That is why John's vision describes the horses' tails as being **like unto serpents, and had heads, and with them they do hurt.**

Even the force of the open sixth chakra is not enough to completely purify the physical. According to verse 20, our selfish creations that were not purified (**not killed by these plagues**) did not offer to be transformed from being selfish to being selfless. These are the beliefs and ideas to which we cling (**worship**). It will take more than the cleansing of the first six chakras to fully transform an individual.

Chapter Ten

A Bitter Book

The human being has been the battleground for a synthesis of the physical and the spiritual. As originally created, we were unlimited Spirit; but we then chose to experience the physical and to thereby place restrictions upon ourselves. Our minds or awareness was subdivided into conscious and subconscious aspects because the spiritual was not designed to operate in the three dimensional world. The conscious mind was again split as we chose to emphasize either our masculinity or our femininity. This whole process was one of dichotomy again and again. We are the meeting place of seemingly irreconcilable opposites. Revelation, however, is the story of how one individual in particular (Jesus) and of how we in general are to reconcile these opposites into a unified, coherent whole. We are in the process of creating something new, a combination of spirit and physical in which our total awareness can operate through a new type of spiritualized physical. The Apostle Paul calls it a "spiritual body" in which the flesh itself has been purified and is able to enter into God's presence.

In Chapter 10, we begin to see more of the force which will purify the physical. The divine pattern of the inner self takes control, and the actions necessary for spiritualization are then described. This state of existence is similar to (although more intense than) that of an individual who has just felt a "calling" from God. Such an individual knows that he or she must do something that can manifest the intense feeling or understanding they possess, although the exact nature of that manifestation is not yet able to be articulated. Some typical questions which the individual might ask are: "Should I become a missionary? Should I quit my present job and enter the ministry? What should I do to put God first in my life?" What such an individual is expressing is his or her need to take God's spiritual energy/insight/awareness and use it in the physical world in such a manner that the message from the spiritual realm is properly conveyed into physical consciousness.

This emphasizes the position of human beings in the total scheme of God's creation: We are the only creatures capable of possessing both a spiritual **and** a physical consciousness. We are in the unique position of being a bridge between the two, with one foot in the spiritual and one in the physical. We are in this position to synthesize the two seemingly incompatible awarenesses into something new. To do so will require actions from us – our inner and outer selves working together in harmony. Let's continue to examine this process as described by the vision of Revelation.

Chapter 10:1-7

Scripture

Revelation 10:1

And I saw another mighty angel come down from heaven, clothed with a cloud: and a rainbow was upon his head, and his face was as it were the sun, and his feet as pillars of fire:

Revelation 10:2

And he had in his hand a little book open: and he set his right foot upon the sea, and his left foot on the earth,

Revelation 10:3

And cried with a loud voice, as when a lion roareth: and when he had cried, seven thunders uttered their voices.

Revelation 10:4

And when the seven thunders had uttered their voices, I was about

to write: and I heard a voice from heaven saying unto me, Seal up those things which the seven thunders uttered, and write them not.

Revelation 10:5

And the angel which I saw stand upon the sea and upon the earth lifted up his hand to heaven,

Revelation 10:6

And sware by him that liveth for ever and ever, who created heaven, and the things that therein are, and the earth, and the things that therein are, and the sea, and the things which are therein, that there should be time no longer:

Revelation 10:7

But in the days of the voice of the seventh angel, when he shall begin to sound, the mystery of God should be finished, as he hath declared to his servants the prophets.

Symbolism/Meaning

mighty angel - the spirit of the inner self.

heaven - consciousness or awareness.

clothed with a cloud - clothed in mystery.

rainbow was upon his head - the message deals with the mind and the understanding of self.

face was as it were the sun - the consciousness of this message brings life.

feet as pillars of fire - the strength of the message is that it provides a firm foundation based upon the purification process explained thus far.

in his hand - the mighty angel has control of the understanding.

little book - understanding of self.

open - the self (body, mind, and spirit) is now understood.

right foot upon the sea, and his left foot on the earth - symbolizes the position of humanity: a link between the spiritual (sea) and the physical (land).

loud voice, as when a lion roareth - sounding his authority.

seven thunders uttered - the purified body supports and answers the mighty angel.

lifted up his hand to heaven - a symbol of truth.

there should be time no longer - the purification of the body has been fulfilled.

Commentary

Chapter 10 is a new step in the ongoing, soul development cycle. Remember, this is the sixth trumpet, before the blowing of the seventh, so something new is added to this ever-spiraling progression. Here we are shown a vision of the divine pattern of the inner self (**mighty angel**) whose nature was still partly hidden from John (**clothed with a cloud**). John could see that the divine inner self had complete understanding of who it was (**rainbow was upon his head**[1]) as an individual who radiated God's light (**face as it were the sun**) and that this pattern of the self was strong in its ability to complete the purifying process (**feet as pillars of fire**).

This divine inner nature is in control of the physical, emotional, and mental processes in the body, as the person now becomes like an open book (**a little book open**). The individual, now purified, with the chakras open, begins the process of bridging the spiritual (**right foot on the sea**) and the physical (**left foot on the earth**). The cry which the angel makes is the voice of authority which is affirmed by the seven spiritual centers (**seven thunders**). The exact nature of this authority and what it entails can only be understood by someone whose development has reached this level of attainment. John, in being told not to write down what he heard, expresses the individualized nature of this message. In addition, since this divine self was in the process of combining the spiritual and the physical (**stand upon the sea and upon the earth lifted up his hand to heaven**), it would be impossible for anyone who was just beginning to struggle with these two extremes to understand how they could be combined. Without the Christ Consciousness directed self being aware of itself as a divine entity, the two extremes of spirit and flesh seem to be just that: irreconcilable extremes. It is only "in Christ" that the two may be reconciled. This is the reason John was told not to write it down.

This divine pattern of the inner self then acknowledges (**sware**) that for the individual who reaches this level of attainment, there shall be no more delay (**time no longer**). It is now time for that individual's potential as a child of God to become manifest (**should be finished**). "[T]ime as we know it no longer exists, for all things ... are known as one thing (holistically) and there is nothing but God."[2] However we understand the phrase, it seems to be related to the synthesis of the spiritual and the physical into a new creation that exists in a new awareness combining that of eternity in which there is no time and the physical in which time exists.

Chapter 10:8-11

Scripture

Revelation 10:8

And the voice which I heard from heaven spake unto me again, and said, Go and take the little book which is open in the hand of the angel which standeth upon the sea and upon the earth.

Revelation 10:9

And I went unto the angel, and said unto him, Give me the little book. And he said unto me, Take it, and eat it up; and it shall make thy belly bitter, but it shall be in thy mouth sweet as honey.

Revelation 10:10

And I took the little book out of the angel's hand, and ate it up; and it was in my mouth sweet as honey: and as soon as I had eaten it, my belly was bitter.

Revelation 10:11

And he said unto me, Thou must prophesy again before many peoples, and nations, and tongues, and kings.

Symbolism/Meaning

Take it and eat it up - make it a part of you.

It shall make thy belly bitter - application of what is learned brings problems.

in thy mouth sweet as honey - sweet in the expression.

prophesy - tell what you know.

Commentary

John is now commanded to strengthen his true inner self by gaining a greater understanding of the self (**Take** the book). He must gain this self understanding from the divine perfected image of the inner self (**the angel which standeth upon the sea and upon the earth**) that came down from Heaven. Notice in the earlier description of this angel that it was made up of nothing but heavenly materials: clouds, rainbow, sun, fire. This mighty angel represents humanity as we were first created: spiritual beings. Since our sojourn into the physical, though, we have become something new, consisting of both physical and spiritual. As we cleanse our chakras and memories and begin to remember our spiritual heritage by allowing the Christ Spirit to be in control, we are once again allowed access to our spiritual nature. By taking the **book** from the **angel**, John is symbolizing his taking control of his own spiritual nature. God allows the cleansed and purified physical body to have this controlling access to its spiritual awareness.

This access is quite a privilege for anyone, yet it is a privilege that brings along with it many responsibilities. As John is allowed access to an awareness of being a spiritual entity, he tastes the sweetness of this knowledge (**in thy mouth sweet as honey**). As he swallows this spiritual message of self, though, he discovers that it lies as a heavy burden within in him (**my belly was bitter**). Having been given this revelation, John must now tell others (**prophesy**) that they, too, are spiritual in nature as well as physical and can be brought to a remembrance of their true nature.

Because the culture and people of his time were not ready for this new awareness and all it meant for the development of the soul, the admonition to prophesy was bitter for John. It was difficult enough for the people of his time to accept the concept of a Messiah who did not come as a warrior to save the Jewish people from the Romans, but came rather to bring the whole person to God. it was bitter because he was unable to tell others of this wonderful new knowledge. But John fulfilled his command to prophesy by writing down this vision in symbolic terms, allowing humanity the time to grow and develop until we were ready to expand our consciousness and embrace this new awareness. The Revelation is John's manifestation of the command to **prophesy about many peoples and nations and tongues and kings** as he tells us of ourselves.

Chapter Eleven

Witnesses of the Mind

The concept of time and events in Revelation resembles a spiraling ascent (or descent) in consciousness, rather than a linear progression of events. The spiral of sevens within the vision lavishly illustrates this ancient world view: the sixth event in each cycle introduces a radically new item so that the seventh event is both a completion of the old as well as the genesis of the new concepts, events, etc.

Even though the book of Revelation was not originally divided into chapters, Chapter 11, the halfway point in the book, serves as a dividing line between the previous discussion of the inner person (the process of cleansing and opening the chakras and of spiritualizing the physical) and an explanation of how the new human being (an integration of the spiritualized physical with the spiritual self and the Mind of God) manifests and fulfills its divine purpose on earth. Like the spiraling cycles, it begins with something old – a discussion of the physical – and then continues to something new – a discussion of the mind's role in helping to bridge the distance between God and humanity.

In the previous chapter, John was given a message to swallow about the spirituality of self. As he swallowed this message, it became a bitter experience in his life; yet, it could become sweet once again upon his lips through the retelling of the message. The retelling of this message, along with the vision that inspired it, begins in Chapter 11 of the Revelation.

Chapter 11:1-2

Scripture

Revelation 11:1

> **And there was given me a reed like unto a rod: and the angel stood, saying, Rise, and measure the temple of God, and the altar, and them that worship therein.**

Revelation 11:2

> **But the court which is without the temple leave out, and measure it not; for it is given unto the Gentiles: and the holy city shall they tread under foot forty and two months.**

Symbolism/Meaning

rod - standard by which the self is to be judged.

Rise- to rise in consciousness.

measure - to give boundaries or limits to.

temple of God - that which has been built from the mental application of spiritual energy.

altar - place of self sacrifice within .

them that worship therein - the ideas, ideals, beliefs, etc. held by the self: the mental and emotional aspects of self.

court which is without the temple - all who are not under the influence of self.

theGentiles - influences over which we have no control.

tread under foot - outside influences predominate and rule in the absence of the ChristConsciousness.

forty and two months one-half of seven– a "half time" (see discussion in commentary).

Commentary

In Revelation 2:27, we read about the **rod of iron,** which was also spoken of in conjunction with the **nations,** just as it is here associated with the **Gentiles**. In the earlier reference, the Christ Spirit told John that those who remain faithful to the end will be given power over the nations and will be able to rule them with a **rod of iron**: The iron symbolized the strength of the ability to rule. We are reminded of the comforting characteristics of this Christ Spirit as we notice that the term **rod** is joined with the term **staff** as it is in the Twenty-Third Psalm ("Thy rod, and thy staff, they comfort me.") Often we are afraid of coming under the rod: We fear the discipline or the loss of freedom. David the psalmist realized that the rod of God is a symbol of protection and comfort that liberates us from the burden of karma and allows us to ascend in consciousness back to the Creator. It is in possessing the mind of Christ – the Christ Spirit – that we discover the freedom to release the captive inner self and bind the restrictive ego.

John is commanded to **rise** (ascend in consciousness) and to compare (**measure**) several items: **the temple of God**, the **altar**, and those who worship there. Measuring is a way of defining the limits of an object through the process of comparing that object with another. According to 11:1, John has been **given a reed, like unto a rod,** which is to be the standard by which all is to be measured. What is this standard? It is the Christ Spirit itself. John is to measure his physical, mental, emotional, and spiritual bodies (**the temple of God**) and see how well it compares to this standard. Do the actions, thoughts, and feelings of John reflect the presence of the Christ Spirit?

John is also asked to compare (**measure**) the place of self-sacrifice within him (**altar**) to the Christ Spirit. Is he sacrificing his own desires (the ego) in order to express the God-given desires inherent in the spiritual energy he receives?

To be thorough in his comparison, John must also measure **them that worship therein**. Who are these who worship within us? These are the ideas, concepts, beliefs, and habits that we have formed over time: They are our own creations. John, as well as each of us, must set these self creations next to the Christ Spirit and see how well they measure up. Notice that we are not required to measure or judge anything outside of ourselves: **the court which is without the temple leave out, and measure it not**. We do not have control over any forces or conditions that originate within other people. The measuring rod of the Christ Spirit is for each individual to apply only to self, not to others. The **court** symbolizes those conditions or forces that do not originate within us: We are not to judge (**measure**) anything outside of our own selves at this time. There is a distinction between Chapter 2 where it says we will rule the nations (outside influences) and Chapter 11, where we are not to judge the outer influences. Although the Christ Spirit gives us a power stronger than the outside influences, we do not use this power to make judgments on those ideas, thoughts, beliefs, actions, etc., that do not originate within us. In this manner we refuse to accept the karmic baggage that those outside influences possess, and thus we do not take on any new karma. Those outside influences (**Gentiles**) have to experience their own karma (**the holy city shall they tread under foot**) until they work through it and learn the lesson inherent in the experience.

The time period which is allowed for the external karmic experiences is **forty and two months**. In numerology this represents a time of completion (**forty**[1]) intensified by two. This time span is also three and one-half years or one-half of a cycle of seven. If you remember the illustration used to describe the cyclic nature of the events in Revelation, in which a complete cycle from God's point of view is seen as a circle, then a half-cycle represents the time it takes to go around half the circle (180°). In other words, a half-cycle is the time it takes to completely change your direction and to head back in the direction from which you came. It is not the complete journey, yet at least it points you in the opposite direction! It has often been noted that the ministry of Jesus lasted three and one-half years. By showing us that we are heading in the wrong direction, Jesus' ministry serves as an example for us to copy if we also wish to change our direction. In 11:2, the forty two months represent the part of the cycle in which the outer influences make their choices and create the conditions necessary for their own karma. It is their time of turning away from the ultimate Source of Life and coming to the realization that they are not what God intended.

The number forty two can also symbolize the earthly forces (four) intensified by ten (10 x 4) with the two added to double the intensity of the earthly influences. In this sense, the forty two months, or three and one-half years, represent a complete physical cycle (as opposed to the spiritual cycle of seven). Even though this can be viewed as a complete cycle in the physical, it is complete only because some event is concluded in that amount of time. Notice that the consequences of that event are not included in the physical cycle. Thus the physical view of events is actually incomplete since only the event itself is considered, whereas the wider results of that action are seldom envisioned as part of the event. For example, the act of copulation, while often viewed as an event in itself by many human beings, may result in the birth of a baby. And the event does not end there: The baby must be nourished and loved; the responsibility of rearing the child must be considered; then, as the child grows and matures, the actions of that child and the results of those actions become part of the event of copulation years ago. Our physical consciousness is not sufficient to view or imagine all the possible ramifications of one event as it happens. It takes a greater awareness – that of the consciousness of the Christ Spirit – to see the connections between physical events. This is why the physical cycle of forty two months is incomplete when viewed from the spiritual sense.

Chapter 11:3-6

Scripture

Revelation 11:3

"And I will give power unto my two witnesses, and they shall prophesy a thousand two hundred and threescore days, clothed in sackcloth.

Revelation 11:4

These are the two olive trees, and the two candlesticks standing before the God of the earth.

Revelation 11:5

And if any man will hurt them, fire proceedeth out of their mouth,

and devoureth their enemies: and if any man will hurt them, he must in this manner be killed.

Revelation 11:6

These have power to shut heaven, that it rain not in the days of their prophecy: and have power over waters to turn them to blood, and to smite the earth with all plagues, as often as they will.

Symbolism/Meaning

two witnesses - the two unknown halves of the total human being – the subconscious and the superconscious

prophesy a thousand two hundred and threescore days - a "half time."

clothed in sackcloth - repentance and dependence upon God.

two olive trees and the two candlesticks - symbols of illumination and healing

God of the earth - the self under the direction of the Christ Spirit.

fire proceedeth out of their mouth - they are purified in their intent.

power to shut heaven - close off connections with the source of life.

that it rain not - no life energy given.

have power over waters to turn them to blood - to take the life force (water) and turn it to physical life (blood).

smite the earth with all plagues - to force learning experiences through karma.

Commentary

In this section, John is introduced to **two witnesses**. The number two is the number for an adequate witness (see Appendix B). Since these two witnesses agree, this symbolizes that the truth is being witnessed to in this section. They are allowed to **prophesy a thousand two hundred and threescore days**, which is another half-cycle. By expressing the event in these terms (1,260) rather than as 42 (months) or 3 $^{1}/_{2}$(years), a different emphasis is given to the event. In numerology, complex numbers are reduced to a single digit [2] to capture the essence of the number. This is accomplished by adding the different digits in a number. In this example, 1,260 reduces to 9 (i.e., 1 + 2 + 6 + 0 = 9). By looking up the meaning of the number 9, we can better understand the larger number. In this case, nine represents "finality or judgment" (see Appendix B). From this we understand that this period of prophecy by these two witnesses deals with a time of testing, after which comes judgment. Who are the witnesses? To whom are they prophesying, and to what are they witnesses?

According to Rev. 11:4, these two witnesses are **the two olive trees and the two candlesticks standing before the god of the earth**. The **olive tree** is an "ancient symbol of the Holy Land, peace, love, and the path of healing and regeneration."[3] The **candlestick** symbolizes that which holds illumination. Together, the olive trees and the candlesticks symbolize that which brings the light of healing and renewal. In the context of what we have been studying, these two witnesses must be the new awareness brought about through the cleansing of karmic influences in the chakras and the uniting of the subconscious with the superconscious. When the subconscious and superconscious agree to allow the Christ Spirit to sit upon the throne of our lives and to have control over the lower chakras (**of the earth**), then these two parts of the mind, in an attitude of true repentance (**clothed in sackcloth**), agree in their witness to the truth contained in their new awareness.

The combined forces of the union give new powers to the individual; they work together to prevent the lower, physical self (the ego) from receiving any life energy or force and misusing it (**to shut heaven**). Instead, the Christ Conscious self can take the life force (**waters**) and manifest it directly as physical life (**blood**): an experience which forces the body (**earth**) to face its karmic needs. If the body is to be a part of the developing spiritualized human, then the body must meet itself in its karmic weaknesses (**plagues**) and learn the lessons most needed.

This is often experienced as those "dry, desert days" in the spiritual life when we quit receiving spiritual messages or when we feel forsaken. During such a time in my own life, I was struggling with the process of meditation: I performed the rituals I had used for months that had always given me a rich return in the form of feedback and synchronicity.[4] Now such events had dried up; I did not feel the presence of the Christ Spirit. Just as I was about to give up the struggle, I had a dream about the servant's quarters. I found myself in a wooded, mountainous area near a large castle-like structure. There was a friend with me who was giving me a tour. As we went through the stone gateway entrance into a small courtyard, my friend directed me into the front door of the "modest stone structure," as he described it, and we entered the house. As we walked in, it was quite evident that the interior was being remodeled and redecorated. Workers were everywhere, scurrying around with ladders, paint, furniture, hammers, saws, etc. Every room on the first floor was being completely redone. In one room, the walls were being sculptured into three-dimensional relief and then painted to bring out the shadows and depth. In another, a plush carpet was on the floor, and a writing desk, bookcases, and reading room chairs dominated one end.

Every area in this house was being remodeled. In one room we entered, the workers had just finished, and they were celebrating by performing a choreographed game of basketball. At this point I realized that these rooms were huge. The servant's quarters seemed like a mansion to me! My friend and I entered one unfinished room and took a thin stain and applied it as a wash over all the walls of the room. I was afraid that this style would not fit in with the master architect's plan, and I feared that he would be upset with what we had done. Instead, he responded with pleasure and said that it gave that room "a primitive look" that was needed in the house.

About this time I entered the grand gallery (remember, this is the servant's quarters!) and decided to go up to the second floor and look around. On this higher level, the work was definitely in its early stages, with scaffolding, ladders, unfinished drywall, bare floors and fewer people moving about doing the work.

Wanting to go even further up, I scampered up the large spiral staircase to the third floor, right under the dome. At this level, the lights were off, no one else was around, lumber was lying about, and dust lay on the bare walls and the floor. As I wandered about, I saw my footprints being left in the dust, and I thought, "They will know I have been here." After going back down the stairs, I left the house and admired the gorgeous mountain scenery all about me, marveling at the complexity of all that I had seen.

Once awake, I joyfully realized that I remembered the dream. As a minister, people often telephoned me late at night with emergencies. I had taught myself over a period of twenty years to become instantly awake and conscious for the other person, no matter how soundly I had been asleep. For this reason, I often forgot my dreams. So whenever I remember a dream, I know it is an important one.

Because this dream was still active in my conscious mind, I was ecstatic! Finally I had broken my dry time of no spiritual messages. Now that I remembered the dream, the challenge facing me involved understanding it. This dream was one of both encouragement and warning. My soul (the servant's house) was experiencing changes and growth. It was larger and more glorious inside than I had ever imagined as viewed from the outside, physical world. What I was doing in my life was good and on target, though it seemed "primitive" at times. Yet, even with the growth that I was experiencing within, there were still new levels to climb, explore, and refurbish. The "me" which left the footprints on the third floor was my conscious mind. My friend, the subconscious mind, did not leave footprints; although always with me, he was never seen. He invited me into the house for the tour. Knowing that the conscious mind needed the reassurance of what was going on in the soul, it allowed me (the conscious mind) to enter the abode of the subconscious. This was why I remembered the dream: My conscious mind had been allowed – invited – to share the dream with the subconscious.

In a similar manner, when the subconscious mind and the superconscious mind unite and are guided by the Christ Spirit, their power to let the flow of spiritual energy either enter or be shut off from the physical is great. Their powers can be used to help cleanse some of the remaining bodily cells by allowing them to face their karmic patterns (**smite the earth with all plagues as often as they will**).

Chapter 11:7-14

Scripture

Revelation 11:7

And when they shall have finished their testimony, the beast that ascendeth out of the bottomless pit shall make war against them, and shall overcome them, and kill them.

Revelation 11:8

And their dead bodies shall lie in the street of the great city, which spiritually is called Sodom and Egypt, where also our Lord was crucified.

Revelation 11:9

And they of the people and kindreds and tongues and nations shall see their dead bodies three days and an half, and shall not suffer their dead bodies to be put in graves.

Revelation 11:10

And they that dwell upon the earth shall rejoice over them, and make merry, and shall send gifts one to another; because these two prophets tormented them that dwelt on the earth.

Revelation 11:11

And after three days and an half the Spirit of life from God entered into them, and they stood upon their feet; and great fear fell upon them which saw them.

Revelation 11:12

And they heard a great voice from heaven saying unto them, Come up hither. And they ascended up to heaven in a cloud; and their enemies beheld them.

Revelation 11:13

And the same hour was there a great earthquake, and the tenth part of the city fell, and in the earthquake were slain of men seven

thousand: and the remnant were affrighted, and gave glory to the God of heaven.

Revelation 11:14

The second woe is past; and, behold, the third woe cometh quickly.

Symbolism/Meaning

beast - lower self or ego.

Sodom - sin.

Egypt - bondage or release from bondage.

people and kindreds and tongues and nations - influences from all sources.

three days and an half - a half cycle.

that dwell upon the earth - self created influences, thoughts, habits, etc.

send gifts one to another - share their life force.

Spirit of life from God - spirit.

Come up hither - ascend farther into consciousness.

they ascended up to heaven in a cloud - given proper recognition and honor.

Commentary

In this next section of Chapter 11, we meet **the beast** ascending from **the bottomless pit**. As the mental aspect of our selves comes into alignment with the (the subconscious and the superconscious – the two witnesses), it meets opposition from the lower self or ego. There are still habits and actions which we perform that are contrary to the higher ideals of the Christ Spirit. Yet, even in the midst of knowing what is right, we continue to follow our old habits and to repeat our old sins. As the Apostle Paul noted in Romans 7:15-25, our bodies refuse to act out the instructions (**testimony** of the two witnesses) that our new consciousness gives us. There is an inner struggle in which the physical wins the battle over the new consciousness (**shall make war against them and shall overcome them**). When this happens, it will seem like our new consciousness did not help us in the battle: We are filled with questions, anger, and doubt. Why, when we know what is right, did we continue to do what was wrong? Even Paul succinctly describes what is happening in Romans 7:19 when he states, "For the good which I would I do not: but the evil which I would not, that I do." Yet Paul then continues in the next verse to distinguish between his new consciousness (which he identifies as the true self) and the lower, physical urges that he describes as the "sin that dwelleth within me" (Rom. 7:20). Paul experienced this war between his mental self (the alignment of the subconscious and superconscious minds) and his physical self (the physical urges). As he says in Romans 7:23, "But I see another law in my members, warring against the law of my mind, and bringing me into captivity to the law of sin which is in my members."

The experience of Paul is, of necessity (according to Revelation), the experience of each of us. For the duration of our struggle (**three days and an half**), it will seem that the physical has conquered over the mental. The purpose of this time is to make us aware of our bondage to our lower nature (**Egypt**) before we are to leave this bondage behind us. Just as the Hebrew people were led out of Egypt to begin their journey to the Promised Land, so too will we be led out of our bondage to our lower nature and sin (**Sodom**), as we travel to our promised awakening in consciousness. Before this happens, all that we have created in the physical (our desires, attachment to objects, etc.) **rejoice** over the apparent victory they have over the Christ Spirit. We feel the satisfaction in the physical as its needs and lusts are met, even though such satisfaction is gained only by the exchange of our life force – kundalini – from one physical need to another (**send gifts one to another**). No new energy is entering at this time. One physical need is met at the expense of another.

At this time in our lives we need to simply "keep on keeping on." During the desolate times when it seems the Spirit is not in us, we must remain faithful. For after the completed time of desolation and dryness (**the three and an half days**), life will again be given to the subconscious mind and the superconscious mind to vindicate their acceptance of and cooperation with the Christ Spirit (**ascended up to heaven in a cloud**). When this combined mental aspect of the self rises in consciousness, then a great number of the physical desires will be destroyed (**in the earthquake were slain of men seven thousand**) while the remaining desires will serve God's higher purpose for our lives. This reviving of the two witnesses and their ascension into heaven symbolizes the self's ability to take control of its true nature and to once again express this nature in the daily activities and thoughts of a life lived for others.

The second great step (**woe**) in our soul's growth has occurred. There is but one more to come.

Chapter 11:15-19

Scripture

Revelation 11:15

And the seventh angel sounded; and there were great voices in heaven, saying, The kingdoms of this world are become the kingdoms of our Lord, and of his Christ; and he shall reign for ever and ever.

Revelation 11:16

And the four and twenty elders, which sat before God on their seats, fell upon their faces, and worshipped God,

Revelation 11:17

Saying, We give thee thanks, O Lord God Almighty, which art, and wast, and art to come; because thou hast taken to thee thy great power, and hast reigned.

Revelation 11:18

And the nations were angry, and thy wrath is come, and the time of the dead, that they should be judged, and that thou shouldest give reward unto thy servants the prophets, and to the saints, and them that fear thy name, small and great; and shouldest destroy them which destroy the earth.

Revelation 11:19

And the temple of God was opened in heaven, and there was seen in his temple the ark of his testament: and there were lightnings, and voices, and thunderings, and an earthquake, and great hail.

Symbolism/Meaning

the dead - not yet possessing the Christ Consciousness.
shall be judged - measured, compared to.
temple ... in heaven - the concept of the new body.
ark of covenant - the promise from old.

Commentary

Beginning with the blowing of the seventh trumpet, the old cycle is ending and the new is appearing in full force. Recognition is made of the growth in consciousness and awareness of the soul's oneness with God. Additionally, there is the acknowledgment that the physical and the spiritual have combined to become something new: **the kingdoms of this world are become the kingdoms of our Lord and of his Christ**. Mastery over the physical is now in the hands of the Christ-centered self. The sensing of both the physical and the spiritual worlds through the channels of the 24 cranial nerves (**24 elders** [see Chapter 5]) no longer must come through the filter of the ego. All input to the brain is direct and consists of the full and true reality rather than the distorted and partial awareness provided by the ego. (This would account for the ability by some saints and others to sense and know that which is beyond the grasp of simply the physical. People who have reached this stage in their spiritual development often have psychic abilities which science has yet to understand.[5]) Because of this direct contact with reality, the senses praise God (Rev. 11:16-18).

In their statement of praise, the 24 elders speak of the time for the dead to be judged and the time for rewards as well as destruction. The **dead** in this context refer to our past actions and thoughts: It is time for seeing if what we have done with the spiritual energy given to us has been for self or for others. If our thoughts, actions, and motivations have been tempered with the desire to be for others, then they will find their reward in their intended purpose. On the other hand, if they were for the self, then they have been guilty of draining the physical of its life-force and were to be destroyed just as they attempted to destroy the body (**destroy them which destroy the earth.**).

The last verse of Chapter 11 describes the opening of God's temple **in heaven**. Jesus referred to his own body as "the temple of God" (John 2:19-21). This last verse continues that theme by describing the unveiling of a spiritualized physical body. At this point in Revelation, the spiritualized physical body exists in the Mind of God (since it is **in heaven**), and it is not fully physically manifested in the life of the individual.

Chapter Twelve

The Individual is Born

Jesus, when speaking to his disciples immediately before his crucifixion said, "But the Comforter, which is the Holy Spirit, whom the Father will send in my name shall teach you all things, and bring all things to your remembrance, whatsoever I have said unto you" (John 14:26). At the end of the previous chapter of Revelation, the subconscious and superconscious minds had joined together in acknowledging and accepting the Christ Spirit as their guiding principle (i.e., the individual has taken on the mind of Christ). When this occurred, it "opened up the door" for the Holy Spirit to fully enter into the life of the individual. To understand this image of an open door, we must remember that the subconscious mind controls the glandular centers associated with the seven chakras. The sixth chakra, the Pineal center, was referred to in Chapters 2 and 3 as being the door which can be either open or shut. When this door is opened, the kundalini or prana may flow, bringing life and energy to the individual. Not until we possess the mind of Christ is this door permanently opened wide, granting the Holy Spirit free access to all parts of the body and the mind.

Chapter twelve begins the story of what happens when the Holy Spirit comes fully into our lives. It is a story filled with symbols and images. It is also a tale of remembering all that has happened to the soul. A description is given of the soul's history showing the influences that have occurred as the soul enters into the flesh. This story is different from the usual interpretation of this portion of Revelation because, instead of happening outside of us in past or future history, it describes what has or will occur to the soul which we are: It is not only history (His story), it is also our story.

Chapter 12:1-6

Scripture

Revelation 12:1

And there appeared a great wonder in heaven; a woman clothed with the sun, and the moon under her feet, and upon her head a crown of twelve stars:

Revelation 12:2

And she being with child cried, travailing in birth, and pained to be delivered.

Revelation 12:3

And there appeared another wonder in heaven; and behold a great red dragon, having seven heads and ten horns, and seven crowns upon his heads.

Revelation 12:4

And his tail drew the third part of the stars of heaven, and did cast them to the earth: and the dragon stood before the woman which was ready to be delivered, for to devour her child as soon as it was born.

Revelation 12:5

And she brought forth a man child, who was to rule all nations with a rod of iron: and her child was caught up unto God, and to his throne.

Revelation 12:6

And the woman fled into the wilderness, where she hath a place prepared of God, that they should feed her there a thousand two hundred and threescore days.

Symbolism/Meaning

great wonder - the soul, as created in the Mind of God.

a woman - the feminine, life-giving principle of the soul.

clothed with the sun - the life force itself is draped around the soul.

moon under her feet - ability to reflect.

crown of twelve stars - the twelve characteristics, and attributes of the human body (see Appendix E).

child - the true state of the soul.

birth - the soul moves into materiality.

great red dragon - conscious self, principle of rebellion.

seven heads - seven chakras.

ten horns - aggressive power.

seven crowns upon his heads - chakras controlled by the ego.

tail drew the third part of the stars of heaven, and did cast them to the earth - the results of selfishness brought a loss of heavenly consciousness.

dragon stood before the woman - the self confronts the soul.

for to devour her child - the self wishes to control the true state of the soul.

man child - the active consciousness of the soul (superconsciousness).

caught up unto God - the superconsciousness aspect of our soul remained with God.

woman fled into the wilderness - the remaining aspects of the soul became confused and lost (subconscious).

Commentary

The Holy Spirit begins our remembrance of all things by first showing us a **great wonder**: the vision of the soul as created by God in the very beginning. The soul is seen as **a woman** because it realizes that, although it is separate from God, it is still one with the Creator, and it has the potential of bringing new expressions of the Creator's handiwork into manifestation. The soul is seen as having a creative nature and is thus portrayed as being feminine. This creative soul is also envisioned as being surrounded with the life-giving force of the physical plane (**clothed with the sun**) to emphasize that this soul is one which is choosing to manifest into the physical. It has been endowed with the ability to reflect upon its choices (**moon under her feet**), and it fully understands the perfect nature of the physical being (**upon her head a crown**). The **crown of twelve stars** symbolizes the twelve-fold characteristics of the human body (see Appendix E). All of this was understood by the soul from the very beginning.

Now the soul was **with child**: She was pregnant with the potential of the physical existence. To take on the physical form would mean a loss of heavenly consciousness and the possibility of being lost in materiality. Thus the soul cried out in her pangs of birth, in anguish for delivery. Physicality was something the soul desired, yet it came at a painful price.

While this soul was writhing in her anguish over the myriad possible results of entering the physical, another event was happening in the spirit realm. Returning for a moment to the story of Adam and Eve in the Garden of Eden, you remember the serpent which tempted and deceived them into disobedience. In Revelation, that serpent is seen as a fully grown **great red dragon**. In both instances, it symbolizes the development of the ego through the agency of the spirit of selfishness. The danger to the soul lies in the ego's desire and potential to control the seven spiritual centers (the **seven crowns** upon the **seven heads** of the dragon). The power of the ego is great, as symbolized by the **horns**, and the number **ten** (complete, nothing wanting) amplifies that power. This false self then uses its **tail** to sweep down a **third of the stars of heaven**. This image symbolizes the activity and purpose of the ego-directed self: In its attempt to control a person, the ego will cause him to lose awareness of his heavenly estate. The physical manifestation of this spiritual occurrence was recorded most clearly in the Old Testament book of Job. Satan, one of the heavenly beings, is given permission by God to first take away the physical possessions of Job (Job 1:8-22) and then to destroy the physical beauty and comforts of the body itself (Job 2:1-10). If Job's awareness had consisted only of the conscious mind and if he had thought of himself as simply a physical creature, he would have been totally destroyed by Satan's actions and would have had no hope in a God who allows destruction of His creation. Remember, however, that only **one third** of the stars of heaven had been swept away; the physical human being still had access to two thirds of the heavenly consciousness. But the nature of the selfish ego is such that it is never satisfied. It **stood before the woman**, hoping to **devour her child**.

When the **woman**, or soul, gave birth, she **brought forth a man child**. The male represents the active force in any manifestation. Here, it symbolizes the superconscious mind of the soul, which remains in direct consciousness of God, apart from the rest of the soul (**caught up to** God). The soul has now given up one aspect of itself in order to be born into the physical, and because it is no longer complete, it is confused: It finds itself to be in a state of existence **prepared of God**, yet surrounded by a **wilderness** totally unlike what it had known before. This is a description of the birth process: A soul gives up its direct awareness of God in order to find itself in a bewildering, but God-given, limited body. It has to learn how to use its new physical body to communicate with others and to eventually manipulate its environment. The soul is now a human being.

At this point in the story of the soul's sojourn into the physical, a related vision occurs which explains more of the role that the dragon plays in this drama. This short vision is described in the next section.

Chapter 12:7-12

Scripture

Revelation 12:7

And there was war in heaven: Michael and his angels fought against the dragon; and the dragon fought and his angels,

Revelation 12:8

And prevailed not; neither was their place found any more in heaven.

Revelation 12:9

And the great dragon was cast out, that old serpent, called the

Devil, and Satan, which deceiveth the whole world: he was cast out into the earth, and his angels were cast out with him.

Revelation 12:10

And I heard a loud voice saying in heaven, Now is come salvation, and strength, and the kingdom of our God, and the power of his Christ: for the accuser of our brethren is cast down, which accused them before our God day and night

Revelation 12:11

And they overcame him by the blood of the Lamb, and by the word of their testimony; and they loved not their lives unto the death.

Revelation 12:12

Therefore rejoice, ye heavens, and ye that dwell in them. Woe to the inhabiters of the earth and of the sea! for the devil is come down unto you, having great wrath, because he knoweth that he hath but a short time.

Symbolism/Meaning

war in heaven - struggle between the oneness of Christ Consciousness and the ego.

neither was their place found any more in heaven - ego could not exist alongside of oneness.

Devil, and Satan - Biblical references to the accuser, here seen as the ego.

cast out into the earth - only in the physical (earth)can the ego exist.

accuser - reference to Satan's role as portrayed in Job.

overcame him - reference to the work of Jesus who was the first to attain oneness in the physical.

Woe to the inhabiters of the earth and of the sea - the body and the emotions suffer the results of the ego.

Commentary

It seems strange to say that was **war in heaven**, for we are taught that heaven is supposed to be a place of peace, tranquility, and harmony. This image serves a purpose for understanding our own soul development. The ancients had a saying that describes the concept of the microcosm and the macrocosm: "As within, so without. As above, so below."[1] The macrocosmic physical universe has its analogous components within the microcosmic physical body; whatever happens in the physical existence outside of the body has a corresponding happening within the body. In a like manner, whatever happens in the physical world has a corresponding previous action in the spiritual realm. Therefore, a **war in heaven** describes not only a heavenly event but also foreshadows an event happening within the human consciousness (heaven in the microcosmic). This war between the **dragon** and the **male child caught up unto God** manifests itself as a struggle within the superconscious to rid itself of any influence of the ego. The **dragon** and **his angels** could no longer abide in heaven where the superconscious now exists, because of the potential for influencing this aspect of the human soul that, in God's plan, had to remain untouched by the ego.

The selfish influences were then **cast out into the earth**: that is, their sphere of influence was limited to the physical and the emotional. This sphere is exactly the limits of Satan's influence over Job. This limitation occurs when we contact the superconscious (the God within) and become aware of this great difference between our conception of ourselves as physical creatures and the superconscious knowledge of ourselves as companions to God.

Notice that even though we are able to still contact that superconscious aspect of ourselves, the ego still exists and still has reign over the body and the emotions (**Woe to the inhabiters of the earth and the sea.**). In fact, the body and emotions are most vulnerable at this time to the selfish destruction by the devil self or ego.

Chapter 12:13-17

Scripture

Revelation 12:13

And when the dragon saw that he was cast unto the earth, he persecuted the woman which brought forth the man child.

Revelation 12:14

And to the woman were given two wings of a great eagle, that she might fly into the wilderness, into her place, where she is nourished for a time, and times, and half a time, from the face of the serpent.

Revelation 12:15

And the serpent cast out of his mouth water as a flood after the woman, that he might cause her to be carried away of the flood.

Revelation 12:16

And the earth helped the woman, and the earth opened her mouth, and swallowed up the flood which the dragon cast out of his mouth.

Revelation 12:17

And the dragon was wroth with the woman, and went to make war with the remnant of her seed, which keep the commandments of God, and have the testimony of Jesus Christ.

Symbolism/Meaning

he persecuted the woman - attempted to control the human body and conscious mind.

two wings of a great eagle - fly away from the trap of materiality through the process of reincarnation.

nourished - strengthened for the task of living as a human being.

cast out of his mouth water - floods the body with emotions.

earth helped the woman - the physical body absorbs the abuses of the dragon.

remnant of her seed - the thoughts, attitudes, beliefs, actions which we produce.

Commentary

As the story of the soul's journey picks up again, we discover that the false self (**dragon**) next attempts to control the soul's conscious and subconscious minds (**he persecuted the woman**). Even though the dragon, as Satan in the book of Job, was not given permission to harm the mind, he knew it was that aspect of the soul in the earth which was most like his (Satan's) own existence; it would therefore be the easiest aspect of the soul to influence. But God provided the conscious and subconscious minds with a hiding place (**wilderness**) where they could be **nourished** for a half cycle. This **wilderness** could be the time of adjustment that the mind must take as it learns how to control the body during infancy and early childhood. In almost every manual on child psychology, you can read of the typical growth stages of the mind as it begins to interact with its environment and those around it. When this development reaches a certain stage, the ego begins to emerge and assert itself. The early time of growth, before the emergence of the ego, is one in which the infant is overwhelmed with a flood of inner emotions in response to information originating in the physical world outside of itself (**cast out of his mouth water as a flood after the woman**). Even though extreme trauma at this time can have lasting effects in a child's life, the body and mind of a child can absorb much of the outside influence and adapt to it as simply the "way things are," while continuing to grow and develop (**the earth opened her mouth, and swallowed up the flood**).

An example of this phenomenon that has always been a marvel to me involves my youngest son. When he was three years old, he was involved in an automobile accident which damaged his spinal cord and left him a paraplegic with no feeling or control over his ankles and feet as well as some of his bodily functions. Rather than lament this handicap and possess a "poor me" attitude, he has been able to recognize his condition as a given and to look at life with the attitude "look at what I am able to do!" He doesn't dwell upon his condition – he puts it behind him and goes on. And with his braces and crutches, he moves faster and further than I can! If the accident had occurred after the ego was fully developed, I doubt that his attitude would have been the same. The infant human body and mind is a remarkable creation in that it can absorb a lot of impact and still keep right on going.

In John's vision, the woman was given **two wings of a great eagle** to transport her away from the false self. The wings can symbolize the ability of the consciousness to fly away, while the number two implies that this source of transportation is just adequate for the job. Because these are the wings of a **great eagle**, it has a special significance. In ancient times, the eagle was sometimes given the qualities of the phoenix,[2] a bird consumed in the fire only to rise again, fresh, young and full of life. This bird is symbolic of reincarnation. In reincarnation, the soul incarnates into the flesh until the flesh vehicle is removed by death. The soul's experience in the flesh is evaluated at that time, and a choice is then made as to how, when, and if, the soul incarnates again. With acceptance of this concept, this section of Revelation takes on a new meaning: The **wilderness** to which the soul retires for nourishment refers to those times between physical incarnations, where the false self cannot harm or influence the soul, since it has permission to influence only the physical aspects of humanity (see Job 1 and 2). The conscious "self," i.e., ego personality, is that which perishes at the death of the physical. Since it does not exist, it cannot harm the soul in between incarnations. The earth swallowing the river which the dragon had poured from his mouth refers to the physical body's application of the lessons that it is learning in order to absorb the flood of emotions that the ego unleashes upon the physical.[3] What is important to note at this point is that God has prepared a way for us to survive – and to grow – even in the face of the ego's destructive acts.

In 12:17, it is not a surprise to see the **dragon** become angry (**wroth**) with the woman (soul), since the ego's only source of power would prove to be ineffectual against the growth of the soul into the Christ Spirit, that state of consciousness of being for others. In its anger, the self then turns against the physical manifestations of the soul's attributes in the world: that is, our traits and temperaments

(make war with the remnant of her seed).[4] Meanwhile, in the beginning of Chapter 13, the ego stands before the **sea** of the emotions ready to summon its greatest weapon to wreak havoc upon the soul.[5]

Chapter Thirteen

The Beast Within

III. Vision Two: The Scroll in Heaven	4:1 - 16:21
D. Signs, Beasts, Angels, Interludes and Plagues	12:1 - 16:21
3. The Beast Out of the Sea	13:2 - 10
4. The Beast Out of the Earth.	13:11 18

In Chapter 13 we enter the confusing story of the two beasts, one arising out of the sea (verse 1) and the other arising out of the earth (verse 11). In the macrocosm (the outer, physical world) the beasts are associated with the Anti-Christ, and there is speculation as to "Who (or what) is the Anti-Christ?" and "Whose name is equal to the number 666?" Since our view of Revelation looks at the microcosmic inner world of each individual rather than the outer world, the questions we ask are different: What do the two beasts symbolize within us? What significance does the number 666 have in understanding ourselves? We have already seen, in Chapter 12, that the influence from Satan (spirit of rebellion), symbolized by the dragon, has been with us from the time we, as souls, first realized we were separate from God. The Satan Consciousness is the process of choosing (or attempting) to be entirely separate from God in all respects. The Christ Consciousness is the knowledge that one's true self is separate from God, yet one with God. The story of Revelation is the story of our progress from the Satan Consciousness back to the Christ Consciousness.

Chapter 13:1-8

Scripture

Revelation 13:1

And I stood upon the sand of the sea, and saw a beast rise up out of the sea, having seven heads and ten horns, and upon his horns ten crowns, and upon his heads the name of blasphemy.

Revelation 13:2

And the beast which I saw was like unto a leopard, and his feet were as the feet of a bear, and his mouth as the mouth of a lion: and the dragon gave him his power, and his seat, and great authority

Revelation 13:3

And I saw one of his heads as it were wounded to death; and his deadly wound was healed: and all the world wondered after the beast.

Revelation 13:4

And they worshipped the dragon which gave power unto the beast: and they worshipped the beast, saying, Who is like unto the beast? who is able to make war with him?

Revelation 13:5

And there was given unto him a mouth speaking great things and blasphemies; and power was given unto him to continue forty and two months.

Revelation 13:6

And he opened his mouth in blasphemy against God, to blaspheme his name, and his tabernacle, and them that dwell in heaven.

Revelation 13:7

And it was given unto him to make war with the saints, and to overcome them: and power was given him over all kindreds, and tongues, and nations.

Revelation 13:8

And all that dwell upon the earth shall worship him, whose names are not written in the book of life of the Lamb slain from the foundation of the world.

Symbolism/Meaning

sand of the sea - edge of the emotions.

beast - ego.

sea - emotions.

seven heads - symbols of the ego as related to the seven chakras.

ten - completion.

horns - symbols of power.

crowns - symbols of mastery over whatever is in your domain.

name of blasphemy - selfishness.

like unto a leopard, and his feet were as the feet of a bear, and his mouth as the mouth of a lion - characteristics of the influences arising from the ego (see also Daniel 7 for a similar vision relating to the macrocosm, physical world).

as if it were wounded to death - possessed the appearance of having had life taken away

worshiped the dragon - give homage to the spirit of rebellion and selfishness.

speaking great things and blasphemies - boasting of the ego.

make war with the saints - to have influence over righteousness.

book of life - the record of all that is righteous and holy.

Commentary

As the vision of this chapter begins a beast ... having seven heads and ten horns, and upon his horns ten crowns, and upon his heads the name of blasphemy rises out of the sea. If this image is not confusing enough, we also learn that the beast is "... like unto a leopard, and his feet were as the feet of a bear, and his mouth as the mouth of a lion..." What does this jumble of images represent?

The usual method of understanding this section of Revelation is to turn back to the seventh chapter of Daniel where a vision with similar images occurs. In that chapter, not only Daniel's vision is described, but also an explanation of the symbols is given. Instead of one beast, Daniel views four beasts: a lion with eagle's wings (Daniel

7:4); a bear with three ribs in its mouth (Daniel 7:5); a leopard with four wings and four heads (Daniel 7:6); and a fourth beast with iron teeth, ten large horns, and one small horn, which uprooted three of the large horns (Daniel 7:7-14). This vision is said to pertain to the rise and fall of four kingdoms that we know of as Babylon, Medo-Persia, Greece, and Rome.[1] Since these symbols are similar to those found in Revelation, and the explanations of these symbols are included in Scripture, it seems reasonable to use the same concepts when interpreting Revelation. This is the basis behind the Historicist and Futurist methods of interpretation as described in the Prologue. While acknowledging the validity of this method (and recognizing the plurality of such discourses in recent years, each attempting to give the "correct" explanation), the attempt of this author is to go deeper into an understanding of these symbols as they relate to the soul development of each of us in our lives as spiritual beings. Once we understand the dynamics occurring within ourselves, we can better understand external events as related to these symbols.

Returning to the scripture, let us examine the images and attempt to decipher their symbolism. In 13:1, the first **beast** arises out of the **sea** of emotions and is given its validity by the spirit of rebellion within us (**the dragon gave him his power, and his seat, and great authority.**). Rebelliousness interacts with the physical, churning our emotions (**sea**) and creating the desire to express our separateness from God. As we then express our "self-ness," we create a conscious mental image of who we are: We are of a certain height and weight; we possess a certain degree of intelligence; we like some things and despise others, etc. This image grows until, without any warning or announcement of when it happens, we come to believe that this image of ourself is our true self. We think, "This is who I am and no one can change that (**Who is like unto the beast? Who is able to make war with him?**)." We name this image our "ego." We hand over the reins of our life to this ego and allow it to control the actions of the seven spiritual centers (**seven heads**). The ego has the power to direct these centers and to allow the flow of kundalini to be used for selfish purposes, rather than for the purposes that God intends. The ego receives information from the physical world through the five physical senses. Since we have created the ego from both the physical and the mental, the five senses are each expressed twice: once to represent the physical world, and again to symbolize the mental representation of that physical object. For example, when we look at an object, the image of that object is projected upon the retina of the eye and stimulates the rods and cones located there (Figure 13.1). Our brain then deciphers and interprets the signals received from these stimulated rods and cones as a physical object outside of ourselves. Thus there is both the physical object and our mental interpretation of that object.

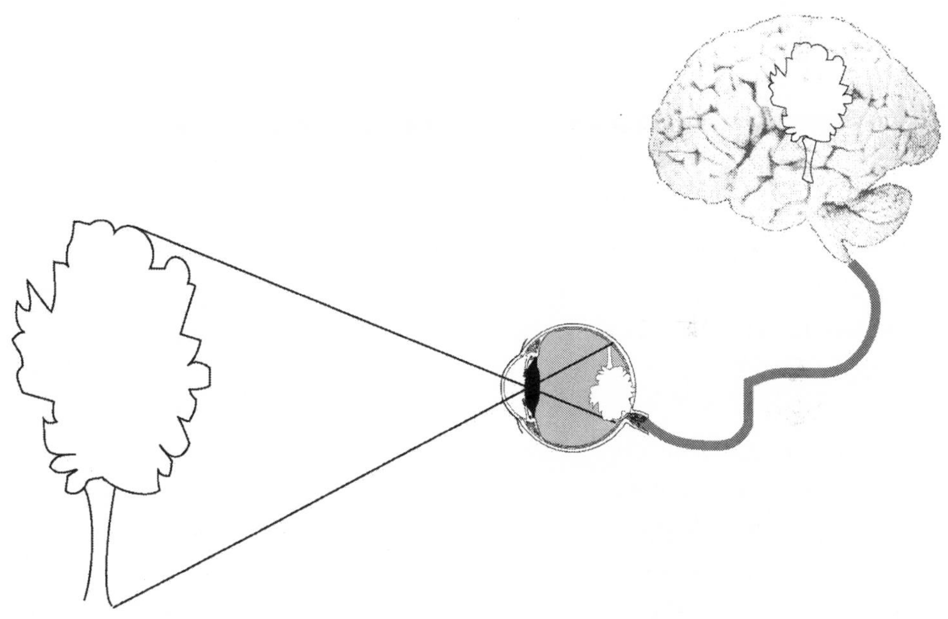

Figure 13.1

Because of this doubling of the physical world through the five senses (a physical object and a mental representation of that object), the beastly or selfish and emotional aspect of ourselves, known as the ego, is viewed as having ten **horns**: i.e., ten powerful influences, with each influence reigning supreme (**diadems upon its horns**) in its arena of influence.

The ego possesses a cunning intelligence (**like unto a leopard**), crushes others with its overbearing words and actions (**feet of a bear**), and tears cruelly into anyone or anything who would threaten its rule (**... mouth of a lion**). These characteristics suit the purpose of our rebellious spirit (**dragon**), and thus it gives the ego its **power and seat, and great authority**.

The seven chakras are envisioned as **heads,** because it is through them that the energy is given form and purpose for the ego's selfishness. It is the ego's bent toward self-preservation and physical expression which lends the blasphemous name to each of the seven chakras. The true purpose of the chakras is to facilitate the full expression of spiritual energy in the physical realm. When the ego controls these creative, spiritual energy transformers, it alters their purposes and they act for self, thus blaspheming their original purposes.

One of the chakras (**heads**) had a mortal wound which **was healed**, and the **all the world wondered after the beast**. Since the original purpose of the chakras was to serve as vortices for the transformation of spiritual energy, when the ego restricts the amount of that energy that can come through the chakras, then it is indeed wounding their ability to function in their natural manner. But why is only one chakra wounded? And how was it healed? To answer these questions we must realize that just as a head is that part of the physical body that houses the thinking apparatus (the brain), the chakras are more than just doors that open or close in the presence of spiritual energy. They also have associated with them physical regions of the body that take the spiritual energy and begin to manifest it in the physical plane through the application of the highest level of consciousness available to them. When we were created, our highest consciousness was that of being one with God and with others. When we lose that spiritual consciousness of oneness, we experience the first death and believe ourselves to be separate and alone. To prevent ourselves from experiencing severe depression and slipping into solipsism, we allow the ego to use the will – the free will that God has given us – to express the ego's desires. The ego thus is creative in its expression, but its creativity is for self rather than for others.

By allowing the ego to influence the perception of self through the use of free will, we are able to develop a stronger ego that may help us to survive in the physical and emotional turmoil of our world. Thus, what the ego does is for its own survival and growth and, from the point of view of the physical, its actions are both essential and justified.

From Revelation's viewpoint, the chakra associated with the will (the fifth chakra) first appeared to be mortally wounded when it no longer had contact with God's will to give it direction and life. But when the ego used kundalini in conjunction with giving new purpose to the self, the chakra once again could be active – even though it was now acting solely for the benefit of self. The physical body is grateful for the action of the ego (**all the world wondered**), because it allowed the physical body to survive and even to have the feel of power and control. The body at first worships the spirit of selfish rebellion (**worshiped the dragon**), which gives its power to the ego. Then the body begins to worship the ego itself (**worshiped the beast**) for its seemingly invincible mastery over outside influences. This, in turn, puffs up the ego, which now boasts of its strength (**speaking great things and blasphemies**). At this time the ego is allowed to rule for one-half cycle (**forty and two months**), using all its resources to increase its influence for selfish purposes.

As verse six shows, the ego attempts to assert its control by blaspheming **against God**, even **to blaspheme his name, and his tabernacle, and them that dwell in heaven.**. If you remember, in the story of Job, Satan was given permission to harm Job's physical condition, but not to harm his life. In Revelation we see that the beast, having the spirit of Satan as its creator and not being allowed to harm the life force of an individual, attempts to assert its influence by making every aspect of the individual reflect the purpose of self rather than that of the Christ Spirit. The ego even attacks the concept of God within us where the body is the temple of God (**his tabernacle**), as well as the consciousness of being heavenly creatures with God (**them that dwell in heaven**). Although its influence does not extend to those areas, the ego, which exists within, is still able to place temptations in the pathways of all who have not yet reached the consciousness of being one with God. Even living as a saint in the physical does not prevent the ego's influence from being present (**make war with the saints, and to overcome them**). The ego's power is so strong that we believe it is the true self; we **worship it** and would do anything to hold on to it. When we grasp the ego so tightly that we identify our self with it, then we are denying the spiritual connection between our higher self (the **man child** taken up to Heaven in Chapter 12) and God. In denying that connection, we are denying ourselves the way out of our fallen condition (our loss of spiritual consciousness). When this happens, our names are not written ... **in the book of life of the Lamb.**

Chapter 13:9-10

Scripture

Revelation 13:9

If any man have an ear, let him hear

Revelation 13:10

He that leadeth into captivity shall go into captivity: he that killeth with the sword must be killed with the sword. Here is the patience and the faith of the saints.

Symbolism/Meaning

If any man has an ear, let him hear - a road sign that says, "Pay attention!"

killeth with the sword must be killed with the sword - a statement of karma.

Commentary

Verses nine and ten comprise a two verse interlude between the two beasts These two verses are actually a warning: The ego is indeed a beast that has the potential of taking over our thoughts and dictating our beliefs and actions according to what seems best for the ego's continuance, but the actions of the ego actually lead to a life of accumulated karma. If we allow the ego to be a proxy for the higher self, then we become slaves to the physical (**captivity**). If we cut ourselves off from our higher self, then we are cutting away our true source of life (**slays with the sword ...**).

Chapter 13:11-18

Scripture

Revelation 13:11

And I beheld another beast coming up out of the earth; and he had two horns like a lamb, and he spake as a dragon.

Revelation 13:12

And he exerciseth all the power of the first beast before him, and causeth the earth and them which dwell therein to worship the first beast, whose deadly wound was healed

Revelation 13:13

And he doeth great wonders, so that he maketh fire come down from heaven on the earth in the sight of men,

Revelation 13:14

And deceiveth them that dwell on the earth by the means of those miracles which he had power to do in the sight of the beast; saying to them that dwell on the earth, that they should make an image to the beast, which had the wound by a sword, and did live.

Revelation 13:15

And he had power to give life unto the image of the beast, that the image of the beast should both speak, and cause that as many as would not worship the image of the beast should be killed.

Revelation 13:16

And he causeth all, both small and great, rich and poor, free and bond, to receive a mark in their right hand, or in their foreheads:

Revelation 13:17

And that no man might buy or sell, save he that had the mark, or the name of the beast, or the number of his name.

Revelation 13:18

Here is wisdom. Let him that hath understanding count the number

of the beast: for it is the number of a man; and his number is Six hundred threescore and six.

Symbolism/Meaning

earth - the physical.

two horns - double-mindedness of the ego (either for self or for others).

like a lamb - gentle, following meekly .

spake as a dragon - purpose was that of selfishness.

power of the first beast - actions come from selfishness of the ego.

fire come down from heaven - destruction or zeal

image to the beast - the selfish personality.

give life unto the image - give life to the personality.

a mark in their right hand, or in their foreheads - actions (hand) or thought (forehead) are selfish and egocentric.

buy or sell - participate in actions which are purely physical and for self.

Six hundred threescore and six - selfishness or self

Commentary

In this next section, beginning with verse 11, we are introduced to the second **beast**. This beast arises out of the **earth** rather than the **sea**. Since the **earth** symbolizes the physical world, we are able to see the dual nature of the rebellious spirit: It can influence the emotions (**sea**) as well as the physical (**earth**). Remember that the ego, as the first beast, is the perception of who we think we are. We even come to believe that the ego is the true self rather than our created image of who we are for this lifetime. As we allow the ego to possess our strength and to act (through the emotions) for the true self that we hide deep within, we discover that our actions (the results of our thoughts, beliefs, emotions, etc.) may be applied in two ways: for self or for others. Our purposes sometimes seem to be worthy of God, but, at other times, we are ashamed of our selfish actions. This double-mindedness[2] is a result of the dragon's influence: His duality of action is symbolized by the **two horns**. Notice that Revelation 13:11 states that this beast has horns **like a lamb**. Since young sheep (**lambs**) do not have horns, this image reveals that the power or strength of this second beast is concentrated in our actions, which often seem to be gentle and innocent. Moreover, since the ego, or first beast, is the source of this second beast's power (**power of the first beast**), it might be said that the second beast (our actions) "... follow its master just like a lamb – for self or God – following and doing the bidding of its master."[3] Our actions flow as a natural result from our purposes. If we allow the ego to determine our purposes, then our actions will speak of this egocentricity which originates from the rebellious spirit within (**spake as a dragon**).

This descriptive use of symbols in John's vision helps us to understand how the ego works: We form the ego from the desire to express our self-ness. We then bestow authority upon our created "self" to act in our place. It does so by creating this second beast to be the active agent that manifests the spirit of the dragon within the physical world. By believing that we, as individuals, are purely physical, we convince ourselves that the selfish actions of the second beast are to our benefit and thus are justified in strengthening the ego (**causeth the earth and them which dwell therein to worship the first beast**), even though the actions of the ego take us further away from God. We tend to hold on to the conscious identity given to us through the ego and to hide our true identity deep within the subconscious. Now we can believe that our actions are those of the ego within us, and that therefore we do not have to accept responsibility for our actions. We can say "the Devil made me do it" and not feel any guilt or need for repentance. The truth is that we have taken the gift of free will which God gave us and have turned it over to the ego as it masquerades its own desires as ours. We must still accept responsibility for these selfish desires, although they were given power by the dragon (Satan) and did not originate within our true self. These selfish desires and actions are ours by virtue of our choice to emphasize our separateness and individuality rather than our oneness and unity with God. As we concentrate on and direct our attention to certain thoughts or ideas, we give power and energy to those thoughts and ideas. By choosing to emphasize our self-ness, we give power to the ego. With this power, the ego can then do **great wonders**. Even when one seems to be on the right path and in communion with the God within, this power to do wonders can easily be misused. Revelation 13:13 (makes **fire come down from heaven on the earth in the sight of men**) is reminiscent of 1 Kings 18 where Elijah, closely in touch with God, calls down fire to burn up the water-soaked sacrifice he had set up to disgrace the prophets of Baal in front of all the people. All this was well and good, but Elijah did not stop there. Overwhelmed with his power, he then commanded that all the prophets of Baal be assassinated on the spot to satisfy his zeal. Again, this is the temptation of the double nature of the ego – it can result in service for others, or it can result in self-aggrandizement. These displays of power may seem to be what is best at the moment, but they later result in more problems.[4] The **fire** coming down from heaven could also symbolize the destructive zeal of one who uses spiritual power in selfish ways.

Whatever they may symbolize, the **great wonders** of the ego are for deceptive purposes (**deceiveth them that dwell on the earth**). This display of power causes the self to create a self-image (**make an image to the beast**) of what it believes itself to be. This image is known as our personality – that which we project outward for others to see. The personality, created by the desire and influence of the ego, becomes so important to us that we think of this personality as being the essence of who we are – all of our beliefs, desires, and thoughts rolled up into one creature. We breathe life into this image of ourselves (**give life unto the image of the beast**) and allow it to speak for us. Other people see the actions and hear the words of our personality. They come to know this projection and believe that this projected image is the true us. When people talk about someone, they are actually referring to that person's personality. How many times have we conjectured as to the probable actions of another person based simply upon our understanding of that individual's personality? Or how many people have been hurt by another's image of who they are? I remember quite distinctly the feeling I had as I read the comments about me written by my friends in my senior yearbook. Although their image of me was not a bad one, it was not the one I held. Nevertheless, I consciously accepted and projected their image of me as my true self. I began to worship the ego's projected image (my personality), rather than to hold on to the inner knowledge of who I really am. In other words, the inner part of me that held on to the truth was slain, because it did not worship the ego's image (**cause that as many as would not worship the image of the beast should be killed**).

By desiring the approval of others more than I desired the truth, my ego subtly strengthened its hold on me. My mental image of me gradually changed from that of a spiritual-minded being to that of a physical creation: I desired the physical image more than the spiritual truth; I became more concerned with my physical appearance; I hoped for a reward in heaven after I died, rather than for the manifestation of a truly selfless existence of service for others while incarnate in the physical. For this reason, I was not able to commune with my true self for the wisdom and knowledge I needed. I called upon God, but it was the God outside of me, transcendent and "Wholly Other."[5] This God did not seem to be near me or to be concerned about my problems. He would not talk to me, except as I became aware of external events and the messages they contained.

Even though I thought I was "good" (i.e., righteous), deep within me I knew that something was missing; however, I did not take the time to search for what it might be. My habits and inclinations kept me too busy attempting to uphold my projected image. This condition is precisely what is meant by the **mark** of the beast as described in Revelation 13:16-17: to possess a certain pattern of thoughts and actions which reflect their egocentric origins within. This mark is found in both the actions (**right hand**) and the thoughts (**forehead**) of those who are controlled by the ego. Unless we possess that **mark, or the name of the beast, or the number of his name**, we are not able to **buy or sell**. Both buying and selling are human conventions that we have created for the sole purpose of satisfying our physical comforts. One who lives in the spirit is able to trust in God for "our daily bread," rather than believe we must engage in the process of buying or selling. [6] I realize that most people are not capable of living wholly on trust, but that simply strengthens the message of Revelation.

Even when we examine the number of the beast, **666**, we discover this same concept: The number six is sometimes viewed as a symbol for sin, since it is short of God's perfection (i.e., seven symbolizes God's perfection and six is one less than seven). Since three is also a number representing perfection, three sixes would symbolize perfect sin. Of course, this explanation would need to be altered if we accept the alternate number of 616 [7] When this number is used, we look at the placement of the numbers: the number one hemmed in by two number sixes. The placement of the two sixes (which represent not only sin but also the mentality of humankind, which attempts to exclude any thought of God) around the number one (symbolizing God) shows how we attempt to hide God within our own selfishness. We want only our selves to show, both front and back, and we attempt to hide the God within. But the One is still there, deep within ourselves, awaiting the time when our selfishness, projected through the ego, will be cast away.

The infamous number of the beast, which is also the number of man, therefore symbolizes the human expression without the awareness of God. Whenever we have the mentality of being separate, physical creatures, all alone in our journey in the universe, then our actions, beliefs – even our thoughts – reflect the narrowness to which we have restricted ourselves. By denying our true self-expression, we are the ones who stop short of the perfection of God. This is the story of our lives in the ego. And yet, as hopeless as it might seem, there is a way out of our self-deception. Chapter 14 begins with a description of the way back to God.

Chapter Fourteen

The New Person

Having been given the picture of our present condition (i.e., lost in our own selfishness) and the reasons for this condition, John is shown a picture of our hope in Christ. Chapter 14 is a summary of the actions by the seven chakras as they are cleansed and completely opened by the acceptance of our spiritual state (i.e., companions with God) guided by the Christ Spirit.

Yet there is a difference between the functions of the chakras at this point and their functions as described in Chapters 2 and 3. In our spiritual journey, the chakras perform as spiritual transformers, taking the spiritual energy provided by God and changing it into manifested thoughts or actions in the physical world. When the Christ Spirit is allowed full reign in one's life and the chakras have been cleansed and fully opened, then the chakras themselves undergo a transformation. No longer are they simply points of contact between the physical and spiritual realms: They develop and evolve into consciously aware entities that are capable of activity within the mind and the physical body of an individual. It is as if the chakras become aware of themselves as separate individuals and begin to take a more active part in the development of the whole. This awareness can be likened to a little league baseball team whose outfielders have been running and catching fly balls for several years. Suddenly, they realize that they can more fully contribute to the success of their team if they use their knowledge of the outfield to hit the ball when they are at bat. Hence, they play a more active role in the team's success: Rather than only waiting for a ball to be hit to them while they are in the outfield, they take control and begin strategically hitting the ball during their times at bat. In the same manner, the chakras that are ruled by the Christ Spirit do not just wait for energy to be given to them: They actively apply certain principles to the energy passing through them, assisting in the transformation of an individual into the 'glorified body' spoken of by the Apostle Paul in his writings.[1]

Associated as they are to the seven endocrine centers, the seven chakras connect the spiritual to the physical through the mind and the consciousness. This process may be observed by the workings of the endocrine centers. These glandular centers are influenced by the mind. For example, when we are badly frightened, the adrenal glands pump more adrenaline into the blood stream to give the body the extra burst of strength needed to face whatever it is that frightened the individual. This is the familiar "fight or flight" reaction. When we ask "Why was the adrenaline released?" the only satisfactory answer we can supply is that the individual believed that such a response was needed, and this belief (which is a function of the mind) caused the mind to act upon that belief and to send a message to the proper glands (the adrenals). Thus we see that the mind is the active agent, dispensing the proper commands to the bodily organs. Since none of the process was consciously directed, we conclude that the subconscious mind is in control of the adrenals. (The autonomic nervous system is controlled by the subconscious mind.)

By taking this line of argument one step further, we gain insight into the marvels of the human body. In order to influence or direct anything, the mind must operate through consciousness. This consciousness must be present both in the mind and in the object receiving the mind's influence. Thus the physical body organ(as the adrenals in the previous example) must have a certain level of consciousness in order to be influenced by the mind. Indeed, this consciousness extends even to the cellular level. Each physical cell possesses a type of consciousness that allows the mind (a nonphysical force) to have influence over the physical cell itself. Like any consciousness, this cellular consciousness may be raised to a greater level of awareness. Chapter 14 speaks to this increase in consciousness of the physical human body.

Chapter 14:1-5

Scripture

Revelation 14:1

And I looked, and, lo, a Lamb stood on the mount Sion, and with him an hundred forty and four thousand, having his Father's name written in their foreheads.

Revelation 14:2

And I heard a voice from heaven, as the voice of many waters, and as the voice of a great thunder: and I heard the voice of harpers harping with their harps:

Revelation 14:3

And they sung as it were a new song before the throne, and before the four beasts, and the elders: and no man could learn that song but the hundred and forty and four thousand, which were redeemed from the earth.

Revelation 14:4

These are they which were not defiled with women; for they are virgins. These are they which follow the Lamb whithersoever he goeth. These were redeemed from among men, being the first fruits unto God and to the Lamb.

Revelation 14:5

And in their mouth was found no guile: for they are without fault before the throne of God.

Symbolism/Meaning

looked - concentration of one's consciousness.

Lamb - Christ Spirit

Mount Sion - spiritual level of consciousness (e.g., a "mountain-top" experience).

a hundred and forty four thousand - the bodily cells which have remained in perfection.

name written on their foreheads - possessing the Christ Consciousness.

voice from heaven - a thought in consciousness from the true, inner self.

as the voice of many waters - abundant, spiritual life.

as the voice of a great thunder - dynamic, with authority.

voice of harpers harping with their harps - purposeful, accompanied by action or a story of action.

not defiled with women - remain, whole, balanced.

first fruits unto God and to the Lamb - the first to reach the physical perfection.

in their mouth was found no gile - never put on false pretenses.

Commentary

John begins this chapter by concentrating his attention toward the vision that now appears (**I looked**). Mount Sion, the mountain upon which the temple was built, was considered to be one of the "high places" of the Hebrew faith. These high places were sacred areas of worship where one could be in the presence of God. Symbolically, Mt. Sion represents a high level of spiritual awareness – the level of consciousness where an individual is in the presence of the Christ Spirit (**Lamb**). By seeing the **Lamb** standing on **Mount Sion,** John is aware of the prominent position of the Christ Spirit. The individual is in the very presence of God and, since choosing to be guided by the Christ Spirit and to have the "Mind of Christ," is becoming aware of its oneness with God.

In addition to the Christ Spirit, John also sees in this vision **a hundred and forty- four thousand**. These are the bodily cells that have always had the full consciousness of being one with God (**having his Father's name written in their foreheads** [see Revelation 7:4-8]) and that serve as the catalyst or example for all other cells in the body to imitate. These 144,000 have held within themselves the awareness of being one with the Creator. This pattern of consciousness, held safely within these cells, carries the Divine spark into the physical. Without these 144,000, the awareness of our true self would be lost.

In this state, where the individual has chosen to be guided and controlled by the Christ Spirit, John hears a **voice from heaven**. This voice is the true self, speaking with authority (**loud thunder**) and filled with life-giving power (**many waters**). This voice is describing how the spiritual energy is to be made manifest in the physical. The symbolism of the **voice of harpers** playing on their harps points to the ideal of all bodily cells being attuned to the God-given intentions of the spiritual energy. The **harpers** playing on their harps refers to the activity of the 144,000 cells that are in tune with God. They sing a new song which is the song of cooperation and obedience to the will of God. This song is presented to the Christ Spirit now dwelling upon the **throne** and to the earthly aspects of our humanity (**four beasts**). Since it is sung before the elders, it encompasses all the senses – both physical and spiritual.

This new song, or level of awareness, could only be learned by those who have not attempted to combine the spiritual and the physical through selfish desires and lusts. The phrase **they which were not defiled with women; for they are virgins**, refers to the often overlooked reference in Genesis where "... the sons of God saw that the daughters of men were fair; and they took to wife such of them as they chose" (Genesis. 6:2). This is a reference to the spiritual beings ("sons of God") who desired the pleasures of the physical and thus attempted to join the physical and the spiritual together in a manner that God never intended. The Book of Enoch speaks of this event, stating many unforeseen and undesirable consequences of this selfish desire.[2] Without getting lost in the details of this event (which also relates to the fallen angels), the point of concern for us is that it was their selfish desires that led them astray. They did not **follow the Lamb** (the Christ Spirit) and learn how to properly combine the spiritual and the physical.

Yet the 144,000 remain true to the Christ Spirit and never attempt to bypass God and hurry His will (**are without fault**). The meaning behind this symbol is that there exists within each of us a part that never sinned, that never participated in the worship of the beast (the development of the ego), and that therefore has remained in contact with God. Many of us today would say, "Yes, that part of us is our soul, or that divine spark within our soul." Yet John's vision seems to say that it is more than that: somehow, there exists within us physical cells that have a heightened consciousness and that have always worked to bring about God's will "in earth" (the physical) "as it is in heaven" (the spiritual). These cells are built into us and have existed there since before the Fall (or loss of one's awareness of being spiritual), keeping themselves untainted from the desires and lusts of the physical or the ego. These are physical cells, yet they are spiritualized, because they never gave in to the demands of the flesh. This **new song** that only these 144,000 cells could sing is symbolic of that heightened awareness or increase in consciousness.

The subconscious mind has always had control over the cellular level of consciousness, so it is first to recognize what makes this song **new** – a heightened awareness. It, too, is raised to a higher level of consciousness now that it comprehends how the spiritual desires of God may be manifested in the physical without the need of an ego. The subconscious now realizes that the Fall was necessary for the spiritual soul to understand the physical and to make the physical a part of the soul's total experience. Without the Fall, this new combination of flesh and spirit could never happen! After eating the fruit, Adam and Eve suddenly become conscious of the physical ("then the eyes of both were opened, and they knew that they were naked" [Genesis 3:7]) and unaware of the full range of their creative abilities. Prior to the Fall, they had been spiritual, godlike creatures inhabiting a physical body and knowing God (Elohim) on an intimate basis. Now they understood themselves to be physical creatures who relate to the Lord God

(Elohim-Jehovah) as if they were subordinates afraid of the "Big Boss" (Genesis 3:8-10). Since that time, the story of humanity has been a struggle to answer the question "Who – or what – are we?" During the ages of our struggle, we have carried along with us a cellular memory of those days in the Garden of Eden when we possessed a spiritual consciousness (**the one hundred and forty four thousand**). But the majority of the cells in our bodies have no consciousness of the spiritual state; they only know themselves to be physical. As we choose to increase the God-consciousness within our awareness, the spiritualized cells become a catalyst for disseminating the message of our spiritual origins (**sing a new song**) to our other cells in an attempt to also raise their consciousness.

Chapter 14:6-11

Scripture

Revelation 14:6

And I saw another angel fly in the midst of heaven, having the everlasting gospel to preach unto them that dwell on the earth, and to every nation, and kindred, and tongue, and people,

Revelation 14:7

Saying with a loud voice, Fear God, and give glory to him; for the hour of his judgment is come: and worship him that made heaven, and earth, and the sea, and the fountains of waters.

Revelation 14:8

And there followed another angel, saying, Babylon is fallen, is fallen, that great city, because she made all nations drink of the wine of the wrath of her fornication.

Revelation 14:9

And the third angel followed them, saying with a loud voice, If any man worship the beast and his image, and receive his mark in his forehead, or in his hand,

Revelation 14:10

The same shall drink of the wine of the wrath of God, which is poured out without mixture into the cup of his indignation; and he

> **shall be tormented with fire and brimstone in the presence of the holy angels, and in the presence of the Lamb:**

Revelation 14:11

> **And the smoke of their torment goes up for ever and ever; and they have no rest, day or night, these worshipers of the beast and its image, and whoever receives the mark of its name."**

Symbolism/Meaning

another angel - controlling force of the first chakra (Gonad center).

everlasting gospel - the true message of who we are.

preach unto them that dwell upon the earth - the physical and earthly/mental is the recipient of the new awareness.

hour of his judgment -the consequences of the new awareness will be experienced through the service of the individual.

another angel - controlling force of the second chakra (Leyden center).

Babylon - the self projected by the ego.

fornication - the desire for self.

And the third angel - controlling force of the third chakra (Adrenal center).

wine of the wrath of God's - accepting responsibility for our own actions.

tormented with fire and brimstone - continually being purged of our desire for self.

in the presence of the holy angels, and in the presence of the Lamb - having an awareness of the true state of our soul.

Commentary

The first angel spoken of in this next selection of scripture (beginning with verse six) (**another angel**) symbolizes a new influence within the body, dwelling first within our consciousness (**in the midst of heaven**). This new angel brings a new consciousness to the first chakra: the consciousness of the spiritual origins and creative capabilities within the physical body. The desire of this first chakra now is to make the new consciousness available to all cells in the body (**them that dwell on the earth, and to every nation, and kindred, and tongue , and people**). This chakra, as noted in the commentary on Chapter 2, serves as a motor to raise the prana or spiritual energy within the body and to disperse that energy to all other chakras. This is the perfect chakra to **preach** this **everlasting gospel** to all other cells! The message distributed is one of instruction (**Fear God and give glory to him**) as well as announcement (**for the hour of his judgments is come**). The consciousness directing this first chakra now becomes one which tells the other cells that they can praise God for allowing them to experience the physical as they come to recognize their spiritual origins. It is also a message of great importance, because it is an attempt to awaken the total body to an actualization of its creative potential. The hour of judgment refers to whether the body takes the prana and uses it for others or for self. We must take an active part in manifesting God's will in the physical for it is this same will – or creative forces – that **...made heaven, and earth, and the sea and the fountains of water**. These creative forces are there to work through us, and they are infinitely more powerful than any of the creative forces arising from within ourselves. This should produce a sense of awe within us as we realize the power available to us – the same power that **made heaven, and earth, and the sea and the fountains of water**. Such awe should also raise within us the desire to serve others through our manifestation of God's energy.[3]

Jesus, because he completely submitted his will to God's will, was blessed with freely flowing prana and kundalini throughout his chakras. This powerful combined creative energy allowed Jesus to perform healings and other miracles, all of which Jesus attributed to "the Father who dwells in me does his works" (John 14:10)."[4]

As the first chakra begins to take on this new consciousness of direction represented by the first angel, we also begin to see some of the new directions of the individual who comes to this stage in their growth and awareness. The life of such a person will be characterized by a desire to serve others, by an understanding of the power available to them, and by a respect for the responsibilities that come with such power. The **judgment** spoken of in verse seven is simply this: recognition of God's energetic power, our ability to manifest that power in the physical, and a commitment to bring to physical manifestation the unadulterated expression of that energy. Our judgment comes with our level of understanding and how well we cooperated with God's creative forces.

Verse eight mentions **another angel**, symbolic of the second chakra. Earlier, we learned that this second chakra is where we place value upon what we create. We give our creations more or less value depending upon the degree we invest our own life-force in them. By investing ourselves in our many creations, we discover that we have created a multitude of life forms (ideas, thoughts, desires, physical objects, organizations, etc.), all of which have a little of our personality inherent within them. Many of these self-creations are selfish in nature and were created so that the ego could be physically sustained and its existence could continue. In his vision, John saw all of these selfish ego creations as a busy city: **Babylon**, a city synonymous with sin and self-indulgence. As we constantly give of our life-force (kundalini) to our creations, we create a city where the many aspects of our personality (**nations**) feast upon the selfish actions of our ego (**drink the wine of the wrath of her fornication.**).

Yet, this city of one's self, which the ego has constructed, begins to fall (**is fallen, is fallen ...**) because of starvation. Since there is no need to invest our own life into the new spiritual energy flowing through the second chakra, the whole of our created self (selves?) begins to die because of lack of sustained life-force. Without a constant investment of our life in what we desire to manifest (since God's intentions for this spiritual energy is intact, we simply let it flow through us, bringing it into manifestation as God desires, not as we desire), the second chakra's previous job is no longer needed. Thus, our selfish personality begins to crumble as we manifest the greater characteristics and will of God, rather than our own creations. Our actions point to God, and not to ourselves!

The third **angel**, symbolizing the new aspects of the third chakra (the adrenal center) speaks with a commanding **loud voice**. Since we learned in Chapters 2 and 3 that it is through the third chakra that we accept responsibility for our actions of changing or imposing our will upon the energy flowing through it, it is no surprise that this new characterization of the third chakra also refers to such activity. We are told through the authority symbolized by the **loud voice** that any cells that continue to **worship the beast and his image ... shall drink of the wine of the wrath of God**. This is a warning that those cells which do not advance in consciousness and that continue to hold on to and value the ego and its creations, will also continue to experience the results of its karma. As long as they claim responsibility for the continuance of the selfish ego's actions, they must also reap the consequences of those actions. These consequences, at this point in one's development, will not be buffered by the tender mercies of God. To know what is good and not to do it is sin,[5] and this sin (or error in judgment) must be dealt with quickly and decisively if the body, mind, and spirit are to claim their spiritual destiny. The desire for the ego's way must be purged from the consciousness of the individual. To be **tormented with fire and brimstone** is the symbolism of this purging process. It is accomplished as the new consciousness grows within the presence of the already spiritualized cells of the body (**in the presence of the holy angels**) and as the Christ Consciousness (**the presence of the Lamb**) begins to dominate the mental as well as the physical aspects of the individual. This process of quickly receiving the consequences (karma) of our selfish actions, thoughts, desires, etc., along with the growth of our awareness of being spiritual companions with God, seems painful to those who are carnal-minded. Yet to those who are aware of their true nature, the goal for which they strive overshadows any physical pain or discomfort. For anyone who is not of the mind of Christ, karma – the reaping of what we have sown – is a continual process that never ceases (**the smoke of their torment goes up for ever and ever; and they have no rest, day nor night**), as long as we refuse to allow the Christ Spirit to totally occupy our being. Even when we are not aware of its process, we still experience karma as we punish our bodies with worry, anxiety, stress, and general dis-ease. In this section of Revelation, John is shown that when we acquire a heightened awareness of the Christ Spirit, then the karma process becomes more evident to us – even at the cellular level. We become more aware of the consequences of our selfish actions and their consequences. No wonder the "life for self only" seems less and less desirable as our spiritual awareness increases. It is this awareness of karma in our lives that prompts the warning found in the next couple of verses.

Chapter 14:12-13

Scripture

Revelation 14:12

Here is the patience of the saints: here are they that keep the commandments of God, and the faith of Jesus.

Revelation 14:13

And I heard a voice from heaven saying unto me, Write, Blessed are the dead which die in the Lord from henceforth: Yea, saith the Spirit, that they may rest from their labours; and their works do follow them.

Symbolism/Meaning

patience of the saints - process of striving toward total Christ Consciousness.

Write - symbol meaning that what follows is important!

dead which die in the Lord - to die while possessing the awareness of one's true self.

Commentary

As we begin to grow into Christ Consciousness and to become aware of the process of karma within our lives, we tend to grow discouraged as we realize more acutely that our selfish actions have caused the pain our bodies and mind experience. The extent of our suffering seems overwhelming, even though the only change we might experience from our previous life is the increased awareness of the karma operative in our lives. At first, we are not aware of karma's consequences. Afterward, we despair because of the extent of karma's destructive force upon our bodies. This period of despair may occur at an early stage of our increased awareness, before we have had time to realize that we have always experienced the effects of karma and that now we have the power to do something about karma's influence. Therefore, John is given the **call for the patience of the saints.** By enduring the despairing thoughts we have as we grow in awareness, the chakras will then assist in breaking the tight grip which the ego has upon each of us. The tendency toward despair is the ego's way of asserting its own influence over us for its continued existence. The ego's actions, however, lead to karmic influences that destroy the physical and deceive the mental. As the Apostle Paul says, "The wages of sin is death."[6] There is a double meaning to this concept: first, that the consequences of the selfish ego's actions lead to the death of the physical body; secondly, that it is only through the death of the selfish (i.e., ego- directed) consciousness that the Christ Consciousness can bring us to an awareness and manifestation of the eternal life which is ours by birthright.

It is no surprise, then, that the Spirit speaks to John from his higher self (**voice from heaven**) and tells him to **write** down an important message. As previously noted, whenever John's vision is interrupted in this manner, the message is of extreme importance. Notice what the message says: "**Blessed are the dead which die in the Lord from henceforth.**" On the cellular level of consciousness, this refers to the death of the ego consciousness and the birth of the new Christ Consciousness within the cells. On a more macro level, the death of enough of our old cells may lead to the physical death of the body. Yet the higher level of consciousness remains with us beyond death: **... and their works do follow them**. To **rest from their labors** refers to the breaking free from the constant cycle of selfishness-karma-despair-selfishness which we travel in our ego-led existence. Once we begin to live in harmony with our true nature, then there is no need for the karmic repercussions that attempt to teach us and to direct us to God's intentions rather than our own. Thus, those who have the Christ Consciousness no longer must continue to face karma. Their struggles are over as they allow God's energy to flow through them and become manifest in the physical as God intended, not as we selfishly intend. In addition, no longer do we have to expend our energy in order to sustain our selfish creations. God's energy now empowers what we unselfishly manifest.

Chapter 14:14-20

Scripture

Revelation 14:14

And I looked, and behold a white cloud, and upon the cloud one sat like unto the Son of man, having on his head a golden crown, and in his hand a sharp sickle.

Revelation 14:15

And another angel came out of the temple, crying with a loud voice to him that sat on the cloud, Thrust in thy sickle, and reap: for the time is come for thee to reap; for the harvest of the earth is ripe.

Revelation 14:16

And he that sat on the cloud thrust in his sickle on the earth; and the earth was reaped.

Revelation 14:17

And another angel came out of the temple which is in heaven, he also having a sharp sickle.

Revelation 14:18

And another angel came out from the altar, which had power over fire; and cried with a loud cry to him that had the sharp sickle, saying, Thrust in thy sharp sickle, and gather the clusters of the vine of the earth; for her grapes are fully ripe.

Revelation 14:19

And the angel thrust in his sickle into the earth, and gathered the vine of the earth, and cast it into the great winepress of the wrath of God.

Revelation 14:20 And the wine press was trodden without the city, and blood came out of the winepress, even unto the horse bridles, by the space of a thousand and six hundred furlongs.

Symbolism/Meaning

white cloud - collective unconscious or a hidden truth.

upon the cloud one sat - master of this level of consciousness.

like unto the Son of man - the fourth chakra representation (thymus center).

crown - in control and possessing power.

sharp sickle - symbol of harvest.

another angel - directing force of the fifth chakra (thyroid center).

came out of the temple - now directed by the higher self.

Thrust in thy sickle, and reap - a command of the will to the lower centers to work in service for others.

harvest of the earth is ripe - time to manifest in the physical what the harvest of the spiritual brings.

And another angel - directing force of the sixth chakra (Pineal center).

he also having a sharp sickle - ready to reap the harvest.

another angel - 7th center (the pituitary) .

came out from the altar - purifying aspects of the Christ Consciousness.

power over fire - control over all forces, including that of purification.

clusters of the vine of the earth - the fruits of service.

winepress of the wrath of God - that which separates or strains.

blood - life.

horse's bridle - control point

one thousand six hundred furlongs - a period of time.

Commentary

In these final verses of Chapter 14, John's vision continues with an overview of the activities of the four higher chakras as these new angels, or forces, begin their influence. In verse 14 John saw one like **a Son of man**, seated on a **white cloud**, wearing **a golden crown** on his head and carrying **a sharp sickle** in his hand. This angel is described as bringing the previously hidden truth of our spirituality from the realm of the collective unconscious to serve us as we grow in spirit. The **white cloud** represents the unconscious or what is hidden, and being seated on the **cloud** symbolizes the mastery of the fourth chakra over the unconscious.

Remember, in the commentary upon the fourth chakra in Chapter 2, the Christ Spirit, speaking to this chakra, refers to himself as the "Son of God." Here, we have the angel of this chakra described as one **like unto the Son of man**. This is to remind us that it is around this chakra that the spiritual forces and the earthly forces revolve and are brought into balance. The angel of the fourth chakra now wears a **golden crown** to signify the heavenly power of this chakra to bring about the necessary balance. It has achieved this power by going through the physical experience, by meeting the karma generated by this experience, and then by returning to the awareness of its spiritual nature through its choosing to follow the Christ Spirit. It carries in its hand a **sharp sickle** signifying that it is now ready to restore balance by bringing into physical manifestation the new experiences that will result from having the purpose and ideals of Christ. The time is now to reap the results of a life led by the Spirit!

The fifth chakra (the thyroid center), represented by **another angel** (verse 15), comes out of the temple of the soul and directs the fourth angel to begin reaping the results of a life directed by the Christ Spirit (**Thrust in thy sickle, and reap**). This fifth angel, symbolizing the fifth chakra, is the angel of one's will. By using the will, we make decisions and choices as to how or whether we serve ourselves or others. That is why this angel, influenced by the higher self, is viewed as giving directions to the lower chakra. As long as the chakras are guided by the Christ Spirit, it is time (**the time is come for thee to reap**) to take God's spiritual energy and transform it into physical action. In so doing, we allow God to reap the results of His energy flowing through us that is being transformed into a physical manifestation. That is the meaning of "Thy Will be done on earth as it is in Heaven."

Because of the command of the will, the fourth chakra (dealing with the earthly forces even while balancing the spiritual and earthly forces within the individual) **thrust in his sickle on the earth and the**

earth was reaped. The earthly portions of the body were prepared to be an ambassador for God and represent the spiritual God of Heaven in the physical world. The human will, now at one with the will of God, directs the physical to manifest God's intentions. The result is the Logos made flesh.[7] It is for this reason that Jesus could say, "... the Son can do nothing of his own accord, but only what he sees the Father doing; for whatever he does, that the Son does likewise (John 5:19)." The body that has been cleansed by the will of the Christ Spirit has no desires of its own (i.e., selfish desires). Therefore it will take the spiritual energy given to it by God and perfectly manifest it in the world. God's intention for that energy becomes the Son's intention for it also.

The decision of the angels to choose the will of God also extends to the sixth chakra, as is shown in verse 17. This center, symbolizing the pineal center in the body, is characterized in Chapter 3 as representing the Mind of Christ within us. It is this center that has a direct link to the second chakra and that can open or close the passage of the spiritual energy flowing through the body. Again, this angel carries a **sharp sickle**, symbolic of its desire to open the way and to reap the results desired by God.

The seventh angel, representing the pituitary center and the seventh chakra, then emerges **from out from the altar**. Since the **altar** is a place of sacrifice, this is symbolic of the sacrifice of the ego. Remember, the seventh chakra is the one which receives the energy flowing through the other six chakras and then directs the body to respond to this energy in a manner consistent with the nature of the energy. The seventh chakra does not change or influence the energy. If the ego had influenced the energy, the response would have been a physical thought, urge, or action that was at least partially selfish in nature. Since the ego's influence had been sacrificed for the greater good of the Christ Consciousness, the energy reaching the seventh chakra is pure and unchanged, still containing the intention for that energy which God had placed within it originally. The new angel, or controlling influence for this chakra, is described as having **power over fire**. This description refers to the purity of the energy now received. In Chapter 3 the original angel of this chakra advised John to

buy gold refined in the fire, referring to the passage of God's spiritual energy (**gold**) through the chakras, so that God's intention is strengthened (**refined in the flame**), as it moves toward physical expression. In this passage, the seventh angel instructs the sixth angel to **Thrust in thy sharp sickle** (physically manifest the spiritual energy – i.e., act out God's will) and to gather **the clusters of the vine of the earth** (reap the results of service toward others). Now that the Christ Spirit is in control of the individual, the physical world of nature works in harmony with God's intentions. The individual can therefore command "the winds and the waves to obey,"[8] as did Jesus, and may even perform miracles. This agreement between the overall purpose of God's physical creation and that of the spiritual energy being manifested by someone possessing the Mind of Christ is described in John's vision through the words **its grapes are fully ripe**. The time for manifestation of God's will is when the energy possessing His will has fully matured within the individual.

As John watches in this vision, the individual transformed the spiritual energy into physical action (swung his sickle) and allowed God's will to produce the desired result (**gathered the vine of the earth**). This result was then honored as God's, because it was fulfilled in the manner which God intended. The **winepress of the wrath of God** is symbolic of allowing God's will to be manifest in all actions. We are not to draw out our own intentions from the actions made manifest while using God's energy. We are to allow God to use our actions to perform His will. Even though sometimes it might seem as if God is angrily punishing us, in actuality He is lovingly correcting us. God's **wrath** is a process of purifying us so we may return to Him filled with purity and cleansed of any egotistical tendencies. This is another reason that the seventh angel has **power over fire**: the Christ Consciousness helps to squeeze out the dross and to leave only pure life within us. Because of the physical service for others performed within the world and external to our bodies (**without the city**), an abundance of life force is produced (**blood came out of the winepress**). This life is given in service to others as the true, controlling point in our lives. This is the symbolism behind the image of the **horses' bridles**. The bridle is the instrument used to guide a horse or to command a horse to obey. Thus the **blood** (life) being as deep as the **horse's bridles** refers to the life of service as now controlling our actions. The **one thousand six hundred furlongs** symbolize the extent of influence such a life would have. Its influence would extend far beyond that which our own selfish actions might produce.

Chapter Fifteen

The Responsibility to Become

In the previous chapter, we were introduced to the concept of the **wrath of God**. It is important to fully comprehend this imagery if we are to understand the symbolism of the next few chapters. The word "wrath" means anger. Psychologically, anger, even righteous anger, is the fear of being hurt by what others say, do, or think. The hurt can be a physical, a mental, or a spiritual injury. If there is no perceived injury, then there can be no anger.

When we talk about the wrath of God, we must first remember that God can not be injured by any of his creation. To injure another is to have power over them, and God is omnipotent – no one can have power over God. Since we cannot injure God, His wrath can contain no hint of anger toward any creature. We may strike out at God, but He does not perceive any threat from us. What, then, is meant by the phrase **the wrath of God**?

To answer this question, imagine that you are an all-powerful God looking down at a tiny ant who is lashing out at you, attempting to hurt you in some way. What kind of emotion do you feel? Because you cannot be hurt, you will not feel anger; however, you might feel pity or compassion for that tiny ant, since the only one being hurt is the ant. Your only response toward it would be love. This is the only response God can have for us.

Thus the actions of the angels in both this chapter and the previous chapter are actions of God's love for us, not his anger and punishment toward us. It might seem to be punishment from the physical point of view, but from the spiritual point of view, everything is "for good for those who love the Lord."[1] What Jesus experienced in the last few hours of his life on earth was interpreted as painful and agonizing by those watching him, but, to Jesus, it was simply "bearing his cross" for the greater good. In fact, Edgar Cayce, in one reading, stated that Jesus laughed and joked even while on the way to Calvary.[2] Jesus was bearing the "wrath of God" in order to bring about a new level of consciousness into the physical. For him everything was an act of love, because he had the Mind of Christ, i.e., the Christ Consciousness.

Let us now begin our examination of Chapter 15 and its description of God's wrath.

Chapter 15:1-8

Scripture

Revelation 15:1

And I saw another sign in heaven, great and marvelous, seven angels having the seven last plagues; for in them is filled up the wrath of God

Revelation 15:2

And I saw as it were a sea of glass mingled with fire: and them that had gotten the victory over the beast, and over his image, and over his mark, and over the number of his name, stand on the sea of glass, having the harps of God.

Revelation 15:3

And they sing the song of Moses the servant of God, and the song of the Lamb, saying, Great and marvelous are thy works, Lord God Almighty; just and true are thy ways, thou King of saints.

Revelation 15:4

Who shall not fear thee, O Lord, and glorify thy name? for thou only art holy: for all nations shall come and worship before thee; for thy judgments are made manifest.

Revelation 15:5

And after that I looked, and, behold, the temple of the tabernacle of the testimony in heaven was opened:

Revelation 15:6

And the seven angels came out of the temple, having the seven plagues, clothed in pure and white linen, and having their breasts girded with golden girdles.

Revelation 15:7

And one of the four beasts gave unto the seven angels seven golden vials full of the wrath of God, who liveth for ever and ever.

Revelation 15:8

And the temple was filled with smoke from the glory of God, and from his power; and no man was able to enter into the temple, till the seven plagues of the seven angels were fulfilled.

Symbolism/Meaning

another sign in heaven - an aspect of consciousness.

seven angels - dealing with the seven chakras and the total person.

last - no need for any more changes or growth.

in them is filled up the wrath of God - A fulfilling of this type of God's love.

sea of glass mingled with fire - purified emotions.

them that had gotten the victory over the beast, and over his image, and over his mark - those without a selfish ego.

harps of God - in harmony with God. **song of Moses** - a song of victory.

song of the Lamb - a song of victory.

temple of the tabernacle of the testimony in heaven - an awakening to the awareness of the spiritual significance of all that we have done.

seven angels - the purified intelligences of the seven chakras.

one of the four beasts - representative of the physical senses.

golden vials - containers of spiritual essences.

wrath of God - the love of God.

smoke - results from the plagues.

no man was able to enter into the temple - - a necessary condition.

Commentary

This chapter begins with John being shown **another sign in heaven**. Since this is again in heaven, we know that it deals with consciousness. It is an important discovery for John, because he describes it as **great and marvelous**. Why would he describe **seven angels having the seven last plagues** as being **great and marvelous**? Most people would consider a creature carrying a plague as being a devil rather than an angel! The difference between seeing them as angels and devils is the difference between the physical consciousness and that of the spiritual or Christ Consciousness. Surgery is often viewed with fear and trepidation, even though it will bring relief from a lingering or life-threatening illness. In the same way, John, still possessing his physical consciousness, sees the angels' burdens as plagues. On the other hand, he is also sufficiently aware that, from a spiritual viewpoint, they are blessings.

John also states that these **plagues** are the last, **for in them is filled up the wrath of God**. If the wrath of God is really His love for us, then what does it mean to say that His wrath **is ended**? Could that mean that God's love for us is over? No, the symbolism behind this phrase goes deeper than that, with its roots deep within the human being as described in Revelation.

Throughout Revelation John has been shown how the human being must be cleansed. The chakras have been the target of this cleansing, because the purposes and ideals of the individual have affected the energy flowing through the chakras. We have also seen how God intends to "spiritualize" the cells of the physical body in order for them to be pure enough to form a synthesis of the physical, mental, and spiritual. These final plagues deal with this process of purifying the bodily cells. The cells are a repository of memories. Previously we learned that each cell has consciousness, even though it might be at a rudimentary level. The consciousness of our cells carries the patterns of existence that we place within them. If you have ever been cut, for example, your body will have a scar. This scar can be thought of as the memory of the time you were cut. If you have abused your body with drugs or alcohol for a long period of time, your body remembers that abuse, and you bear the results in your appearance as well as in your weaknesses. There are many times in our lives when we have done the selfish thing, and our body's cells have remembered our actions, even though our conscious mind has long forgotten. The karmic effects of our actions are there with us long after we have forgotten the incident. When such consequences of our actions return to us in karmic effects, and we have forgotten the actions, then we wonder, "Why is this happening to me?" It takes a leap of faith to realize that we are responsible for our condition, even though, in the physical sense, we see no connection between what is happening to us and what we have done to deserve our fate. If we accept the premise that karmic results can transcend a lifetime and may return to us in a different lifetime (i.e., accept reincarnation), then we see the necessity of accepting responsibility for our present condition if we are to reach the stage of possessing the Christ Consciousness. After all, did not Jesus bear the responsibility of "the sins of the world" and accept the consequences for those sins? How can we not accept the responsibility for our own condition and expect to be of the Mind of Christ? Thus, when John states that the wrath of God is ended, he is saying that the need for God to continually arrange for us to receive our karmic consequences is no longer needed: We are able to accept responsibility for whom we are and what we do. No wonder John states that this **sign in heaven** is **great and marvelous**!

As John begins to describe this vision, he sees **as it were a sea of glass mingled with fire**. Again John uses the terms "appeared to be," signifying that what he sees in this vision is not a real sea of glass mingled with fire, but rather it points to the purpose or intention of the vision. The **sea** symbolizes the emotions, and the **glass** symbolizes the crystallization of those emotions. The phrase **mingled with fire** to bring out the purifying aspects of what is intended. Remember, since this vision deals with the actual purification of the body now that the chakras are purified, and the body must deal with the karmic influences that we have built within the very structure of the cells, John is viewing the crystallized cellular memory of past actions, thoughts, and desires that are in the process of being purified. This process of purifying the cells involves revealing these subconscious memories to the new Christ Consciousness and accepting responsibility for them, thus releasing the cells from their bondage to these memories of selfish actions and desires. The cells that have not lost their consciousness of God (see Chapter 14) stand beside this **sea of glass** and vibrate in harmony with God's will (**having the harps of God**), serving as examples for the remaining cells to imitate. These cells, which had not succumbed to the beast, its image, or the number of its name, are singing the **song of Moses**. This song, found in Chapter 15 of Exodus, is the song that Moses sang after the Egyptian army had drowned in the Red Sea. It is a song of victory and a song of the glory of God. It is a song which celebrated the release of the Hebrew people from their bondage to the fleshpots of Egypt. For that reason, it is an appropriate song for the perfected cells to sing as they celebrate the upcoming release of the bodily cells from their bondage to the physical. The victory over the desire for only the physical is represented by the symbolism of **the song of the Lamb.**

Once the song is sung (verses 3 and 4), John's awareness is directed to a new sight: **the temple of the tabernacle of the testimony in heaven was opened**. What is this new sight that will command John's attention for the remainder of Chapter 15 and all of Chapter 16? What is the significance of this **temple** now being **opened**?

Consider an ancient concept brought out in a reading made by Edgar Cayce:

> Q-6. Is the temple or tabernacle of testimony, Rev. 15:5, referring to Akashic Records?
> A-6. That as you may term the Akashic Record, or the Book of Life, or the Book of Revelation: that is, of the individual, see? 281-36

According to Cayce, this **temple of the tabernacle of the testimony in heaven** refers to an ancient belief that there exists a record of the events of each soul's journey through time and space. This record is a "Book of Revelation" for each individual and describes not only what the soul did, but also what it gained or lost in its spiritual journey. In other words, each of us has our own personal diary of our struggles toward becoming one in consciousness with God. This concept makes sense in this context, because the cells of the body must face their karmic past and conquer the tendencies to be selfish and physical. We cannot conquer the past if we are unaware of that past. When this personal record is **opened**, the karmic memories will be presented to our awareness.

This is the imagery behind the opening of this temple and the emergence of **the seven angels** with **the seven plagues**. We have already noted that the **plagues** are not events to be feared, but are rather the working out of God's love for us. By becoming aware of our personal history, we will be able to conquer it. The dress of the angels (**pure and white linen, having their breasts girded with golden girdles**) symbolizes the pure, heavenly love by which these so called plagues are delivered.

The earthly portion of the individual (**one of the four beasts**), realizing the importance of becoming purified at the physical, cellular level, offers God's love (**golden vials full of the wrath of God**) to the angels. This is John's way of describing the body's willingness to endure the plagues while recognizing them to be a means of God's love. In practical terms, this is when we stop and say "Thank you, Lord" in the midst of what may seem to be terrible or terrifying circumstances from the physical point of view. To be able to say this, and mean it, is one way of purifying the very cells of the body to become one with God.

In the final verse of this chapter, John comments that the **temple was filled with smoke from the glory of God and from his power**. This smoke is simply the result from the purification of the bodily cells and symbolizes the glory given to God through this process. This final step of enduring the plagues with joy is a necessary step, for without it **no man was able to enter the temple**: No one is able to return to God without taking the glorified physical body back with them. We all must become not only like Christ, we must become Christ!

The Rainbow Promise

Chapter Sixteen

Plagues of Love

In Chapter 16 we return once again to the seven angels of the seven churches, only this time we see the activities of those centers in relation to the cellular cleansing. The images are presented as plagues, but we must remember that these "plagues" are blessings from God, as we are presented with memories of our past selfishness and are given a chance to accept responsibility for our situations. By responding to these plagues in a positive, joyful, thankful manner, we expand our consciousness as well as cleanse the body. Whenever the ego places upon God's spiritual energy a new directive that is different from God's intention for that energy, the body responds by carrying out our desires rather than God's. We give our life to our creations. The energy of God that does not get expressed is left behind in the physical body, mixing with our selfish desires. This mix of conflicting desires adds stress to the cells of the body, pulling them in different directions and bringing "dis-ease" to our physical selves. These are the memories of our selfishness, and they can only be cleansed by our becoming aware of them and releasing them through our thankful acceptance of our present situations. Thus, that which plagues us must be accepted.

Chapter 16:1-7

Scripture

Revelation 16:1

And I heard a great voice out of the temple saying to the seven angels, Go your ways, and pour out the vials of the wrath of God upon the earth.

Revelation 16:2

And the first went, and poured out his vial upon the earth; and there fell a noisome and grievous sore upon the men which had the mark of the beast, and upon them which worshipped his image.

Revelation 16:3

And the second angel poured out his vial upon the sea; and it became as the blood of a dead man: and every living soul died in the sea.

Revelation 16:4

the third angel poured out his vial upon the rivers and fountains of waters; and they became blood.

Revelation 16:5

And I heard the angel of the waters say, Thou art righteous, O Lord, which art, and wast, and shalt be, because thou hast judged thus.

Revelation 16:6

For they have shed the blood of saints and prophets, and thou hast given them blood to drink; for they are worthy.

Revelation 16:7

And I heard another out of the altar say, Even so, Lord God Almighty, true and righteous are thy judgments.

Symbolism/Meaning

great voice out of the temple - message of importance.

pour out...upon the earth - influence the physical, earthly qualities.

the vials of the wrath of God - that which brings purification.

first - symbolizes the first chakra (the gonad center).

noisome and grievous sore - pain from the misuse of creative energy.

second angel - symbolic of the second chakra (the Leyden center).

sea - life - e.g., the life we give to our creations.

as the blood of a dead man - the image of our lives in the physical.

every living soul **died in the sea** - the condition of humankind when only the physical consciousness is operative.

third angel - symbolic of the third chakra (the adrenal center).

rivers and fountains of water - sources of true life within the cellular memories.

and they became blood - the cellular memories became the new source of life for us.

given them blood to drink - the life God gives us is given through the system of karma.

Commentary

At the start of this chapter, John hears the true or higher self speaking to the angels, telling them to **Go...and pour out the vials of the wrath of God upon the earth.** The higher self, which knows the history of the soul, is in the **temple** containing the record of the soul's experience. It is this Christ Spirit led self that gives the chakras permission to cleanse the body (**the earth**) through this process of becoming aware of all past experiences. The higher self knows the **vials of the wrath of God** are the way of cleansing the body and cutting the ego off from its source of life.

The **first angel**, when it pours its **vial on the earth**, causes **noisome and grievous sores** to come upon **the men which had the mark of the beast and upon them which worshipped his image**. Those cells that had lost the consciousness of the Christ and are consumed in their selfishness are the recipients of this plague. As the first angel symbolizes the gonadal center within our bodies, its work also concerns the purposes of that center. As noted in Chapter 2, this center raises the spiritual energy throughout the rest of the body and its chakras. If there is selfishness contained within this chakra, then the energy raised by it will not be pure. Thus it is essential that this center be completely free of any selfish desires or thoughts. This is also the center for the origin of our creativity, whether in the form of human procreation or in its ability to raise spiritual energy to expression through moments of creative insight. The image of boils (**grievous sores**) arising from this plague is appropriate when you realize that a boil is the body's way of spewing such a festering pocket of disease away from our systems. A boil collects that which is poisoning us and attempts to remove it from the body. This plague attempts to take the selfishness, which is poisoning our bodily cells and polluting our spiritual energy, and to forcefully and purposely eject such material from our bodies. We only have to look at the scriptural reference to Job to see his reaction to a literal enactment of this verse (see Job 2:7-10). Faced with a body covered with "sore boils from the sole of his foot unto his crown," Job refused to curse God: "What? shall we receive good at the hand of God, and shall we not receive evil?" Notice that Job did not blame anyone else not even Satan. Job did not understand why God would allow this "plague" of boils to come upon a man who had led a righteous life. Yet Job accepted his situation (to a certain point, anyway). Although difficult to accept from the physical view, such a "plague" as this was a blessing for Job, because it gave him the opportunity to come to God face to face. In a like manner, the higher self realizes that it is only through such facing of our own decisions that we can come to God face to face as co-creators with Him.

The **second angel** next pours **his vial upon the sea**. The **sea** is often seen as a symbol for either the emotions or the source of life within us. In this case, it represents the second chakra (the Leyden center), the center which is associated with the word "temptation" in the Lord's Prayer (see Appendix D). Because the Leyden interstitial cells are those that produce testosterone and estrogen, many of the changes occur through the sexual temptations arising from this center. In Chapter 2 we also discovered that it is in this center that we place value upon what we create. The things pertaining to this center bring a storm of emotions into our lives. The "plague" of this angel is directed toward the **sea** of emotions which resides within us.

As the angel pours out his bowl, the sea **became as the blood of a dead man, and every living soul died that was in the sea**. This phrase speaks of that process whereby we give away our life to the objects (thoughts, ideas, desires, and actions) that we create. When we give away our life, we become like a **dead man** and have no life within us. **Blood** is the symbol for life. To become **as the blood of a dead man** means that no longer could we give our life to our creations and no longer could we bestow value upon what we create. The Christ Spirit would direct our creations now that we possess the Christ Consciousness. The value of these creations would be given by God Himself, as we carry out His will: "It is not I who do the work, but the Father within me."

Moreover, the sense of personal pride, which came from the ego's ability to manipulate the emotions, would be lost. Thus **every living soul died that was in the sea**. All our creations (i.e., our selfish desires) to which we had given life and value would no longer exist. Even the desire to be selfish would die within us. This "plague" turns out to be the promise of the Christ-like life!

The **third angel** then **poured out his vial upon the rivers and fountains of water, and they became blood**. Here we are dealing with the third chakra, associated with the adrenal system and the acceptance of responsibility for our own creations. The adrenal glands secrete several different hormones such as adrenaline, noradrenaline, and aldosterone. These hormones provide us with the necessary energy for "fight or flight" reactions and regulate the mineral and water balance in the body. As this "plague" affects the body through the pathways by which the hormones are disseminated (**the rivers and the fountains of water**), we realize that these glands now begin to secrete substances that provide us with more life force: **they became blood**.

The symbolism of this angel's actions also affects our acceptance of responsibility for our creations. It is through the acceptance of responsibility for all of our past actions and thoughts that we come to find true life (**blood**). Only when we are able to say "My actions have placed me here, and my choices have led me to this place" can we realize that we have the power to either remain there or to move away from such circumstances and toward the Christ-like life.

It is no wonder that the angel reflects upon God's judgment in verses 5 and 6. In reality, this judgment is God's mercy, for we have taken the spiritual energy and have tried our best to destroy God's intention, replacing it with our own (**have shed the blood of saints and prophets**). Our "judgment" is that God gives us true life (**blood to drink**) so that we realize what we have done. That realization or awareness of who we are and what we have done is our "just reward" (**for they are worthy**). In verse 7, the **altar** itself reiterates this stance of God's **true and righteous** judgments. This voice, coming from the altar, is symbolic of all the spiritual intentions of God that we sacrificed in our zeal to accomplish our own will instead of God's will. God, in submitting the spiritually advancing individual to such judgments, proves that He is a God of love and mercy.

Chapter 16:8-11

Scripture

Revelation 16:8

And the fourth angel poured out his vial upon the sun; and power was given unto him to scorch men with fire

Revelation 16:9

And men were scorched with great heat, and blasphemed the name of God, which hath power over these plagues: and they repented not to give him glory.

Revelation 16:10

And the fifth angel poured out his vial upon the seat of the beast; and his kingdom was full of darkness; and they gnawed their tongues for pain,

Revelation 16:11

And blasphemed the God of heaven because of their pains and their sores, and repented not of their deeds.

Symbolism/Meaning

fourth angel - symbolic of the fourth chakra (Thymus region).

sun - source of light, heat, judgment.

scorch men with fire - the trial by fire of our created images.

great heat - intensity of trial.

blasphemed the name of God - the purely physical understand the trial to be a plague from God.

Repented not - our physical creations could not glorify God nor serve others.

fifth angel - the fifth chakra (Thyroid center).

seat of the beast - directed toward the rebellious attitude of will within us.

darkness - absence of light or insight.

gnawed their tongues - unable to express their will or desire.

Commentary

These next three verses (continue describing the blessings of God in the guise of plagues. The **fourth angel**, or the thymus center chakra, pours his bowl on the **sun**. Recognizing from Chapter 2 that this center is a balancing point between the upper three chakras and the lower three chakras, and that the ego accomplishes much of its operation at this center, we realize that the **sun** is used here as a symbol for the source of life for our own creations: that is, the sun represents the ego. By pouring the bowl of God's wrath upon the ego itself, the force of this plague is directed toward the ego. The ego took over the identity of the self when the true self withdrew behind its projected identity. Then, as the ego created our ideas, thoughts, and desires, it (and we) slowly began to identify our true self with the ego. Now it is the time for the ego's work to be evaluated. The creations of the ego must endure a trial by fire to see if they are sufficiently for others instead of simply for self. This trial by fire is symbolized by the phrase, **to scorch men with fire**. The **men** are the ego's creations and they must endure this trial. The result of this trial is that these creations, due to their selfish nature, **blasphemed the name of God, which hath power over these plagues, and they repented not to give him glory**. From their point of view, these are indeed plagues, and they lash out at the One who allows such events to happen. They did not **repent** (or re-think) their selfish purpose, because, being creations of the ego-self, they were unable to choose a different pathway. What could have been a gentle, warm breeze, turned out to be unendurable heat and pain for the ego's creations.

While this may seem harsh from a physical point of view, if the ego's creations will not change, then they must suffer the consequences of their actions and their purposes. If these have been purely selfish, they must lose their source of life for these actions, even if by so doing, they suffer pain and die. What this means to us as individuals is that, when God provides us with spiritual energy to serve others, we must learn not to impose our values or ego-directed purposes upon this energy. When we are led by the Christ Spirit, we act because it is God's will, not our own. This means that there are no objects or desires that we can call our own in terms of having originated within our ego. This type of life may not be acceptable to some people who still desire the pride of ego, but it is the type of life one will lead when the Christ Spirit is the directing force. Everything we do will be directed by God in order to **give him glory**.

This same thought continues as John describes the **fifth angel** pouring **his vial on the seat of the beast**. The fifth chakra is the thyroid center, which involves our self-will, the ability to choose and make decisions. The battle is centered on this aspect of ourself. It is here that we choose whether or not to enhance the ego or God's directives. This is the seat of the matter (**the seat of the beast**) where the decision to be for self or for others is chosen. As noted in Chapter 14, this chakra directs the four lower chakras in their actions upon the spiritual energy flowing through us. This chakra, and the choices we make here, gives directions to all we do, say, think, and desire. When the **fifth angel** pours out this bowl of God's wrath, the **kingdom** of the beast **was full of darkness**. Through these terms, John symbolizes the removal of the ego's power to make selfish decisions and to have them stick. No longer can the ego use the self's will: The creations of the ego suddenly lost their ability to express their desire (**gnawed their tongues for pain**). Without the backing of the will, the ego's creations have neither direction nor force of their own. For the reasons stated above, they **blasphemed the God of heaven because of the pains and their sores, and repented not of their deeds.**

Chapter 16:12-16

Scripture

Revelation 16:12

> **And the sixth angel poured out his vial upon the great river Euphrates; and the water thereof was dried up, that the way of the kings of the east might be prepared.**

Revelation 16:13

> **And I saw three unclean spirits like frogs come out of the mouth of the dragon, and out of the mouth of the beast, and out of the mouth of the false prophet**

Revelation 16:14

> **For they are the spirits of devils, working miracles, which go forth unto the kings of the earth and of the whole world, to gather them to the battle of that great day of God Almighty.**

Revelation 16:15

> **Behold, I come as a thief. Blessed is he that watcheth, and keepeth his garments, lest he walk naked, and they see his shame.**

Revelation 16:16

> **And they assembled them at the place which is called in Hebrew Armageddon**

Symbolism/Meaning

sixth angel - the sixth chakra (Pineal center).

river Euphrates - source of beginnings.

water thereof was dried up - preparing a passageway for a new beginning.

kings of the east - those which recognize the new consciousness.

unclean spirits like frogs - unclean.
dragon - the spirit of rebellion or selfishness.
beast - the ego.
false prophet - the conscious mind.
spirits of devils - their purpose is to torment and destroy.
working miracles - marvelous and miraculous actions.
kings of the earth-ruling influences over the physical and selfish.
Armageddon - the place of the great battle.

Commentary

In the next verse, the sixth angel poured out his vial upon the great river Euphrates. In the creation story, the Euphrates River flows out of the Garden of Eden (see Genesis 2:14). Thus this river symbolizes new beginnings. We may view the actions of this sixth chakra, therefore, as dealing with the new beginning of an individual who is purified even to the cellular level; who possesses the Christ Spirit; and who is aware of who he or she has been, is now, and will be forever. As this vial or bowl of God's wrath (love) is poured out, this river of beginnings is dried up. Whenever a river dries up, it provides a pathway for travel across it, such as seen in the events at the Red Sea and the Jordan River. In this first event, the Hebrew people made the transition from being slaves to the physical in the fleshpots of Egypt to being a people led by God. It took 40 years to accept this new consciousness, but the trip across the Red Sea was its beginning. In the same manner, the Hebrew people traveled across the Jordan River in order to enter the promised land of Canaan. This was another time of consciousness changing as they accepted their new position as possessors of land rather than as traveling nomads. Here, in Revelation, the individual is at the beginning of a new consciousness as a co-creator and companion with God. The symbols of the Euphrates River and the drying up of the water both emphasize the importance of this event. In addition, the image of the kings of the east preparing to cross that river emphasizes the coming into consciousness of the knowledge and truth of those who already recognize this new state of awareness. Just as the kings from the East who welcomed the birth of the Christ Child knew of the significance of the One who was born, so, too, the symbolism here in Revelation points to the knowledge of the significant event that is happening within the individual.

Next, within this sixth angel's activity, John sees **three unclean spirits like frogs** coming from the mouths of the **dragon,** the **beast,** and the **false prophet.** We have already met two of these characters, the **dragon,** symbolizing the spirit of rebellion or selfishness within us, and the **beast,** symbolizing the ego, which we created to express who wanted to be and what we wanted to do. It is this third entity, the **false prophet** that is introduced at this point, as if we already knew who or what it is. What we can learn about the false prophet from this scripture is that it is in league with the other two and thus partakes of the spirit of selfishness: that it, like the other two, is a **spirit of the devil** (i.e., its ultimate purpose is to torment and destroy that which would cause its destruction); that it helps to assemble all those that rule in the world of selfishness (**the kings of the earth**) for a **battle of the great day of God Almighty**. From 19:20, we also learn that the **false prophet**, in the presence of the beast, **wrought miracles before him, with which he deceived them that had received the mark of the beast, and them that worshipped his image**. This reference is to 13:13-14 where the beast performed great signs that resulted in the development of the personality. It is this clue that finally allows us to understand the symbolism behind the **false prophet**: In order to develop the personality, the beast had to utilize the conscious mind of the individual. The conscious mind is capable of great deception as anyone can attest to when remembering a time when self- justification was needed to convince (deceive) one's self that the actions just carried out were "right" and "correct." We have to convince ourselves many times to believe that we have done a selfless act, when, if we were honest with ourselves, we know that such an action was for selfish reasons. The conscious mind is the active agent behind such deception. It provides the reasons (**signs**) that allow the ego to deceive us. Since this conscious mind will perish at physical death, it sides with the dragon and the beast in an attempt to prolong its life.

Verse 15 in this chapter is a statement from the Christ and is similar to that found in 3:3. Yet, in this context, talking about the conscious mind and its connections with the selfishness of the ego, this verse would seem to be directed toward the mind and its dual nature: the conscious and the subconscious. The admonition is to the subconscious mind that has merged with the conscious at this point. The subconscious, being aware of the soul's spiritual heritage, must be careful not to be lulled back into a subordinate position again. The conscious mind is about to be stripped of its ability to deceive, and if the subconscious were to slide into the background again, then the conscious mind would indeed be **naked** and be seen exposed. The subconscious must be ready to support the individual during the shame of its self-deception. As I have mentioned before in this book, one of the most devastating events in my life involved the conscious awareness of my own mind's deceptive abilities in regard to my so called "memory" of an event that I remembered clearly, but discovered that not one of those who participated in that event had any remembrance of the events, as I recollected them. My mind, in that incident, was rendered **naked** and exposed in its deception.

The final verse in the section involving the sixth chakra mentions that dreaded place **Armageddon**. Before talking about the symbolism involved in that word, we must first look again at some of the aspects of this sixth chakra. Associated with the pineal center, this chakra also has a close connection to the mind. The pineal center "controls or is a major influence to the intellect or what is called the mind."[1] As the lower chakras (especially the Leyden center) send their influences upward to the pineal center, it uses these influences to affect or control what the mind does. These relationships are relevant in this discussion because of the part played by the mind in the previous verses discussed. The sixth chakra deals with the mind and the forces at work there, directed toward and from the other chakras and the physical body. Since this bowl of the wrath of God is concerned with the mind, the battle of **Armageddon** must also deal with the mind. In other words, this place where the **kings of the earth** assemble is none other that within our own minds! Each one of us must fight this battle. It is a battle of God's will against our will, and we must ultimately surrender our will to God's.

If you remember from Chapters 2 and 3, the pineal center or sixth chakra contains the key that can either open or close the door to the energy that enters or passes through the second chakra. The door at that level was closed when the soul chose to become centered on the physical rather than the spiritual. It was as if the soul closed behind it the door to spiritual awareness, shutting out the Light of God, and choosing to live in darkness. With the reemergence of spiritual awareness, the higher self brings the key to that door back to the soul and opens the door, allowing the kundalini to flow from below up to the higher chakras and to meet the prana or spiritual energy coming down from above. Yet this open door also brings with it the clash of the images, ideas, and attitudes of the physical with the purposes and direction of God. This is the battle of **Armageddon**, and we must endure this battle as old habits and desires fight for their survival at the hands of the newly chosen will directed by the Christ Spirit.

Chapter 16:17-21

Scripture

Revelation 16:17

And the seventh angel poured out his vial into the air; and there came a great voice out of the temple of heaven, from the throne, saying, It is done.

Revelation 16:18

And there were voices, and thunders, and lightnings; and there was a great earthquake, such as was not since men were upon the earth, so mighty an earthquake, and so great.

Revelation 16:19 And the great city was divided into three parts, and the cities of the nations fell: and great Babylon came in remembrance before God, to give unto her the cup of the wine of the fierceness of his wrath.

Revelation 16:20

And every island fled away, and the mountains were not found.

Revelation 16:21

And there fell upon men a great hail out of heaven, every stone about the weight of a talent: and men blasphemed God because of the plague of the hail; for the plague thereof was exceeding great.

Symbolism/Meaning

seventh angel - the seventh chakra (the Pituitary center).

air - who we are in totality; the spirit of our being-ness.

It is done - the plagues (blessings) have been poured out and the soul has come back to its spiritual home

voices, and thunders, and lightnings - symbols of consciousness recognizing the event which has happened.

earthquake - the shaking up of old to generate the new.

great city - the self

three parts - body, mind, and soul.

Babylon - the selfish self.

to give unto her the cup of the wine of the fierceness of his wrath - the physical must fulfill all the law to be spiritualized.

island, mountains - selfish concepts within consciousness.

fled away - purged and purified, no longer present.

A great hail - fixed concepts.

weight of a talent - heavy burdens.

men blasphemed God - the physical still does not understand the blessing of the plagues.

Commentary

The seventh angel, representing the seventh chakra, has been associated with the pituitary center within the body. The pituitary gland has been called the "Master Gland," because it seems to have some control, or can affect, the other glands. Its purpose seems to be directive in nature, as it offers directions for the other glands to follow. This activity of the pituitary gland is echoed in its activity as a chakra center. It offers direction to the other chakras that depend upon the ideals held by the individual and the fulfillment of those ideals in the physical activity of the individual. It receives the energy sent to it from the lower chakras and distributes the influences that effect change within the chakras and their purposes. When it receives the spiritual energy unchanged from its passage through the lower chakras, the seventh center directs the body into a physical result that is the will of God. If the lower chakras alter that spiritual energy, then the body is directed into a selfish act that is the will of the ego.

When this angel **poured his vial into the air**, it was the seventh chakra releasing the energy that had been flowing through the other chakras and bringing about their cleansing. It is poured out **into the air** to symbolize the totality of what has happened. Just as the air surrounds us totally and is everywhere even though we do not notice it, our oneness with God in consciousness is now total and is part of our very being-ness when we reach this level. The **great voice** is the voice of the higher self emanating from the center of our being-ness, **out of the temple of heaven, from the throne,** which represents the true seat of the soul. This self announces, with finality, this merger of the spirit and the physical (**It is done!**). This is the same awareness expressed by Jesus upon the cross when he acknowledged the accomplishment of his victory over the physical and the ego. Just as Matthew records the physical manifestations that happened at the death of Jesus ("and the earth did quake and the rocks rent" Matthew 27:51), John describes the event within us in similar terms (**voices, and thunders, and lightnings; and there was a great earthquake**). It is as if everything with the higher self is being shaken up in a radical and new way. No longer will we view our life from the physical point of view. Everything will be seen from the perspective of God, for we will recognize our oneness with God. We will know that we are spiritual rather than purely physical. And the events of life will be seen as having a greater purpose the purpose of God. This event in our life will be likened to the same event in the life of Jesus. It will mean the death to the physical and the resurrection to the spiritual. The true self (**the great city**), although knowing oneness with God, undergoes its spiritualization and union process. First, it will be **divided into three parts**: the physical body, the mind, and the soul. The unspiritualized physical desires, urges, and thoughts (**the cities of the nations**) will fall away and be subjected to the complete purification process as they experience the full force of the transformation (**to give unto her the cup of the wine of the fierceness of his wrath**). The totality of these physical aspects undergoing transformation is called **Babylon**, reminding us of the Jewish reference to that country to symbolize self-centeredness. Other previous images John uses refers to those ideas and concepts that we tenaciously cling to, regardless of the consequences, as the **island**(s) and **mountains** within us. Yet, unlike previously, here the islands and mountains don't just shake a little bit: **every island fled away, and the mountains were not to be found**! He tells us that our crystallized ideas and beliefs (**hail**) are great burdens (**every stone the weight of a talent**) that now rain down upon us from our spiritually aware consciousness (**heaven**). Because so many individuals take it personally when their faults 'rain down upon them', the great plague of hail is perceived as a curse rather than a blessing, and **men blasphemed God**.

The description of our transformation from an egocentric physical existence to a spiritually aware perception of us as companions and co-creators with God is terrible; however, these are plagues of God's love.

Chapter Seventeen

The Prostitution of Self

John has seen the process whereby the complete individual – the physical, mental, and spiritual aspects of our selves – will be (or was, in the case of Jesus) purified and spiritualized in its passage back to God. In this chapter, John is given the reason for the process of purification as he is shown a picture of the self in its state of non-awareness.

Chapter 17:1-6a

Scripture

Revelation 17:1

And there came one of the seven angels which had the seven vials, and talked with me, saying unto me, Come hither; I will shew unto thee the judgment of the great whore that sitteth upon many waters:

Revelation 17:2

With whom the kings of the earth have committed fornication, and the inhabitants of the earth have been made drunk with the wine of her fornication."

Revelation 17:3

So he carried me away in the spirit into the wilderness: and I saw a woman sit upon a scarlet coloured beast, full of names of blasphemy, having seven heads and ten horns

Revelation 17:4

And the woman was arrayed in purple and scarlet colour, and

decked with gold and precious stones and pearls, having a golden cup in her hand full of abominations and filthiness of her fornication:

Revelation 17:5 And upon her forehead was a name written, MYSTERY, BABYLON THE GREAT, THE MOTHER OF HARLOTS AND ABOMINATIONS OF THE EARTH.

Revelation 17:6a

And I saw the woman drunken with the blood of the saints, and with the blood of the martyrs of Jesus:

Symbolism/Meaning

great whore - the self.

sitteth upon many waters - has control over many forces.

kings of the earth - ruling forces over the carnal desires.

fornication - using the forces for self only.

inhabitants of the earth - the results from selfish activities.

drunk - loss of awareness and control.

wilderness - a place of learning.

woman - symbol for the idea of nourishing or "mothering" – a function of the self.

scarlet coloured beast - the selfishness of humanity, nourished by the self.

seven heads and ten horns - the body (seven chakras) and the ego's power (see Chapter 13).

purple and scarlet - symbolic for our thoughts of carnality.

gold and precious stones and pearls - the extravagant methods of decorating our creations.

golden cup... full of abominations ... - filling the precious vessel (our bodies or selves) with selfishness.

Commentary

In the context of this vision, where the soul has lost its spiritual awareness and has descended into the physical realms, only to struggle in its process to awaken and rise again to oneness with the Father, John is now invited to view the way in which we have nurtured the selfish qualities and what this attention to our selfishness has done to us. **The great whore** is the description given to what we have done with the abilities and gifts bestowed upon us by God: We have prostituted our true self, seeking to become like God in our own, selfish ways. This is called the **judgment** of the self, for it offers a vision of not only what the self has done, but the results of its indulgence in the self through the actions of the ego.

First, the harlot is described as being seated **upon many waters**. The **waters** are symbols for the many forces generated within the spiritual realm that contribute to the life forces that sustain us. The process of life is complicated, thus the image of **many waters** rather than just one "River of Life." The symbol of the River of Life, from which we are urged to drink, has become split into many diverse pathways within us, as we have used that life force to give life to our own various creations. We have taken the One and split it into the many. The self is seated upon those waters to show the manner in which we attempt to control our own creations: we sit upon them, attempting to direct their every move and preventing them from doing what we do not want them to do. They are our slaves in addition to our creations. This self is also the one **with whom the kings of the earth have committed fornication**. By this phrase, John conveys the idea that forces which rule over the carnal, physical realm (those forces of selfishness, greed, jealously, etc.) have joined with the self to perform acts for the benefit of the self only (**fornication**). This is the meaning of the term **fornication** in this context to participate together in actions which bring glory only to the self. The glory for self is the **wine** of this fornication, and this false glory has made the **inhabitants of the earth** (our created carnal thoughts, ideas, concepts and actions) **drunk** with a false sense of power and importance. The self loses control of its own creations. It is like a little white lie that gets out of hand. Our created ideas have taken over and led the self into avenues and pathways the self cannot handle.

In verse three, John is carried away in consciousness (**the the spirit**) into **the wilderness**. It is from this position in the spirit that John was able to view the self as God sees it, without the physical desires and emotions coloring His view. A wilderness can be symbolic for a place where one has a learning experience, exemplified by the Hebrew people learning to follow God through their journey of forty years in the wilderness, or by Jesus learning to deal with temptation in his forty day trek through the wilderness. John is taken into the **wilderness** in order to view the activities of the self while he is apart from the self. He would be unable to view the self's activities if he was locked within the self, in a deep darkness brought on because of a lack of light from above.

The images of the **scarlet beast** and **a woman** emphasize that John is viewing the self-indulgent qualities of the self. The **scarlet coloured beast** with its **seven heads and ten horns** represents the powerful forces of self-indulgence as promulgated through the senses and the chakras (see the commentary on Rev. 13:1) while the **woman** represents the nurturing of such forces in order to enhance the self for self's sake; the woman and the beast are united in purpose – abusing the gift of life by willingly defying knowledge of God (**names of blasphemy**).

The woman was **arrayed in purple and scarlet** – two colors which describe the nature of the projected personality. Remember, the personality is that which we project outward toward others, allowing them to believe that our true self consists of that which we project outward. The woman here is **arrayed** to tell us that this is what the self has "put on" for all to see. The two colors chosen tell us that the ideas (**purple** being a color associated with the pineal, or the mind, center) with which we clothe ourselves are from our lower, physical natures (**scarlet** being the color most often associated with anger, selfish desires, sexual exploits, and other physical urges). This vision of the self also includes the **gold and precious stones and pearls,** which add to the gaudiness and extravagant measures we go to in order to dress up our projected image. We believe the outer trappings of what others think about us are more important than the nurturing of the inner, selfless qualities of our true self

Because we have so lowered our awareness to the level of the beastly qualities within us, John sees the image of a **golden cup** (the precious vessel of our physical bodies housing the priceless soul) filled with garbage and the result of our self-indulgences (**full of abominations and filthiness of her fornication**).

We have so misused and misdirected the energies and forces given to us that, unknown to us, we have made it plain, for all who have eyes from the spiritual view, that we are guilty of an unimaginable number of self-indulgent actions. It is as if we have the truth written upon our foreheads for all to see (**And upon her forehead was a name written ...**). We have adulterated the God-given creative energies by using them for selfish purposes. We have earned the dubious privilege of being called **BABYLON THE GREAT, THE MOTHER OF HARLOTS AND ABOMINATIONS OF THE EARTH:** This is the self – and what we have chosen to do with it. John states that he views this self as one that has lost control and that glorifies itself in its ability to take God's spiritual energy and use it for self (**I saw the woman drunken with the blood of the saints**). The ego-directed self believes it has to put to death the selfless principle of service through loving God and others (**drunken with ... the blood of the martyrs of Jesus**). The vision which John sees is not a pretty one: He is seeing the self at its worst, stripped of any attempt to deceive his conscious mind.

Chapter 17:6b-7

Scripture

Revelation 17:6b

and when I saw her, I wondered with great admiration.

Revelation 17:7

And the angel said unto me, Wherefore didst thou marvel? I will tell thee the mystery of the woman, and of the beast that carrieth her, which hath the seven heads and ten horns.

Symbolism/Meaning

wondered with great admiration - John still is attracted to the physical.

mystery - significance

beast that carrieth her - gives direction to.

Commentary

John, in these short transitional verses, reveals his lingering attachment to the physical. He looks at the self and marvels at its abilities and talents under the complete direction of the ego's desires. These actions of the self have an attraction for John just as they have had for us. For example, a student feels an inner call to a certain profession, but he fears it will not sufficiently provide for his material desires. To satisfy the hopes and dreams of his parents as well as his own desire for a certain lifestyle, he follows a different career path that does indeed give him prestige and financial wealth. The emptiness that he sometimes feels because he has not followed his true calling is kept submerged and hidden behind his façade.

The angel, noticing John's reaction, then states that he will tell John the significance (**mystery**) of and the results from the self's ego-directed (**beast ... that carrieth her**) activities. In the #281 series of readings by Edgar Cayce, the question is asked, "What did the angel mean when he said: 'I will tell thee the mystery of the woman, and of the beast that carrieth her'?" The answer given by the sleeping Cayce was as follows:

> (A) That which is understood by those that follow in the way of the Lamb, that come to know how man separates himself through the desires to become as the procreator in the beasts; which made the necessity of the shedding of blood for redemption, for it brought sin IN the shedding – and only through same may there be the fulfilling; and as given, the heavens and the earth may pass, but His law, His love, His mercy, His grace, endureth for

those who WILL seek to know His will. T0281-016
* [Pg 3]

The angel is getting ready to tell John the reason why humanity finds itself separated in consciousness from God (i.e., what we did to place ourselves in this situation) as well as the reason why the shedding of blood was necessary for humanity's redemption. The answers to these questions dwell in humanity's "desires to become as the procreator in the beasts;" that is, in our desires to use the physical world (our beastly, physical natures) to imitate God with our creations. In effect, we have "created" our own world. (Even modern quantum physics states that there must be an observer, or a consciousness, that operates at the quantum level, making choices about the nature of "reality.") We have attempted to become like God in the physical world, using our free will to do what God has done. But by limiting ourselves to the physical realm, we have become self-centered, and our attempts at creation are for ourselves only, instead of for the benefit of the whole of creation. By cutting ourselves off from the consciousness of the spiritual, we have cut ourselves off from the proper reason for the creative act: to love all that exists. We have combined the physical and the spiritual in such a manner that neither the physical nor the spiritual can be fully expressed. In addition, we have created entities which are mixtures of the spiritual and the physical, but serve only the physical (e.g., the ego, the personality, selfish emotions, etc.). It is only by first cutting the ties to the physical (i.e., destroying the self) that the spiritual and the physical can then be rejoined in a manner reflecting God's intended design and desire.

Let us now continue in our journey through John's vision and discover how the images involved tell us the story of humanity's need to destroy the self.

Chapter 17:8-14

Scripture

Revelation 17:8

The beast that thou sawest was, and is not; and shall ascend out of the bottomless pit, and go into perdition: and they that dwell on the earth shall wonder, whose names were not written in the book of life from the foundation of the world, when they behold the beast that was, and is not, and yet is.

Revelation 17:9

And here is the mind which hath wisdom. The seven heads are seven mountains, on which the woman sitteth.

Revelation 17:10

And there are seven kings: five are fallen, and one is, and the other is not yet come; and when he cometh, he must continue a short space.

Revelation 17:11

And the beast that was, and is not, even he is the eighth, and is of the seven, and goeth into perdition.

Revelation 17:12

And the ten horns which thou sawest are ten kings, which have received no kingdom as yet; but receive power as kings one hour with the beast.

Revelation 17:13

These have one mind, and shall give their power and strength unto the beast.

Revelation 17:14

These shall make war with the Lamb, and the Lamb shall overcome them: for he is Lord of lords, and King of kings: and they that are with him are called, and chosen, and faithful.

Symbolism/Meaning

the beast...was, and is not - the self- indulgent self existed within the consciousness, but when the Christ Consciousness took over, that self was banished from the mind.

shall ascend out of the bottomless pit - to rise out of the desire for the physical.

go into perdition - the beastly nature of the self is destroyed.

dwell on earth - the physical desires, urges, etc. created by the old self.

and yet is - a prophecy of the coming new, purified self.

seven heads - chakras.

seven mountains - the foundation for activities.

seven kings-the ruling or guiding functions of the chakras

five are fallen - reference to the selfish use of the five lower chakras.

one is - the pineal center (the center for mind) functioned without selfishness.

the other is not yet come - the full work of the highest chakra has not yet been revealed.

he must continue a short space - the function of the pituitary center, while necessary, is a transitional function.

the beast that was and is not- the old, self- indulgent self.

is the eighth and is of the seven - the self acted as the master of all seven chakras, although it was only expressed through them.

ten horns ... are ten kings - the physical senses (as perceived both for others and for self) have power to rule.

received no kingdom as yet - their power has not yet been granted.

for one hour - the physical senses will rule the self for a short time.

have one mind - work together.

make war with the Lamb - fight against the Christ Consciousness directed Self.

Commentary

As noted above, the **beast** represents the self-indulgent qualities of the self that we have nourished and developed into an entity that we think of as the self. This self- indulgent self existed within us in our mind: We created this image of ourselves. This image of self will be banished from the mind when we accept the mind of Christ (**The beast that...was, and is not**). According to the angel, our new concept of ourselves, a spiritual being designed to be a companion with God, will rise out of the ashes of the old concept of self, a physical creature designed to revel in physical, selfish pleasures for the self only (**shall ascend out of the bottomless pit and go into perdition**). "The beastly mind can be transformed into a higher self and thus shall ascend out of the bottomless pit of self."[1] Our created concepts, whose "lives" depended upon the ego's sustenance (**they that dwell on the earth**), will be amazed at the transformation of the self (**shall wonder...when they behold the beast**). Notice that these created concepts have not existed from the creation of the world, since they are our creations and not God's. Their existence was never meant to be eternal, and thus their names were never **written in the book of life**. They are amazed at the self, for, after being banished from the mind in one conception, it arises again, transformed, as the true self it was meant to be (**was and is not and yet is**).

In the next verse, Rev. 17:9, the angel tells John that the following symbolic description calls for a **mind which hath wisdom**. This phrase serves to set aside what follows as needing some prior knowledge or wisdom in order to decipher the symbols in use. The prior knowledge needed is that involving the seven chakras or endocrine centers along with all that John has been shown thus far in his vision. In both this chapter and Chapter12, we were introduced to the concept of the **seven heads** as representing the seven chakras. Here, that same symbol of the seven heads is repeated with the added explanation that those **seven heads are seven mountains, on which the woman sitteth**. This symbolism makes use of the ancient belief that the flat earth rested upon seven hills or mountains. The **seven mountains** represent the foundation points for the human body. John is being shown that the seven chakras are fundamental to the growth and development of the body, mind, and spirit. They are the foundation points for the self. Without them, we could not exist. We already understand the necessary part played by the endocrine centers of the body, without which we could not physically exist. We are only just beginning to rediscover what the ancients knew: The seven chakras and their spiritual development are necessary for the upward development of the human spirit.

In verse 10, the angel states another function of the chakras: They are the sources of the chemicals and hormones necessary to control or rule the development of the body, mind, and spirit. It is believed by some that the secretions of the various endocrine centers not only control various physical functions and developments, but also aid in the development of the spiritual aspects of humanity.[2] The angel tells John that, when a person reaches this point of being controlled by the Christ Consciousness and has accepted the purification of the physical, then the lower chakras no longer rule over the body: The two highest chakras, represented by the pineal and the pituitary centers, take over and control all the bodily functions as well as the mental and spiritual aspects. The lower five chakras (**five are fallen**) turn over their functions to the upper two chakras, allowing the energy of those two to control what the body does and experiences. This allows the higher mind (the mind of Christ), associated with the pineal center, full expression in directing the lower chakras to be "for others" rather than "for self." The rule of the pituitary center has not yet begun (**and yet is**), hinting at an even greater awareness in store for us. Even then, when the seventh chakra does take over and control the total person, it is to be only a transitional rule, preparing the body for a final transformation into the glorified, spiritual body (**when he cometh, he must continue a short space**).

The angel then refers back to the old self (**the beast that was and is not ...**). According to this angel, the old self, being a concept created by the actions of the un-purified, ego-directed part of the self, attempted to act as if it was the controlling mechanism within the body instead of the chakras. The truth, however, was that the self was a creation of the ego acting through the actions of the chakras (**he is the**

eighth and is of the seven). We use the expression "being our own man or woman" to express the ability to make our own choices and to do whatever we want to do. In truth, we are led and directed by our emotions, our hormones, the external events surrounding us, our internal ego, and self-indulgent self. Even our own created images attempt to persuade and influence our decisions. No wonder we want to abdicate all responsibility and claim "The Devil made me do it!" But, according to the angel who is describing the vision to John, all of these influences must go **to perdition,** as the purified self banishes them from the mind.

Next, the angel tells John that the **ten horns...are ten kings which have received no kingdom as of yet**. These **horns**, symbolic of power, represent the five physical senses and their connections to either bringing in information "for others" or for "self." The physical senses have never had the position of control given to the chakras, even though many individuals claim to "only believe what the senses tell me." The angel prophesies that the physical senses **are to receive power as kings one hour with the beast**. This could refer to the scientific age where we have rejected the spiritual and only accept the physical. We allow the need to satisfy the physical senses to rule us, as we have become more and more materialistic in our outlook. We glorify the physical senses with our multi-media presentations, raising the importance of the senses and their need to be gratified. Whatever the angel meant by the statement, it is true that the physical senses work together (**have one mind**) and **give their power and strength unto the beast**: We seek self-gratification through sensual stimulation.

The angel also tells John that the **ten horns** (physical senses) **make war with the Lamb**. If we are tied so dearly to the physical world through the cord of the senses, then it is only natural that they should resist any attempt to break that tie. Nevertheless, the physical must, and will, be overcome. We cannot allow the desire for the physical to continue to rule our decisions if we wish to be Christ-centered individuals.

Chapter 17:15-18

Scripture

Revelation 17:15

And he saith unto me, The waters which thou sawest, where the whore sitteth, are peoples, and multitudes, and nations, and tongues.

Revelation 17:16

And the ten horns which thou sawest upon the beast, these shall hate the whore, and shall make her desolate and naked, and shall eat her flesh, and burn her with fire

Revelation 17:17

For God hath put in their hearts to fulfil his will, and to agree, and give their kingdom unto the beast, until the words of God shall be fulfilled.

Revelation 17:18

And the woman which thou sawest is that great city, which reigneth over the kings of the earth

Symbolism/Meaning

waters - forces of life.

peoples, and multitudes, and nations, and tongues - the created thoughts and desires within the cells of the body, and the influence their actions have on us

make her desolate and naked - remove their source of stimulus from the self.

eat her flesh and burn her with fire - a source of purification.

God hath put it into their hearts ... - the senses of the body carry out the will of God, even though they are of the physical.

that great city - the self.

Commentary

As John continues to be instructed by the angel, he learns that the source of life which the self has divided into many pieces (**the waters**) has been given to the various created desires and thought patterns of the self (**peoples**). These images are gathered in all the cells of the body (**multitudes and nations**), and they speak out to the self, demanding attention (**tongues**). Then the angel reports what, at first, seems to be contrary to the nature of the physical: ... the **ten horns which thou sawest...these shall hate the whore**. Why would the physical senses (**the ten horns**) and the principle of self-indulgence (**the beast**) hate the self (**the whore**)? Are they not together in their selfish actions? Why would there be hatred between them?

The physical senses are unique in that, although supplying physical information to the self, they must rely upon the source of this information from outside the self, in the physical world. We apply "filters" to the information which the five senses input to the self. Even my wife accuses me of "selective hearing," of only hearing what I want to hear when she tells me something. All the senses work in a similar manner: They supply the evidence of some external stimulus, and our mind, or our self, filters that evidence, retaining only what it deems necessary for the further function of the self. Thus the physical senses have been aware of the self's ego-directed actions all along, since the senses have experienced both the raw data being input, and the filtered, interpreted data which the self retains. This is reason for the **horns**, or source of power for the self, to hate the manner in which the self has adulterated the information they have supplied.

Why does the **beast** hate the true Self? This is more difficult to understand, since it would seem that the self has relied upon the principle of self-indulgence, supplied by the beast, to guide and direct its actions. We must remember that the body is now in a condition of being almost totally cleansed and that the pineal center is beginning to control the five lower chakras. The information which the physical senses bring in to the self no longer can be utilized by the lower chakras for self only. The self begins to understand the physical sensations for what they really are: evidence of the work of either God or of human beings. The senses hate the true self, for it will no longer act upon the input from them to gratify itself. The principle of self-indulgence (**the beast**) does not like (**hates**) this new self's disregard for selfish principles. The lack of regard for the physical stimuli is as if all physical sensations to the body have been cut off (**make her desolate and naked**). The true self must rely upon the direction and information coming from the Christ Consciousness in order to make decisions as to how to act in the physical world. As it is purged and purified (**burn her with fire**) by the actions of the higher chakras, the still physical body feels deprived of its input. The physical sensations craved by the old self, the **whore**, are no longer being supplied to the body. Anyone who has attempted to quit a bad habit understands the body's craving for what it thinks will satisfy it. If we deny the body the physical sensation it craves, we will, in essence, **eat her flesh and burn her with fire**. In this case, the new mind of the self prevents the interpretation of and the need for the physical desires of the body. Furthermore, the angel makes the remarkable statement that the physical senses (the **ten horns**) still carry within their essences the desire to do the will of God (**for God hath put in their hearts to fulfil his will**) – a fact unknown to us before. This means that the physical senses are not purely for self. Their actions were in the physical realm, and they supplied information to the self-indulgent principle (**shall give their kingdom unto the beast)** (see verse 13), but their intention has always been to carry out the will of God.

The angel ends this chapter by stating that the **woman** that you saw **is that great city which reigneth over the kings of the earth**. Again, the self is seen as that which creates the physical thought forms, desires, habits, etc. and gives them its life. It must be emphasized here that, even though the chakras have been cleansed, and the physical body has been emptied of its selfish desires, the body is still physical and still contains those cells and habit patterns which have been built within it through years of self- indulgence. These old thoughts, desires, habits, and intentions can still influence the body, even though the desire for them is no longer within the Christ Consciousness of the new self.

Chapter Eighteen

The End of the Old Self

In Chapter 16 we learned that the selfish creations left behind memories in the cells of the body that must be cleansed and eliminated. The "plagues of love" described in that chapter were part of the cleansing process. Now, in Chapter 18, we come to a similar situation involving the ego and its self-creations. This time, though, it is not enough to simply purify the cells through loving discipline and growth: Our selfishness and the memories of our selfishness must be totally purged and eliminated from the body if the Christ Consciousness is to fully enter and command all aspects of the individual: physical, mental, and spiritual. When the residue of our selfishness is removed, it allows the body to be open to the new consciousness of total unselfishness and of being a co-creator and companion with God. This new consciousness will not enter, though, until the body has completely eliminated the ego and the self, which are separate from God, for this new consciousness is that of being one with God. As long as the body contains even a hint of selfishness within its cells, then the new consciousness cannot totally enter. In effect, the body must be recreated if it is to be one with God. As long as there is selfishness within the cells of the body, or in the conscious mind of the individual, then we look to that selfishness as the reason for more selfish responses and actions. These, in turn, lead to more selfishness, and before we know it, we are back to our old position of thinking about and acting for ourselves instead of others.

The ego-directed self, by its very nature, makes us turn away from the true source of life: God. By applying God's spiritual energy to the activities of that self instead of the spirit-directed self, we shut off the physical's connection to our spiritual source. On the other hand, by eliminating all selfishness from the body, we are also eliminating the body's ego-directed internal and external activity. Our selfish choices, whose creations were strengthened or altered by the activities of the chakras, no longer provide our chakras (or the endocrine system as a whole) with their previous stimulation. The body at first perceives this abrupt change in focus as a loss. This loss, however, changes to joy as the new consciousness enters, and God then dwells with us. Chapter 18 is the story of the body's perceived loss, but Chapters 19 through 22 is the story of our true gain

Chapter 18:1-8

Scripture

Revelation 18:1

And after these things I saw another angel come down from heaven, having great power; and the earth was lightened with his glory.

Revelation 18:2

And he cried mightily with a strong voice, saying, Babylon the great is fallen, is fallen, and is become the habitation of devils, and the hold of every foul spirit, and a cage of every unclean and hateful bird.

Revelation 18:3

For all nations have drunk of the wine of the wrath of her fornication, and the kings of the earth have committed fornication with her, and the merchants of the earth are waxed rich through the abundance of her delicacies.

Revelation 18:4

And I heard another voice from heaven, saying, Come out of her, my people, that ye be not partakers of her sins, and that ye receive not of her plagues.

Revelation 18:5

For her sins have reached unto heaven, and God hath remembered her iniquities.

Revelation 18:6

Reward her even as she rewarded you, and double unto her double according to her works: in the cup which she hath filled fill to her double.

Revelation 18:7

How much she hath glorified herself, and lived deliciously, so much torment and sorrow give her: for she saith in her heart, I sit a queen, and am no widow, and shall see no sorrow.

Revelation 18:8

Therefore shall her plagues come in one day, death, and mourning, and famine; and she shall be utterly burned with fire: for strong is the Lord God who judgeth her.

Symbolism/Meaning

another angel - the new consciousness of the pituitary center.

earth was lightened with his glory - the physical was cleansed.

Babylon the great is fallen, is fallen - the self has been eliminated.

devils ...foul spirit...every unclean and hateful bird- our creations of selfishness.

wine of the wrath of her fornication - the fruit of selfishness.

kings of the earth - our creations which ruled us in egotistical ways.

merchants of the earth - all who had reason to gain from the indulgences in the physical.

my people - the cells which are to be part of the new, spiritualized body.

unto heaven - spilling over into the unconscious.

Reward her even as she rewarded you - the law of karma.

I sit a queen, and am no widow - the self's self- deception

burned with fire - justice shall purge the self.

Commentary

In the first verse, John is introduced to a new awareness (**another angel from heaven**) having the ability to change the beliefs and thoughts of the individual (**having great power**). The power of this awareness to change the individual's life is similar to those eye-opening insights that we occasionally experience and that help to mold our behavior. The difference between those experiences and this one is the degree to which this awareness produces a change within us. In this experience, the physical body itself is cleansed through the process described in this chapter (**the earth was lightened with his glory**).

The angel begins by stating that the old self has fallen from its place of authority over our thoughts, beliefs, and actions (**Babylon the great is fallen, is fallen**). No longer does it rule by taking our physical sensations and creating a world which serves the ego. Since it no longer has any connection to the physical senses (see the previous chapter for details), the ego relies upon its manipulation of all that it has created in the past, which John sees as **devils, foul spirits,** and **every unclean and hateful bird**, to satisfy its needs. But there is a problem. In the past, the ego had fed the kundalini within us to these selfish desires. Now, the ego's connection to that source of energy has been cut away, and there is no longer a steady supply of life energy for the self's creations. This means that no longer do we place value upon our selfish actions. At one time, we lavished our attention upon ourselves and selfishly wasted our life force. The ego's desire for itself (**wine of the wrath of her fornication**) led to our being ruled by our emotions and desires (**the kings of the earth have committed fornication with her**). This attention upon ourselves gave the physical much wealth (**the merchants of the earth have waxed rich through the abundance of her delicacies**), but it was a wealth of deception. The physical cannot endure without the spiritual, and all the "wealth" of the ego was selfish indulgences without the benefit of spiritual principles or God's life-giving energy to sustain it.

Therefore, the angel calls to the physical cells that never gave in to selfishness and to those desires, beliefs and thought patterns that remained faithful to God's intentions to **Come out of her, my people, that ye not be partakers of her sins.** This is a call to these faithful, which have been bound by the strength of selflessness, to come out and express themselves. How many times in our lives has someone "pulled the string" that started us into a senseless argument with that individual? Maybe our parents, our spouse, our children, or someone close to us knows how to quickly involve us in an argument, which, if we were honest enough to look deep within, we would realize was senseless and brought on through our emotions rather than a legitimate reason. Sometimes we even have a small desire to cease our argumentative state; yet we are not able to act upon that desire, so we continue to argue. It is to that small desire deep within us to break through the argument with a simple "I'm sorry" and to banish our need for self-justification that the angel in this verse is calling: "**Come out** and be expressed. Do not let the selfishness of the self overwhelm you." The ego's selfishness has even reached the unconscious mind (**her sins have reached into heaven**) and has attempted to rule even there.

The only justice for the ego is to allow it to experience its own karma (**Reward her even as she rewarded you**). The ego must endure what it has chosen, and no amount of deception will save it from its karma. The ego continues to deceive only itself (**I sit a queen, and am no widow**), refusing to change its ways, therefore bringing on the consequences of its excessive waste of the life force (**her plagues shall come in one day**) as it is purged (**burned with fire**). At this point in John's vision, the ego is being completely destroyed.

Chapter 18:9-20

Scripture

Revelation 18:9

> **And the kings of the earth, who have committed fornication and lived deliciously with her, shall bewail her, and lament for her, when they shall see the smoke of her burning,**

Revelation 18:10

Standing afar off for the fear of her torment, saying, Alas, alas, that great city Babylon, that mighty city! for in one hour is thy judgment come.

Revelation 18:11

And the merchants of the earth shall weep and mourn over her; for no man buyeth their merchandise any more

Revelation 18:12

The merchandise of gold, and silver, and precious stones, and of pearls, and fine linen, and purple, and silk, and scarlet, and all thyine wood, and all manner vessels of ivory, and all manner vessels of most precious wood, and of brass, and iron, and marble,

Revelation 18:13 And cinnamon, and odours, and ointments, and frankincense, and wine, and oil, and fine flour, and wheat, and beasts, and sheep, and horses, and chariots, and slaves, and souls of men.

Revelation 18:14

And the fruits that thy soul lusted after are departed from thee, and all things which were dainty and goodly are departed from thee, and thou shalt find them no more at all.

Revelation 18:15

The merchants of these things, which were made rich by her, shall stand afar off for the fear of her torment, weeping and wailing,

Revelation 18:16

And saying, Alas, alas, that great city, that was clothed in fine linen, and purple, and scarlet, and decked with gold, and precious stones, and pearls!

Revelation 18:17

For in one hour so great riches is come to nought. And every shipmaster, and all the company in ships, and sailors, and as many as trade by sea, stood afar off,

Revelation 18:18

And cried when they saw the smoke of her burning, saying, What city is like unto this great city!

Revelation 18:19

And they cast dust on their heads, and cried, weeping and wailing, saying, Alas, alas, that great city, wherein were made rich all that had ships in the sea by reason of her costliness! for in one hour is she made desolate.

Revelation 18:20

Rejoice over her, thou heaven, and ye holy apostles and prophets; for God hath avenged you on her

Symbolism/Meaning

burned with fire - justice shall purge the self.

kings of the earth - the created desires which have ruled our actions.

bewail her and lament for her - mourn the loss of their life source

no man buyeth their merchandise any more - the body no longer responds to the selfish emotions and baggage carried by the ego.

Revelation 18:12-13 - symbols for greed.

slaves, and souls of men - the key to the actions of the ego: It enslaved the human soul.

the fruit that thy soul lusted after - the desire to become a god in the physical realm.

weeping and wailing- the physical desires mourning their loss.

And every shipmaster, and all the company in ships, and sailors, and as many as trade by sea, - the emotions and all which emanated from them and the unconscious.

wherein were made rich all that had ships in the sea by reason of her costliness - the emotions fed upon the selfishness of the ego

Commentary

Beginning with verse nine, John listens to an extended session of mourning, as the creations of the ego (**the kings of the earth ... the merchants of the earth ... every shipmaster, and all the company in ships, and sailors, and as many as trade by sea**) lament the loss of their energy source. Their selfishness is evident by their unwillingness to aide the self (**stand afar off for the fear of her torment**). The only regret of the ego's creations is that their selfish desires will no longer be met: The body no longer responds to their desires (**no man buyeth their merchandise any more**). In fact, while listing the cargo, the symbols for the satisfying of physical desires, the angel gets to the bottom line: The enslavement of the soul was the true goal of the ego (**... and slaves, and souls of men**).

All the actions of the ego – the satisfying of the physical appetites – were to entangle the soul in the web of the physical so that the soul could not remember its true nature. By becoming trapped in the law of cause and effect (karma), and by denying access to the soul's higher consciousness while in the physical plane, the ego and the dragon of rebellion attempted to perpetuate their existence. They believed they needed the physical and self-gratification to continue the flow of life energy coming to them. For this reason, complicated and convoluted systems of intrigue and deception were developed so that we – that is, the soul that we are – would not find our way out of the physical. Such trappings do not disappear at the death of the individual, for they are woven with the thread of karma: They demand another physical life to reach their fulfillment. Because the conscious mind believes that the body is the most valuable part of the individual, the ego attempts to hold on to the physical, even while the body's life force is being drained by the ego's wasteful extravagances!

All the scheming and desires of the ego come to naught, as it is transformed. Even the soul's desire (**the fruits that thy soul lusted after**) is taken away through the loss of the ego. This desire, to be like God, was the ego's perversion of the desire to be one with God. The true purpose of the soul's creation was to be one with God, yet separate from Him: to know one's self as self, but to be one in Spirit and desire with God. The ego's version of this purpose had been distorted to mean being like God (all knowing and all powerful) in the ego's created world of the physical. We wanted to be gods of our own little worlds, not realizing that we are already capable of being God's offspring on an equal footing with God Himself!

The result of this distortion of our true nature ultimately leads to the destruction of the ego. For only by destroying the ego and revealing the true self, can we come to know God.

Chapter 18:21-24

Scripture

Revelation 18:21

And a mighty angel took up a stone like a great millstone, and cast it into the sea, saying, Thus with violence shall that great city Babylon be thrown down, and shall be found no more at all.

Revelation 18:22

And the voice of harpers, and musicians, and of pipers, and trumpeters, shall be heard no more at all in thee; and no craftsman, of whatsoever craft he be, shall be found any more in thee; and the sound of a millstone shall be heard no more at all in thee;

Revelation 18:23

And the light of a candle shall shine no more at all in thee; and the voice of the bridegroom and of the bride shall be heard no more at all in thee: for thy merchants were the great men of the earth; for by thy sorceries were all nations deceived.

Revelation 18:24

And in her was found the blood of prophets, and of saints, and of all that were slain upon the earth.

Symbolism/Meaning

mighty angel - power of the new consciousness.

great millstone - symbol for a great burden.

cast it into the sea - the ego will be destroyed through purification and transformation

harpers and musicians, and of musicians, and trumpeters - symbolic of those which command our attention.

craftsman - one who is talented at building or doing.

sound of a millstone - influence of burdens.

shall be heard no more at all in thee - the physical and selfish (worldly) demands no longer command our attention.

light of a candle - the influence of the chakras.

bridegroom and of the bride - the ego's attempt to unite the physical and the spiritual

blood of prophets, and of saints - the remnants of God's intentions.

Commentary

The new consciousness is so powerful that it is seen as **a mighty angel**. It has the power not only to present a new outlook toward life, but to actually effect changes within the individual. The consciousness lifts the burden of the ego (**took up a stone like a great millstone**), casting it back **into the sea** of life for reforming or recasting of its creative energies. This action, of course, causes waves, just as would occur if a great millstone were actually hurled into the sea. Because of the infiniteness of life in comparison to the ego, the waves are not destructive, nor are they even noticed. The important item of this symbolism is that the selfish ego is lost forever within the soul's creative principle (**shall be found no more**).

The next two verses describe all that the body loses when the ego is destroyed. **The voice of harpers and musicians, and of pipers, and trumpeters** refers to the vibrations of those thoughts, needs, and desires which were always vying for our attention. Since the chakras no longer have to deal with the process of altering the physical data and spiritual energy flowing through them, these types of interruptions are no longer present (**shall be heard no more at all in thee**). Neither shall there be the creation or building of any object (thought form or action) that will drain the life force of an individual (**no craftsman...shall be found any more in thee**). With the ego purified, the burdening work of the ego, the old self, shall cease (**and the sound of the millstone shall be heard no more at all in thee**). Furthermore, now that the new spiritual consciousness has entered, the chakras, or the candlesticks of Chapter 1, are not being used and no longer give off a light (**the light of a candle shall shine no more at all in thee**). The whole body is, instead, illumined by the light of the new consciousness: a consciousness united with the spiritual and the physical (**bridegroom and bride**) in such a way that the former attempt at marrying those two seemingly incompatibles is annulled. All that remains is the living remnants of our unselfish actions and desires (**the blood of prophets and of saints, and of that were slain upon the earth**). The old self has been destroyed by being purified. Now, we prepare for the new self to enter!

Chapter Nineteen

The Christ Within

In the previous chapter, the egocentric self was purified by the Christ Consciousness, resulting in a disassociation between the physical sensations and the ego. Without the satisfaction derived from the physical urges and desires, the self suffers a period of sensory deprivation: All selfish creations die, because they are cut off from the ego, their source of sustenance. In this process of destroying the egocentric self's purpose for existence, the conscious and unconscious minds have merged into one mind[1] and are ruled by the Christ Consciousness. Also, no longer is the spiritual energy adulterated as it flows through the chakras. Although, the body has been cleansed, it still does not fully understand its new purpose. As we continue our study of Revelation, we will discover the body's reaction to its new condition.

Chapter 19:1-9

Scripture

Revelation 19:1

And after these things I heard a great voice of much people in

heaven, saying, Alleluia; Salvation, and glory, and honour, and power, unto the Lord our God:

Revelation 19:2 For true and righteous are his judgments: for he hath judged the great whore, which did corrupt the earth with her fornication, and hath avenged the blood of his servants at her hand.

Revelation 19:3

And again they said, Alleluia. And her smoke rose up for ever and ever.

Revelation 19:4

And the four and twenty elders and the four beasts fell down and worshipped God that sat on the throne, saying, Amen; Alleluia.

Revelation 19:5 And a voice came out of the throne, saying, Praise our God, all ye his servants, and ye that fear him, both small and great.

Revelation 19:6

And I heard as it were the voice of a great multitude, and as the voice of many waters, and as the voice of mighty thunderings, saying, Alleluia: for the Lord God omnipotent reigneth.

Revelation 19:7

Let us be glad and rejoice, and give honour to him: for the marriage of the Lamb is come, and his wife

Revelation 19:8

And to her was granted that she should be arrayed in fine linen, clean and white: for the fine linen is the righteousness of saints.

Revelation 19:9

And he saith unto me, Write, Blessed are they which are called unto the marriage supper of the Lamb. And he saith unto me, These are the true sayings of God.

Symbolism/Meaning

great voice of many people in heaven - the thought patterns, beliefs, actions, etc., which are either spiritualized or never partook of the self's ambitions.

avenged - God's vengeance is to purify and build up, by allowing His will to be done.

smoke - the consequences of purifying justice.

four and twenty elders - the same as in Rev. 4:4.

four beasts - same as in Rev. 4:6.

God that sat on the throne - the consciousness of the individual is now one with God.

voice - The voice of the self's highest consciousness.

out of the throne - from the center of consciousness.

his servants - the ideas, concepts, beliefs, actions which express the will of God.

small and great - all are a part of God.

great multitude - all parts of the Self.

many waters - much life.

mighty thunderings - stressing their praise.

marriage - the true uniting of physical and spiritual

Lamb - the Spiritual, God-consciousness directed mind.

his wife hath made herself ready - the body has been purified .

arrayed in fine linen, clean and white - the new Christ Consciousness of the body (i.e., the conscious mind).

the fine linen is the righteousness of saints -- deeds being the result, the fine linen is the result of the Christ Consciousness.

Write - signifies importance.

marriage supper of the Lamb - celebration of the marriage of the physical and the spiritual.

Commentary

The first response of the purified body is one of praise. The thoughts, beliefs, actions, habits, etc., that remained pure and true to God's intention (**much people in heaven**) recognize the wisdom of the body's cleansing, and they cry out their praise to God (**Allelujah!**). They recognize the righteousness of what has happened (**true and righteous are his judgments**), knowing that God's "vengeance" is to allow His will to be done. The energy God gave to his intentions has kept them alive (**blood of his servants**), even though the ego-led self adulterated God's intentions by imposing its will upon them (**the great whore, which did corrupt the earth with her fornication**). By using God's selfless intentions for selfish purposes, the ego-led self corrupted the original purpose of the physical body (**the earth**). Originally, the Adamic body was created as the perfect vessel to lead the soul into a full awareness of its spiritual nature. The problem was that the ego entered and began using the self to perpetuate the ego's existence and to keep the soul trapped in the physical with only limited awareness of its true nature. It is no wonder that the first response of the body that had been freed from such limits and restraints is to shout **Allelujah** in praise for its freedom.

As the body rejoices, it remarks, in 19:3, that **her smoke rose up for ever and ever**. This reference to **smoke** refers to 18:18 and signifies the scent of justice which ascends to the new consciousness. The awareness of the body's purity is now permanent and eternal.

Next, the twenty four **elders and the four beasts** worship the newly found God consciousness (**God that sat on the throne**). This shows us (and John) that the mechanisms for bringing information of the physical and the spiritual worlds (**the twenty four elders**) to the brain are still intact, and that the pathways of such information, along with the earthly nature of the physical body (**the four beasts**), recognize the need of the body to be cleansed of all ties to selfishness. The **four beasts**, symbolizing the basic earthly nature of the human body, are not corrupt in themselves. They become corrupted by the ego's selfish use of them to get what it wants, rather than to accomplish God's intentions by the correct use of the physical.

In the next verse, 19:5, a voice cries from the **throne**, telling everyone to **praise our God**. This voice, coming from the throne, is often thought to be that of God, since the previous verse says that the **four beasts ... worshiped ... the God that sat on the throne**. But notice that the voice tells the physical body and its thought forms to **praise our God**, signifying that the voice comes from one who recognizes itself as different from God, yet one with God. This sounds amazingly like the definition of God's intention for the human soul, and, as we shall see in verse 10, the voice comes from one whose purpose is similar to that of John's. So, if God is not on the throne, just who is occupying that spot in the purified self? Let us wait until the commentary on verse 10 to completely answer that question. Simply notice here that the one occupying the throne possesses the same purposes as God.

John next hears what seems to be **the voice of a great multitude**. This **great multitude** consists of all the parts of the purified body praising God for His power and rule. The symbolism used in Rev. 19:6 stresses the abundance of life energy given to them (**many waters**) and the intensity of their praise (**mighty thunderings**). The whole body is now aware of being created for a specific purpose, with each bodily part working in harmony with every other part of the body to bring God's intended Will into physical manifestation. The uniting of the spiritual purposes with the physical body is referred to as the **marriage of the Lamb**. The physical body (**wife**) has **made herself ready** by the process of purification and accepting the Christ Consciousness instead of being ruled by the ego. The body takes on a new understanding of itself when it puts on the Christ Consciousness (**arrayed in fine linen**). John's vision reveals that **the fine linen** consists of the physical manifestation of God's spiritual energy: the action (**righteousness**) resulting from the transformation of the spiritual energy into physical manifestation. The creations of the individual that were not adulterations of God's energy are the **saints,** which help bring about the active results. The body is celebrating. It is now capable of accomplishing the soul's ultimate goal: to be one with God.

Yet the **marriage of the Lamb** is more than just the uniting of the physical body with its spiritual purposes. This image also refers to the uniting of the new consciousness of self (consisting of the purified aspects of the conscious and subconscious minds, which became one at the fall of the ego-driven self) with the unconscious self, or the soul, or the higher self.

If you remember, in the story of creation as described in the Introduction, the fall of humanity involves two distinct steps. In the first step, as we enter the physical plane, our total consciousness is split into a superconscious and a conscious mind (figure 19.1 - figure 19.2). Then, as we enter into a physical body, the conscious mind is further divided into a conscious and a subconscious mind (figure 19.3).

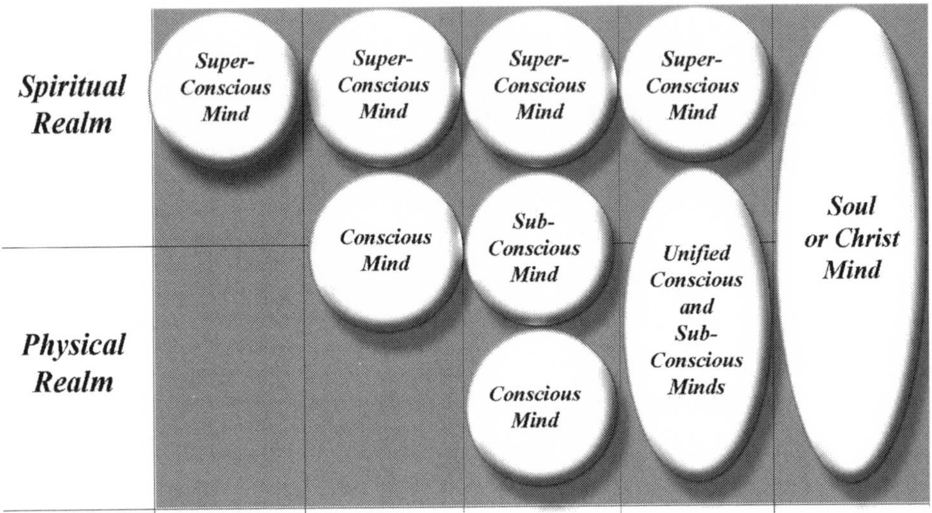

Spiritual Realm

Physical Realm

Super-Conscious Mind

Super-Conscious Mind

Conscious Mind

Super-Conscious Mind

Sub-Conscious Mind

Conscious Mind

Super-Conscious Mind

Unified Conscious and Sub-Conscious Minds

Soul or Christ Mind

Figure 19.1 ***Original Humanity (In the Mind of God)***

Figure 19.2 ***Androgynous Adam***

Figure 19.3 ***Fallen Humanity***

Figure 19.4 ***Purified Humanity***

Figure 19.5 ***The Realized Christ***

The original subconscious mind is sometimes referred to as the soul mind, the superconscious, or the higher self. This part of the mind is normally not knowable in the three dimensional physical world except through glimpses of insight or intuitive feelings and directions brought to the conscious by the subconscious. As the body is purified and the ego-driven self is crucified, the conscious and subconscious minds become one (figure 19.4), and all memories are examined and conquered by facing them and accepting responsibility for them (see previous chapters). This means that the superconscious mind now plays the role previously played by the subconscious mind. Since the body has been raised in awareness, the superconscious mind (or the higher self) is one step closer to the physical body. The connection between the two is now tighter and the higher self has more influence and control over the physical body.

What John's vision refers to as the **marriage of the Lamb** is the complex joining of the physical with the spiritual: body, mind and spirit. Notice in the included illustrations that humanity's final goal, figure 19.5, is to become whole (of one mind), which includes both the physical and the spiritual planes. The marriage of the physical and the spiritual will bring us one step closer to this goal.

Edgar Cayce was once asked the symbolism behind the **marriage of the Lamb** (reading TO281-036):

> (Q) Does the marriage of the Lamb symbolize the complete spiritualization of the body? Please explain.
> (A) As there has been given through the whole portion of Revelation; first how the symbols of the activity of the body mentally, spiritually, physically, are affected by influences in the earth – and as to how now the body has been raised to the realizations of the associations with spirit and matter through mind, the builder, and comes now to that as represented by the Lamb – or the mind, spiritual – that has now so raised the body as to become as a new being; or as was given by Him – the body is the church, the Christ-Consciousness is that activity which motivates same within the individual.

According to this reading, the **Lamb** represents the higher self ("The mind, spiritual"). The conscious mind and the subconscious mind are aware of the soul's original, spiritual state as well as its fallen, broken existence. By the very process of being aware of its condition, the mind can work or build toward the final, unified goal (figure 19.5).

The **angel** in John's vision now tells John to **write ...** (an indication that the following words are of extreme importance and need to be emphasized). The urgent message which the angel relates is as follows: **Blessed are which are called unto the marriage supper of the Lamb**. Then, to underscore their importance, the angel adds, **These are the true sayings of God**. The Greek word used for supper, δειπνον, refers to the chief meal of the day, usually in the evening. A wedding supper was a feast celebrating the union of two individuals. A large wedding feast could last for days, and an invitation to such an event was a momentous occasion in one's life. Such a celebration commemorated the end of one period in one's life and the beginning of a new era. The celebration, in this case, is the joining of the physical and the spiritual. But who would be the **blessed** individuals **invited** to attend that marriage supper? The invitation could not be issued to the physical body and the superconscious mind, for these are the Bride and the Bridegroom. The invitation to that joyful meal could only be issued to the intentions, thoughts, and actions of an individual hungry with the desire to accomplish God's will in a holistic, spirit-filled manner. As Jesus said, "Blessed are they who hunger and thirst for righteousness, for they shall be satisfied" (Matthew 5:6). Even more so will those who hunger and thirst for holiness be satisfied! Every part of the complex entity known as a human being must have the compelling desire to fulfill God's intended purpose for it, in order for the whole person – physically, mentally, and spiritually – to come to the wedding feast (**marriage supper**) of the Christ Consciousness (**Lamb**). This requirement is so important for the spiritual development of each one of us that the angel emphasizes it through the words **these are the true sayings of God**. Since all the words of God are true, the emphasis here is upon their importance in accordance with the vision John experiences and the message this vision imparts.

Chapter 19:10-16

Scripture

Revelation 19:10

And I fell at his feet to worship him. And he said unto me, See thou do it not: I am thy fellow servant, and of thy brethren that have the testimony of Jesus: worship God: for the testimony of Jesus is the spirit of prophecy.

Revelation 19:11

And I saw heaven opened, and behold a white horse; and he that sat

upon him was called Faithful and True, and in righteousness he doth judge and make war.

Revelation 19:12

His eyes were as a flame of fire, and on his head were many crowns; and he had a name written, that no man knew, but he himself.

Revelation 19:13 And he was clothed with a vesture dipped in blood: and his name is called The Word of God.

Revelation 19:14

And the armies which were in heaven followed him upon white horses, clothed in fine linen, white and clean.

Revelation 19:15

And out of his mouth goeth a sharp sword, that with it he should smite the nations: and he shall rule them with a rod of iron: and he treadeth the winepress of the fierceness and wrath of Almighty God.

Revelation 19:16

And he hath on his vesture and on his thigh a name written, KING OF KINGS, AND LORD OF LORDS.

Symbolism/Meaning

thy fellow servant - one who serves God.

testimony of Jesus is the spirit of prophecy - the life of the purified Jesus is a testimony of what can happen to all.

heaven opened - widening or broadening of consciousness.

white horse - purity of the message bearer.

he that sat upon him - the spirit of the Christ.

in righteousness he doth judge and make war. - the Christ Spirit now places value upon the actions of the purified self.

eyes were as a flame of fire - the vision of judgment.

on his head were many crowns - is ruler of all.

name written, that no man knew, but he himself - the Christ Spirit has all power

vesture dipped in blood - symbolic of the breaking of the fleshly tie.

The Word of God - the actualization of God's Will in the flesh.

armies which were in heaven - spiritual energies, imbued with God's Will.

out of his mouth goeth a sharp sword - God's will cuts through any selfishness.

rule them with a rod of iron - a strong, unbreakable rule.

treadeth the winepress of the fierceness and wrath of Almighty God - takes over the activities of the body.

on his vesture - on that which clothes us, i.e., on our new appearance.

Commentary

When John realizes that he has been shown the pathway back to God, he is overwhelmed with joy and thankfulness, and he falls down to worship the angel who has revealed this information to him. But the angel quickly instructs John that he is only to worship the Builder of the pathway (**worship God**). The angel is just a **fellow servant and of thy brethren that have the testimony of Jesus**. According to a reading by Edgar Cayce, it is implied that this "angel" is the higher self of the apostle Peter (or the spirit of Peter) who, preceding John in death, appeared to him in this vision in order to assist John in writing out the information found in Revelation.[2] Whether or not this was Peter's higher self is not of importance: The significance of this angel is that its intentions are in accord with the Christ Consciousness. In this part of the story, the symbols are more generalized than in previous sections of Revelation. This part of the story deals with the universal aspects of spiritual development for humanity as a whole, rather than for an individual, as we have observed before. That is why the angel refers to John and his **brethren that have the testimony of Jesus**. Those Apostles and followers of Jesus did not simply share the stories of what Jesus had done or what he said. They were to be living examples of the ultimate goal of humankind: to become like Christ and to have a unified consciousness directed by the Christ Spirit. Their bodies were being purified by their acceptance of responsibilities for their situations, knowing that the body, mind, and spirit work together to lift them out of the endless cycle of karma and reincarnation. Their egos had been (or were in the process of being) destroyed as they willingly chose to allow God's purpose to be expressed through them without changing or altering that purpose. For example, a careful reading of the four Gospels and the book of Acts will reveal the change in Peter from being a boisterous, speak-first-and-think-later individual with a need to feel important, to being a no-nonsense man of action whose desire was to bring glory to the name of God and Jesus.[3] Those brethren were a **testimony of Jesus** in their actions and words. The **testimony of Jesus**, as the angel said, was **the spirit of prophecy**; that is, the life of Jesus is a prophecy of what can be true for every individual who follows the pathway explained in the book of Revelation and exemplified by the life of Jesus.

After John is instructed in the importance of this vision for all of humanity, the vision broadens in scope (**saw heaven opened**) to become a prophetic picture of the universal aspects of what has been, up to now, a story of our individual struggle to acquire the Christ Consciousness. Now we see a message, pure and unadulterated, coming from the Christ Spirit itself. The **horse** symbolizes the bearer of a message, while its color, **white**, represents the purity of the message or vision which follows. **He that sat upon** the horse (the one with the message) is described in terms that make us think of Christ: **Faithful and true**. We must be careful here to distinguish between the man Jesus and the Christ Spirit. We often speak as if the word "Christ" is the last name of Jesus; we confuse the rich, descriptive concept of the Christ with the person who accepted and became all that the term "Christ" contains. We must remember that the Christ Spirit is a way of understanding all of creation from the eyes of, and with the mind of, God. To accept Christhood is to forsake the consciousness of the physical world and to accept the consciousness of the spiritual. Jesus the man became the Christ through his obedience,[4] as Scripture tells us, and therefore he was able to see and to know the purposes of the soul's existence. He transcended physical laws by applying spiritual laws to the physical, thereby enabling him to perform "miracles." These actions were miraculous to those who saw only the physical side of existence. By accepting the awareness of the universe as seen from God's point of view, "miracles" become simply the physical manifestation of God's intended purpose: the way things are supposed to work!

In these passages of Revelation, we are shown the general, universal results of accepting this Christ Consciousness. The one seated on the **horse** is the new Christ- like self, which shares with Jesus and God the knowledge of the spiritual purposes of creation. This self is **Faithful and true,** because it is at one with God, who is a faithful God and who knows only truth. The new self is the realized pattern of what humanity is to be: Its judgments are righteous because there is no ego to pervert or filter the spiritual intention of God's energy. When the Christ-like self must confront the egocentric self, it does so because it desires to eliminate all selfishness in exchange for selflessness.

The symbolic description of this new, Christ-like self reveals it to be zealous in its desire to see purity in all action (**eyes... as a flame of fire**) and to be in control of all aspects of the body, mind, and spirit (**on his head are many crowns**). The Christ-like self does not attempt to project a personality of being what it is not; it knows itself for what it is, and its name reflects this assurance (**name written, that no man knew, but he himself**). The new self is clothed (**vesture**) in the spiritual consciousness and has broken its connections to the flesh or physical. This is symbolically represented by the reference to the **vesture dipped in blood** – a reminder of Jesus' willingness to accept physical death as an example for all to see the reality of the Christ Consciousness. The Christ-like self is then called **The Word of God**. This name goes back to a previously mentioned passage written by John in his Gospel in which he refers to the Christ Spirit (as exemplified in Jesus) as the Logos (Word) made flesh (John 1:14). The same phrase is used in Rev. 19:13 in a more generalized, universal way to refer to any individual who takes on the Christ Consciousness.

Along with the Christ-like self is an array of spiritual energy imbued with God's Will (**armies which were in heaven ... clothed in fine linen, white and clean**), ready to overcome any hint of selfishness (**smite the nations**) within the body. It is willing to endure any cleansing necessary for the body to be perfect (**he treadeth the winepress of the fierceness and wrath of Almighty God**). In its ability to call upon God's spiritual energy to rule over the physical, the Christ-like self becomes **King of kings and Lord of lords** within the individual. This is the same title used to refer to Jesus as the Christ, because any one becoming one with the Christ Spirit shares in that ability and responsibility.

The new self therefore becomes the Christ within, as its new awareness permeates the body. We need to remember that instantaneous moments of change within an individual may be created; nevertheless, it is still part of a longer process. Since this part of John's vision is more generalized and not specifically directed toward any individual or specific area of one's development, it is difficult to relate to the vision through personal experiences or anecdotes. In addition, we must realize that, in essence, this is a retelling of what John has already seen, although variations and additional information will be included. This will become more evident as we continue in our study of Revelation.

Chapter 19:17-21

Scripture

Revelation 19:17

And I saw an angel standing in the sun; and he cried with a loud voice, saying to all the fowls that fly in the midst of heaven, Come and gather yourselves together unto the supper of the great God;

Revelation 19:18

That ye may eat the flesh of kings, and the flesh of captains, and the flesh of mighty men, and the flesh of horses, and of them that sit on them, and the flesh of all men, both free and bond, both small and great.

Revelation 19:19

And I saw the beast, and the kings of the earth, and their armies, gathered together to make war against him that sat on the horse, and against his army.

Revelation 19:20

And the beast was taken, and with him the false prophet that wrought miracles before him, with which he deceived them that had received the mark of the beast, and them that worshipped his image. These both were cast alive into a lake of fire burning with brimstone.

Revelation 19:21

And the remnant were slain with the sword of him that sat upon the horse, which sword proceeded out of his mouth: and all the fowls were filled with their flesh.

Symbolism/Meaning

angel standing in the sun - since the sun is symbolic for the self, this is a new awareness at the center of self.

fowls that fly in the midsts of heaven - thoughts in the subconsciousness now in consciousness.

supper of the great God - being fed by God.

eat the flesh of kings ... captains ... mighty men...horse sand...all men - the energy inherent in the flesh to be used for God's purposes rather than for selfish purposes.

beast - the now disincarnate ego.

kings of the earth emotions and desires of the flesh which once ruled us.

their armies - the creations of the ego which served to satisfy our physical desires.

false prophet - the old conscious mind, capable of self deception.

lake of fire burning with brimstone - the consciousness of being cleansed and purged.

Commentary

In Chapter 6, we learned that the ego is at the center of our lives when we do not possess the Christ Spirit. The sun was, at that time, the symbol used for the center of one's life. Now that the Christ

Spirit has taken over, John sees this new self as an **angel standing in the sun**: that is, in the center of our lives. This new consciousness then offers a call to **all the fowls that fly in the midst of heaven**. The symbolism of the birds flying in midheaven refers to all the previously subconscious thought-forms that now are part of the new consciousness (figure 19.4). These thought-forms are those that never were brought into consciousness by the egocentric self; therefore, they still carry their God-given directions and intentions. The call by the Christ-like self goes out to these thought-forms to come and feed upon the energies that were once used by the ego to sustain its selfish desires, thoughts, and actions. The raw energies of these selfish creations are now available to be reprocessed for others, rather than for self. This is a recycling of energies for God's purposes.

Next John sees the ego (**beast**), now disincarnate, without a source of power or strength, gathering with all of its creations (**kings of the earth, and their armies**) in order to attempt to overcome the new self. But the ego has no power, since the old self has been destroyed through the process of purification. Because it is powerless, the ego is easily captured by the new self.

Along with the ego, the old conscious mind (**false prophet**), which used its reasoning ability to deceive the self, is captured and **cast alive into a lake of fire burning with brimstone**. While most people see in this image a picture of hell, the symbols tell us a different story. A **lake** can symbolize that reservoir of unformed energy from which life or thoughts emerge. **Fire** has, throughout Revelation, symbolized the process of purification. **Brimstone** (sulfur) is also an agent of purification (as in fumigation). We now see that the ego and the deceptive conscious mind are kept **alive**, but they are subjected to a process that will remove all selfishness from them. Since they depended upon the ego for their life, all of the selfish creations of the ego and the conscious mind are destroyed. Therefore, the new unselfish thought-forms are able to recycle the energies from the old selfish thought-forms (**all the fowls were filled with their flesh**).

Chapter Twenty

Slave or Free?

Within the universal picture of humanity and the true nature of our spiritual existence, we must learn (or remember) our lessons of spirituality and then be tested to see if we can act upon what we have learned. Chapter 20 describes these learning and testing periods in terms of our free will: We learn when we freely give up our will to God, and we are tested when we again receive the ability to make decisions on our own. This process was exemplified in the life of Jesus by his temptation in the wilderness. It was there he chose to exchange his free will for that of God's will until, while on the cross when God's presence was withdrawn from him, he cried out, asking why he had been abandoned.[1] (This is also why Jesus was able to continually state that it was not him who acted, but rather it was God, acting through him.)

This pattern of giving up our free will to God and then having it returned at a later time is to be the universal pattern for each soul as we grow spiritually. The details of this process are given in Chapter 20.

Chapter 20:1-3

Scripture

Revelation 20:1

And I saw an angel come down from heaven, having the key of the bottomless pit and a great chain in his hand.

Revelation 20:2

And he laid hold on the dragon, that old serpent, which is the Devil, and Satan, and bound him a thousand years,

Revelation 20:3

And cast him into the bottomless pit, and shut him up, and set a seal upon him, that he should deceive the nations no more, till the thousand years should be fulfilled: and after that he must be loosed a little season.

Symbolism/Meaning

angel come down from heaven - spiritual awareness.

key of the bottomless pit - key to the physical nature of rebellion.

great chain - to constrain or bind.

dragon - rebellious spirit.

bound - limited or restrained as to influence.

a thousand years - a time of fulfillment.

loosed a little season - limited influence allowed.

Commentary

John becomes aware of a messenger or emissary from God (**angel ... from heaven**). The power of this heavenly messenger is first depicted by his holding the **key of the bottomless pit**. If you remember, the bottomless pit represents the unending cycle of selfishness and rebellion into which our physical nature is capable of throwing us (see Chapter 9). This angel holds the **key** to that unending cycle of physical fulfillment. Could the angel be the same one who was earlier given that key (9:1)? That angel, as previously noted in the commentary, represents our will – our ability to freely choose. The **key** to our physical natures therefore is our free will, which we cherish so dearly. When used properly, free will allows us to choose God's will. When misused, our free will provides the means for expression of our rebellious nature (**Satan**). Thus, this great gift of free will can also be a curse to those who do not control it.

The angel representing the human will also carries a **great chain,** which symbolizes both the ability of the will to limit the influence of the rebellious spirit (**bound him** [Satan]) and to bring about a certain chain of events in the lives of those who reach Christhood. With this **great chain**, the will chooses to constrain the rebellious spirit for a certain amount of time (**a thousand years**) after which that rebellious spirit will be **loosed a little season**. The Christ-like self chooses to bind its free will. Why would the new self choose to limit what many believe to be humanity's crowning glory? Simply, without free will, there is no possibility of choosing selfishly. By binding the self's ability to exercise selfish choices, it allows God's will to be totally expressed throughout the physical. This was the choice of Jesus, the first individual to freely give up his own will in exchange for the will of God. The time period of giving up one's free will is given as **a thousand years**. Using numerology, this number can represent a time of fulfillment or a cycle of three (the three zeros in 1000) coming back to the one[2] (see Appendix B).

In a reading given by Edgar Cayce, this thousand year period is viewed as the time when only those who have banished the rebellious spirit from their lives will be allowed to incarnate upon the earth, thus allowing the Christ Spirit to reign in the earth:

> (Q) What is the meaning of one thousand years that Satan is bound? (A) Is banished. That, as there are the activities of the forty and four thousand – in the same manner that the prayer of ten just should save a city, the deeds, the prayers of the faithful will allow that period when the incarnation of those only that are in the Lord shall rule the earth, and the period is as a thousand years.

> Thus is Satan bound, thus is Satan banished from the earth. The desire to do evil is only of him. And when there are – as the symbols – those only whose desire and purpose of their heart is to glorify the Father, these will be those periods when this shall come to pass.
>
> T0281-037

Whatever the explanation, this will be a period of time without the influence of the rebellious spirit from within either the microcosm (individual) or the macrocosm (physical world). This event comes about through the ultimate expression of free will: the willing surrender of one's own will in exchange for the free expression of God's purpose in our lives, so that all we say and do comes from God.[3]

Until this happens – and not many are willing to freely choose to give up their ability to choose anything other than God's Will – Satan still abounds.

Chapter 20:4-10

Scripture

Revelation 20:4

> **And I saw thrones, and they sat upon them, and judgment was given unto them: and I saw the souls of them that were beheaded for the witness of Jesus, and for the word of God, and which had not worshipped the beast, neither his image, neither had received his mark upon their foreheads, or in their hands; and they lived and reigned with Christ a thousand years.**

Revelation 20:5

> **But the rest of the dead lived not again until the thousand years were finished. This is the first resurrection.**

Revelation 20:6

> **Blessed and holy is he that hath part in the first resurrection: on such the second death hath no power, but they shall be priests of God and of Christ, and shall reign with him a thousand years.**

Revelation 20:7

And when the thousand years are expired, Satan shall be loosed out of his prison,

Revelation 20:8

And shall go out to deceive the nations which are in the four quarters of the earth, Gog and Magog, to gather them together to battle: the number of whom is as the sand of the sea.

Revelation 20:9

And they went up on the breadth of the earth, and compassed the camp of the saints about, and the beloved city: and fire came down from God out of heaven, and devoured them.

Revelation 20:10

And the devil that deceived them was cast into the lake of fire and brimstone, where the beast and the false prophet are, and shall be tormented day and night for ever and ever.

Symbolism/Meaning

thrones - position of power.

judgment was given unto them - the thoughts, beliefs, actions, etc., judged to be unselfish in nature.

souls of them that were beheaded for the witness of Jesus - the unselfish urges within individuals that were not allowed to be expressed because another, more powerful, selfish urge cut it off.

first resurrection - a time of spiritual awareness in the physical plane.

second death - a falling away from spiritual awareness.

priests of God and of Christ - examples and reminders to others of our true nature.

Satan shall be loosed - Satan again has access to us.

go out to deceive the nations - attempt to deceive the desires, emotions, etc.

four quarters of the earth - earthly or physical nature.

Gog and Magog - portions of the land of Israel and therefore symbolically, portions of the physical body of one who seeks.

battle - a fight for control.

camp of the saints - the establishment of God-directed desires, thoughts, actions, etc.

beloved city - the new self.

fire came down from God out of heaven - strength of purity overcame selfishness.

lake of fire - source of purification or purging.

Commentary

Once there is no possibility of choosing to act selfishly, the desires, thoughts, beliefs, etc. that fully express God's purpose are allowed to reign in our lives (**And I saw thrones, and they sat upon them, and judgment was given unto them**). The judgment of these unselfish urges is to allow them to have control. This is the same as what Jesus said: "I do whatever the Father tells me to do." In addition, those unselfish urges which had been suppressed because of the ego's manipulations and substitution of selfish actions, now have the opportunity to express themselves. Without the rebellious spirit to alter God's spiritual energy, our selfish desires (**the rest of the dead**) are unable to be expressed (**lived not again**) until a later time when free will is again restored (**until the thousand years were finished**). This thousand year period is called the **first resurrection,** because it will be a time when we will first be restored to an awareness of our true nature. By acting out God's Will, we will discover by experience the spiritual truths that we now accept only through faith. The Greek term used for resurrection in this passage, αναστασις, literally means a standing up again, or figuratively can be understood as a moral recovery of spiritual truth. By temporarily removing the rebellious spirit from our lives, we choose to recover the truth about our spiritual nature and to wake up from the sleep that is ours by nature of being in the physical plane.

To bind the influence of our selfish nature and remove it from our lives is one of the goals of any individual who is on a journey of soul growth. Through the use of free will, we can come close to that goal, but we are unable to reach it through the use of free will alone. It takes a leap of faith to relinquish our free will and to accept God's Will in its place. Jesus was the first who made this leap of faith, and by accomplishing it, he has shown to all the rest of humanity that it is possible. For us, then, it is not so much a leap of faith, as it is the proper use of will. By using our will to choose God's Will, we effectively bind the satanic rebellious spirit. This is a momentous occasion for any soul (**Blessed and holy is he that hath part in the first resurrection!**). But in verse three and verse five, we learn that this time of blessedness is limited (... **loosed a little season** and ... **until the thousand years were finished**). The reason for this limit will be better understood after studying the subsequent verses in this chapter.

Before examining those verses, we must first look at the reference to **the second death**. Someone reaching this level of spiritual growth is aware that physical death is not the end of life. Even though physical life is enjoyable, such a person would not dread the coming of death: He or she would understand that there will be more to follow, either in the spirit or in the physical again. Death is not viewed as an end as much as a chance to allow the soul to grow and develop further toward the goal of being one with God. In the context of what we have learned from Revelation, the **second death** refers to a loss of awareness of one's spiritual origins through the use of selfish choices leading away from the spiritual and again into the physical. If you reach the **first resurrection** you will not have to worry about losing awareness of your spiritual origins: the ability to choose selfishly is no longer within you, having been given up when you relinquished your free will. By choosing to allow only God's Will to be operative in your life, you become one with God and Christ, and you become Christ-like, serving as an example and leader of others (**priests of God and of Christ**).

Nevertheless, the physical life for such an individual is not completely free of temptations. According to Rev. 20:7, the time of reigning with Christ comes to an end when the selfish use of free will is returned (**Satan shall be loosed out of his prison**). Then the rebellious spirit will attempt to create a new ego to deceive the thoughts, urges, and ideas (**deceive the nations**) that reside within the lower chakras of the physical body (**which are in the four quarters of the earth**). Rev. 20:8 refers to the lower chakras and the selfish physical urges that reside there as **Gog and Magog**. These names, coming from Ezekiel 37-39 (where **Gog** is a king in the land of **Magog**), symbolize greed and worldly concerns. The myriad selfish, physical desires are still present (**their number of whom is as the sand of the sea**), but they are not effective, since there is no longer an ego to direct them. The rebellious side of free will attempts to organize and deceive them, preparing them to battle the Christ-directed consciousness that now occupies the throne at the center of the self. If the individual was being directed by an ego, and the self had abdicated the throne as described in earlier chapters, then the selfish desires would be overwhelming, and the spiritual energy would not be expressed unmolested. Because the true self has firmly taken the throne, and the conscious and subconscious minds have merged into one, free will now has a direct connection with the spiritual and can use spiritual force to destroy the selfish desires (**but fire came down from God out of heaven and devoured them**). This is the proper use of free will: not to choose what our ego may want, but rather to choose what is right for the development of our spirit and for others.

After all selfishness is eliminated from the body, free will itself is given over to be purged (**cast into the lake of fire and brimstone, where the beast and the false prophet are**). Once we come to the stage of allowing God's Will to direct our lives, we realize the ease at which free will could be abused, and we choose not to be deceived again by the selfishness inherent in the ego and it's desires for itself.

It might seem strange to equate free will with Satan, but it is only the misuse of free will that is truly bound and finally cast into the purging lake of fire. At its center, the Judeo-Christian heritage has always been a religion of the will. Emotion, intellect, simplistic belief, etc., are all involved in our faith, but it is the will which is central. From the time Adam and Eve made a choice, to Joshua's exclamation in Chapter 30 of Deuteronomy ("I have set before you life and death, blessing and curse; therefore choose life..." [Deut. 30:19b]), to Jesus' choice in the garden of Gethsemane ("... not as I will, but as thou wilt" [Matthew 26:39]), Christianity has spoken about the choices we must make through the exercise of our will. Even the basic tenant of faith as expressed by many modern-day ministers and priests ("Do you believe that Jesus is the Christ, the Son of the living God, and do you accept him as your Savior?") calls upon us to use our will to make a choice.

This understanding of the will emphasizes its two-fold nature: The will was the means by which we chose to forget our spiritual nature as we made selfish choices, and it will be the means by which we return to our oneness with the Creator. When we make a selfish choice, we jokingly say "the devil made me do it," thereby not accepting the responsibility for our own (not the Devil's) actions. Our misuse of will is "the devil" within us. The importance of recognizing the misuse of will as the Satan that must be bound is the message that Chapter 20 of Revelation imparts to its readers

Chapter 20:11-15

Scripture

Revelation 20:11

And I saw a great white throne, and him that sat on it, from whose face the earth and the heaven fled away; and there was found no place for them.

Revelation 20:12 And I saw the dead, small and great, stand before God; and the books were opened: and another book was opened, which is the book of life: and the dead were judged out of those things which were written in the books, according to their works.

Revelation 20:13

And the sea gave up the dead which were in it; and death and hell delivered up the dead which were in them: and they were judged every man according to their works.

Revelation 20:14

And death and hell were cast into the lake of fire. This is the second death.

Revelation 20:15

and if any one's name was not found written in the book of life, he was thrown into the lake of fire.

Symbolism/Meaning

great white throne - purified center of our lives.

him that sat upon it - the Christ Consciousness.

from whose face the earth and the heaven fled away - separate earthly and spiritual consciousness no longer exists.

dead - past activities, actions, thoughts, concepts, etc.

books - records of our choices and purposes.

book of life - record of our soul's progress.

sea gave up its dead - emotions or subconsciousness revealing their past.

death and hell - concepts of the limited separated consciousness.

second death - a falling away and a purging or purification.

name not found written in the book of life - state of selfishness.

Commentary

In this final section of Chapter 20, beginning with verse 11, John's vision leads us to the very center of our new consciousness (**a great white throne**). It is here that the Christ Consciousness (**him who sat upon it**) dwells as the controlling force behind our actions. The **throne**, or seat of power within the new self, is **white** to symbolize its purity and its freedom from any material or physical bias or selfishness. In the Christ Consciousness, all is in harmony: There is no concept of a physical existence separated from the spiritual. That is why **earth and the heaven fled away** from the presence of the Christ Consciousness: Both the spiritual (**heaven**) and the physical (**earth**) have been constructs of the physical consciousness. The conscious mind sees these as separate and incompatible, yet the new Christ Consciousness sees them as one and inseparable. That is also why **no place for them** was found in this new consciousness. All of creation is one, and a new consciousness demands a new vision of reality.

It is in this new vision that John sees the reality behind Judgment. John tells us that our past actions, thoughts, and concepts (**the dead**) have their purposes and intentions exposed (**books were**

opened) and are judged according to how well we allowed God's intended will to be expressed (**the dead were judged out of those things which were written in the books.**). The **books** are the Will of God that accompanies each bit of spiritual energy. What we have done in our lives (**according to their works**) demonstrated how we manifested that spiritual energy in the physical world. Did we allow God's will to shape the energy and the resultant outcome, or did we impose our own will upon it and wrestle it into some selfish form of expression? Our own use of our will is recorded in the **book of life**. This book is a record of our soul's development, and when it is opened, all of our emotions or contents of our subconscious (**the sea**) and our self-limiting physical consciousness (**death and hell**) are examined and judged according to how well they expressed being for others rather than for self.

Death and hell are concepts that originate in the limited conscious mind. We create both of these concepts to satisfy the ego's desire for a comprehensive explanation of why we seem to have limitations. The conscious mind cannot comprehend death, since the conscious mind does not survive into that state of existence. In order to downplay the importance of the subconscious, the conscious mind creates death as being an unknown, horrible fate, rather than being the state of renewal and evaluation, which it surely is. We learn to fear death rather than accept it as a time of retreat to an existence in the subconscious where we are closer to God. Physical life, rather than being understood as a time of testing our spiritual ideals, is viewed as an end in itself for our ego-driven selves. Rather than understand our life here on the physical earth as a period of testing to see if we have learned our spiritual lessons, we create a "place" after death where the time of testing is transformed into punishment for lessons not obeyed. We call this concept Hades or hell.

Our egos create the concepts of death and hell so that we will not accept responsibility for our loss of spiritual consciousness. By fearing death and dreading hell, we come to believe that the self is all important, and thus we pervert the very reason for physical existence (i.e., to return to God). We no longer wish to return to God and to share our experiences with Him. Instead, we want to remain in the physical and experience the physical for ourselves only. It is no wonder, then, that these two concepts are singled out for a special judgment. After these concepts are examined, they are **cast into the lake of fire**, to be remolded and purged of all selfishness.

The **lake of fire** is described in this vision as **the second death**. As mentioned in the commentary on verse 6, the second death is when we lose consciousness of our spiritual nature and have to begin again in our journey out of the physical consciousness. Any time we have free will and have not chosen to eliminate the selfish use of that free will, there is the possibility of a falling away. Even those who have reached this lofty stage of spiritual development and understanding have the potential to once again desire the selfish aspects of the physical existence. If such desires gain a foothold in the consciousness, then the individual will again forget his or her spiritual nature and be deceived by the ego. In essence, they will return to the earth, to be purged in the fires of testing, and once again attempt to make their way back to God. This, indeed, is the **second death**. The **lake of fire** is the image used to describe this recovery of God's will from the selfishness we imposed upon His spiritual energy. What we have selfishly created will be destroyed and burned away so that what remains will be God's pure will. In the process we must begin all over again to learn our place and purpose in God's creation. This is the meaning of 20:15: ... **if anyone's name was not found written in the book of life, he was thrown into the lake of fire**. This verse also implies that this time of purging and purification (which we often call "hell") refers to the time we spend incarnate in the physical earth! Our time of testing is also a time of purging. Earth can truly be a time of woes and sorrows, or it can be a time of joy and spiritual growth

Chapter Twenty-One

The Christ

Chapter 21 is a description of the New Jerusalem – the Holy City. It is from this chapter that we acquire such images of heaven as the "pearly gates" or the "golden streets." Yet, as we will see, this holy city is not a place where we go after death. Rather, it is an awareness or consciousness within ourselves that allows us to be one with the Creator. This chapter, written in symbolism since we are unable to fully comprehend this state of awareness, describes a new, Christ-like existence that is attainable for all whom so choose.

Chapter 21:1-8

Scripture

Revelation 21:1

And I saw a new heaven and a new earth: for the first heaven and the first earth were passed away; and there was no more sea.

Revelation 21:2

And I John saw the holy city, new Jerusalem, coming down from God out of heaven, prepared as a bride adorned for her husband.

Revelation 21:3

And I heard a great voice out of heaven saying, Behold, the

tabernacle of God is with men, and he will dwell with them, and they shall be his people, and God himself shall be with them, and be their God.

Revelation 21:4

And God shall wipe away all tears from their eyes; and there shall be no more death, neither sorrow, nor crying, neither shall there be any more pain: for the former things are passed away.

Revelation 21:5

And he that sat upon the throne said, Behold, I make all things new. And he said unto me, Write: for these words are true and faithful.

Revelation 21:6

And he said unto me, It is done. I am Alpha and Omega, the beginning and the end. I will give unto him that is athirst of the fountain of the water of life freely.

Revelation 21:7

He that overcometh shall inherit all things; and I will be his God, and he shall be my son

Revelation 21:8

But the fearful, and unbelieving, and the abominable, and murderers, and whoremongers, and sorcerers, and idolaters, and all liars, shall have their part in the lake which burneth with fire and brimstone: which is the second death.

Symbolism/Meaning

new heaven - new concept of spiritual consciousness.

new earth - new concept of physical consciousness.

was no more sea - no more subconscious. The old subconscious unites with the conscious.

holy city, new Jerusalem - the new consciousness of self as one with God.

tabernacle of God is with men - the presence of God is within

wipe away all tears from their eyes - the new consciousness has no place for pain and sorrow.

and there shall be no more death - we are spiritual and cannot die

Alpha and the Omega - see Rev. 1:8.

fountain of the water of life - source of life's spiritual force.

inherit all things - the spiritual consciousness is our birthright.

Commentary

Many people who read this chapter of Revelation readily acknowledge the need for a **new earth**, yet few people question the reason for a **new heaven**. If heaven was truly the place of one's reward for living a good life on earth, then what is wrong with the present heaven that John's vision sees a **new heaven** coming into existence? The new heaven refers to a new spiritual consciousness of being one with God. It can be visualized in figure 19.5 where the soul-mind (or the Christ Consciousness) has united the superconscious and the conscious minds of the purified individual of figure 19.4 into one mind that is able to be fully expressed in both physical and spiritual existence. Because of this union, a new consciousness of physical existence is also needed – the **new earth**. In fact, the new heaven and new earth are inseparable. When the old conscious and subconscious minds, now united in the purified individual, unite with the superconscious, then all parts of the soul's mind are whole again. There is no more subconscious (**was no more sea**). Even the physical and the spiritual are united into one.

This stage of spiritual growth comes about because the purified and spiritualized person described in Chapter 20 makes the choice to never again forget his true spiritual origin: no longer will he express his own will in a manner contrary to God's will. Gone is the possibility of falling away. When that possibility is gone, then the new, spiritualized, glorified individual (the **New Jerusalem**) comes into existence in consciousness (**coming down from God out of heaven**). We will become aware of ourselves as viewed from God's eyes. The beauty of the soul will then shine through, and we will see ourselves as if seeing a **bride adorned for her husband.** Beauty will no longer be skin deep; rather, it will radiate from the complete self.

When this transformation takes place, the self recognizes that God's presence is always with us, because we are one with Him (... **the tabernacle of God is with men** ...). Pain and sorrow are recognized as being false images conjured up by the ego to perpetuate the illusion that the physical alone is more important than the spiritual (**he shall wipe away all tears** ...). The self cannot be hurt, because it is eternal. It is a glorified combination of the spirit and the flesh, which can be created through the exercise of the mind. There will be no need for tears of loss, because we will be incapable of losing anything (**neither sorrow, nor crying, neither shall there be any more pain**). Being eternal and consciously recognizing that we are one with God means that even death will be seen as the illusion it is (**there shall be no more death**).

The Christ Spirit – the Spirit of the Son of God, i.e., the spirit of selflessness – is the vehicle by which this new awareness of self, the Christ Consciousness, comes to pass (**Behold, I make all things new**). When we each become the son or daughter of God by accepting the Christ Spirit and exchanging our will with that of God's, then we will have returned to where we began: oneness with God (**I am Alpha and Omega, the beginning and the end**). This time we will have dominion over the physical, having conquered any selfishness, and we will be capable of experiencing the physical while remaining spiritual beings. We will be a new creation! Once more we will be worthy of receiving God's spiritual energy without any need for limiting the amount (see Chapter 6 and the discussion of the Biblical Flood). This spiritual energy is symbolized by the **fountain of the water of life**, which we will receive without payment.

In 21:8 emphasis is again directed toward those selfish actions that lead to a forgetting and to a period of purging within the fires of a split consciousness (**the second death**). These are the actions that the Christ Consciousness is incapable of performing. They are mentioned here as a further warning to John (and to us) of our fate if we do not choose the path of the Christ Consciousness. Having this warning, John is next given a detailed description of the new creation: the child of God.

Chapter 21:9-14

Scripture

Revelation 21:9

And there came unto me one of the seven angels which had the seven vials full of the seven last plagues, and talked with me, saying, Come hither, I will shew thee the bride, the Lamb's wife

Revelation 21:10

And he carried me away in the spirit to a great and high mountain, and shewed me that great city, the holy Jerusalem, descending out of heaven from God,

Revelation 21:11

Having the glory of God: and her light was like unto a stone most precious, even like a jasper stone, clear as crystal;

Revelation 21:12

And had a wall great and high, and had twelve gates, and at the gates twelve angels, and names written thereon, which are the names of the twelve tribes of the children of Israel:

Revelation 21:13

On the east three gates; on the north three gates; on the south three gates; and on the west three gates.

Revelation 21:14

And the wall of the city had twelve foundations, and in them the names of the twelve apostles of the Lamb.

Symbolism/Meaning

one of the seven angels - the angel of the fifth chakra - the Will.

bride, the Lamb's wife - the new consciousness.

in the spirit - raised in awareness.

great and high mountain - an important insight or the path of the kundalini.

light - power, glory.

like a jasper stone,- valuable.

clear as crystal - understanding

wall great and high - symbol of protection, i.e., faith

twelve gates - openings to the soul (five spiritual + seven spiritual).

twelve angels - guides to the soul.

names of the twelve tribes of the children of Israel - approaches to the soul of the seeker.

east three gates ... west three gates - the soul has access to the physical or earthly in a balanced manner.

foundations that which supports.

names - purposes behind an action or description of the strength of an object or person

the twelve apostles - deriving strength from purposes close to the Christ Spirit.

Commentary

One of the seven angels who had the seven vials of the seven last plagues arrives to give John a detailed description of the Holy City, **the Bride, the wife of the Lamb**. This is a symbolic description (for John is again carried away **in the spirit**) of the individual who has attained the level of Christhood. The angel describes this stage as **the wife of the lamb** to emphasize that becoming the Christ goes hand-in-hand with the sacrifice of one's self will. These two events are married together in a causal relationship.

John first describes this individual as **holy Jerusalem, descending out of heaven from God.** This refers to the new consciousness or awareness (**heaven**) which allows us to see everything as God sees it. This awareness is pure, **having the glory of God**, because it is of God. Its radiance is so bright that it goes beyond white to the **crystal** clarity of understanding the purpose and reason for one's existence. All things will be understood by the individual who becomes one with God.

This state of consciousness is protected from falling into forgetfulness and selfishness by a great, high **wall**, just as any city of John's time placed a high wall around itself for protection from invasion. This protective wall is symbolic of the strong faith that will not allow outside influences to harm the new body-mind-spirit complex that is the new **Jerusalem**. Of course, at this stage, one's faith is no longer the "assurance of things hoped for, the conviction of things not seen," (Hebrews 11:1) but consists rather of the fulfilled promises of Scripture. Having obtained the promises, we know the reality of the Spirit: No longer do we hope for these promises to come true at a future time. That time has come and is now present!

Now that this wall of faith is a reality, John's vision reveals the twelve ways that information reaches the soul within (**twelve gates**). These twelve entrances or gates are guarded by the **twelve angels** whose names (**of the twelve tribes of the children of Israel**) symbolize that the individual is a seeker who has found the way back to God ("Israel" means "one who seeks"). There are three gates in each of the four cardinal directions, indicating a balance in the soul's approach to all worldly and physical aspects of life. In addition, this wall of faith is supported (**twelve foundations**) by the actions manifesting from the twelve spiritual/mental/physical centers (the seven spiritual chakras and the five physical senses) that are now united in purpose. The **twelve names** of the **twelve apostles of the Lamb** describe the strength of a spiritualized person. Since they believed a person's name was a symbol of that individual's totality (as evidenced in the many names for Jesus recorded in the Old Testament prophesies), to have twelve names (where twelve symbolizes perfection) refers to the perfection of that individual. Also, since these names are of the **twelve apostles of the Lamb**, John knew that the individual's strength is derived from having purposes which follow that of the Christ Spirit.

Chapter 21:15-21

Scripture

Revelation 21:15

And he that talked with me had a golden reed to measure the city, and the gates thereof, and the wall thereof.

Revelation 21:16

And the city lieth foursquare, and the length is as large as the breadth: and he measured the city with the reed, twelve thousand furlongs. The length and the breadth and the height of it are equal.

Revelation 21:17

He also measured its wall, a hundred and forty-four cubits by a man's measure, that is, an angel's.

Revelation 21:18

And the building of the wall of it was of jasper: and the city was pure gold, like unto clear glass.

Revelation 21:19

And the foundations of the wall of the city were garnished with all manner of precious stones. The first foundation was jasper; the second, sapphire; the third, a chalcedony; the fourth, an emerald;

Revelation 21:20 The fifth, sardonyx; the sixth, sardius; the seventh, chrysolite; the eighth, beryl; the ninth, a topaz; the tenth, a chrysoprasus; the eleventh, a jacinth; the twelfth, an amethyst.

Revelation 21:21

And the twelve gates were twelve pearls; every several gate was of one pearl: and the street of the city was pure gold, as it were transparent glass.

Symbolism/Meaning

golden reed - the standard by which to compare.

four square - balance between earth forces and spiritual. Also symbolizes balance.

twelve thousand furlongs - intensification of perfection.

a hundred and forty-four cubits - perfection.

pure gold, like unto clear glass - understood and valuable.

jasper ... amethyst - hold spiritual significance for the foundations of humankind (i.e., the growth of the spirit).

twelve pearls - beauty resultant from irritation.

street - the Way or the path into and through the Holy City.

Commentary

In this next section John describes the measuring of the New Jerusalem. To measure something is usually to set limits upon it, yet in this instance, John states that the angel or being that spoke to him carried a measuring rod of **gold** to measure the city and its gates and walls. The golden measuring rod is not a symbol of limitation as much as it is a standard against which something is measured. In this case, since the standard is gold, it symbolizes the highest standard against which to measure any object. The new consciousness (**the city**) demonstrates its perfection no matter how it is measured (**the city lieth foursquare, and its length is as large as the breadth**). This measurement is given as **twelve thousand furlongs**. The number twelve thousand represents an intensified perfected spirituality. The **wall** of faith which protects the spiritualized individual is **a hundred and forty-four cubits** high, symbolizing the perfection of that faith. (One hundred and forty-four is a perfect square of twelve, a number itself symbolizing the unified spiritual and physical aspects of the individual.)

At this point we confront John's curious phrase, **according to the measure of a man, that is, of the angel**. There are several ways of understanding this phrase. First, John could be referring to the spiritualized human being as being equal to that of an angel (remember, in Hebrews 2:7, the author states: "Thou didst make him for a little while lower than the angels ..." This implies that we are to be either equal to or higher than angels when we are perfected.). The work of Jesus in becoming the Christ and the potential of all human beings of reaching that state now places the human soul on par (or even above) with those of angels.

The angel with the golden measuring rod is **one of the seven angels which had the seven vials full of the seven last plagues**. This angel, representing the qualities of one of the chakras, carries John even further into the realm of the spirit (**in the spirit**). The angel most likely to transport John to this realm is the angel of the fifth chakra, whose controlling influence is the will. The self-will of the individual had been freely given up as the body was cleansed of all selfish desires and ego. The cleansed will, which is now able to fulfill God's Will, shows John the characteristics of a person who is totally unified and complete. Such a person would measure everything by the standard of God. This is what Jesus, the man, did as he perfectly carried out the Will of God. Thus the **measure of a man, that is, the angel's** would emphasize the high spiritual aspect of the purified, Christ-like individual.

John next describes the appearance of the purified individual in terms of stones and crystals. It is difficult to understand the symbolism in these images, because the significance of the stones mentioned has been lost in antiquity. (For a modern compilation of data concerning these stones, see Appendix G.) It is interesting, however, that the stones found in the foundation of the new Consciousness (New **Jerusalem**) are mainly the same stones which the Hebrew high priest wore on his breastplate (Exodus 28:17-20). In addition, these same precious stones are mentioned in Ezekiel 28:13 in the following prophetic lament directed toward the then king of Tyre:

> You were in Eden, the garden of God; every precious stone was your covering, carnelian, topaz, and jasper, chrysolite, beryl, andonyx, sapphire, carbuncle, and emerald; and wrought in gold were your settings and your engravings. On the day that you were created they were prepared.

This passage implies that these precious gems had something to do with our beginnings when we were still in the Garden of Eden. Since these stones are associated with the high priest's vestments used when making decisions, and they adorned humanity in the Garden of Eden, we can only conclude that these precious stones represent some qualities of humanity that are evident in our perfection. Many people today will attest to the attunement which they receive while wearing certain crystals or stones. Our modern fashion fascination with precious stones has its roots not only in the economic value of such gems, but also in the inherent, basic desires within certain individuals.

Just watching a couple of hours of the popular "buy-at-home" television networks will verify the desire for such jewelry.

Whatever the origins of such desires within us, we must acknowledge that these gems have significance beyond our present understanding. One attempt at understanding their significance was given by J. Everett Irion. Writing in Interpreting the Revelation with Edgar Cayce, Irion states (p. 178):

> In this context, it seems not unreasonable to compare these stones with the twelve major divisions of the body ... the stones are not just stones; they possess properties, just as the major divisions of the body have special functions and specific works to do.... There is an activity in the body relative to that in the stone worn by the priests as they moved into their inner temples.... these stones must relate to body activities which help in the regeneration or the progress from earth man to the Son of man.

Further research and insight may once again reveal the relationship between these stones and the human body.

Chapter 21:22-27

Scripture

Revelation 21:22

And I saw no temple therein: for the Lord God Almighty and the Lamb are the temple of it.

Revelation 21:23

And the city had no need of the sun, neither of the moon, to shine in it: for the glory of God did lighten it, and the Lamb is the light thereof.

Revelation 21:24

And the nations of them which are saved shall walk in the light of it: and the kings of the earth do bring their glory and honour into it.

Revelation 21:25

And the gates of it shall not be shut at all by day: for there shall be no night there.

Revelation 21:26

And they shall bring the glory and honour of the nations into it,

Revelation 21:27

And there shall in no wise enter into it any thing that defileth, neither whatsoever worketh abomination, or maketh a lie: but they which are written in the Lamb's book of life.

Symbolism/Meaning

no temple when we are one in consciousness, there is no need for a place to store our memories of God and who we are.

no need of sun - no need for an ego or self.

[no need of] the moon - no need for reflection upon either external objects or internal processes.

light - awareness of Oneness.

nations - bodily cells.

kings of the earth - ruling emotions, desires, thoughts.

their glory - the true purposes and functions of serving God.

gates of it shall not be shut at all by day - the self will never again filter what the physical and spiritual senses experience.

no night - no subconscious.

there shall in no wise enter into it anything that defileth...worketh abomination ...or maketh a lie - no temptation to be selfish shall be a part of the new person.

Commentary

The last section of this chapter is used to describe the qualities and attributes of a person who has reached this high level of spirituality. Because the consciousness of such an individual is not divided any longer, and it recognizes its oneness with God, there is no need of a place or **temple** to worship Him. God's presence is a conscious presence within every cell of the glorified body. And since God is light (enlightenment), an individual who allows God to rule within has neither the need of the ego (**sun**) nor its reflection (**moon**) upon our actions. All actions, thoughts, and words (**the nations ... and the kings of the earth**) shall reflect the Will of God and thus add to God's glory. Never again will there be an ego that will filter the physical and spiritual awareness distorting the truth and misleading the self (**the gates of it shall not be shut at all by day: for there shall be no night there**). In short, the spiritualized individual is aware only of God's truth. For such an individual, there is no evil or wrongdoing; the cause of such distortions from within has been eliminated with the cleansing of the body, the unification of the consciousness, and the relinquishing of the free will. Nothing unclean shall enter it, because there is no longer the establishment of an ego within the individual.

Chapter Twenty-Two

One For All

In this final chapter of Revelation, John provides more insight into the nature of the purified, glorified person in Christ.

Chapter 22:1-7

Scripture

Revelation 22:1

And he shewed me a pure river of water of life, clear as crystal, proceeding out of the throne of God and of the Lamb.

Revelation 22:2

In the midst of the street of it, and on either side of the river, was there the tree of life, which bare twelve manner of fruits, and yielded her fruit every month: and the leaves of the tree were for the healing of the nations.

Revelation 22:3

And there shall be no more curse: but the throne of God and of the Lamb shall be in it; and his servants shall serve him:

Revelation 22:4

And they shall see his face; and his name shall be in their foreheads.

Revelation 22:5

And there shall be no night there; and they need no candle, neither

light of the sun; for the Lord God giveth them light: and they shall reign for ever and ever

Revelation 22:6

And he said unto me, These sayings are faithful and true: and the Lord God of the holy prophets sent his angel to shew unto his servants the things which must shortly be done.

Revelation 22:7

Behold, I come quickly: blessed is he that keepeth the sayings of the prophecy of this book.

Symbolism/Meaning

the river of water of life - flow of kundalini/prana energy.

tree of life - symbol of creativity.

twelve manner of fruit - all aspects of the spiritual and physical work together to do the Will of God.

yielding her fruit every month - a continuous process.

leaves of the tree were for the healing of the nations - the transformation of spiritual energy cleanses all the cells of the physical - and when the individual has blossomed to this stage, that individual serves to assist the healing of others.

see his face - be consciously aware of God's presence without distortions.

name shall be in their foreheads - the character of God shall be evidenced from the influence of the seventh chakra.

Lord God of the holy prophets - the originator of the purposes behind what the prophets say and do.

what must shortly be done - the transformation of God's energy into physical manifestations.

I come quickly - the unselfish, all-inclusive totality of God's Will within is soon to be made a reality within the life of the purified individual.

Commentary

As this chapter begins, John sees the **river of** the **water of life ... proceeding out of the throne of God and of the Lamb**. This is a vision of the combined, unhindered flow of kundalini and prana throughout the physical and spiritual centers of the new body of the individual who expresses the Christ Spirit. The point of origin of this life-giving energy is **the throne of God and of the Lamb**: that is, the seventh chakra or the pituitary region. The seventh chakra represents the directing impetus of the soul. Without any distortions of purpose added on by a now vanquished ego, God's pure energies are directed into actual physical actions by this chakra. As noted in the commentary of Chapters 2 and 3, it is from this center that the physical body is directed to respond in kind to the energies it receives, whether from the kundalini or from the prana. In 3:21, the promise given is **To him that overcometh will I grant to sit with me in my throne, even as I also overcame, and am set down with my Father in his throne**. When the individual has reached this level of being one with God in purpose, then the **throne of God** becomes one with **the throne of the Lamb:** The individual's whole life is directed from the desire to do the Will of God. Thus the center of the new individual is in the seventh chakra – the pituitary or master gland – and all physical actions are produced from the pure spiritual energies flowing from this center. These physical actions are fully other-directed rather than self-directed, since there is no more ego.

This flow of selfless energy, **clear as crystal**, glows with the light of God from within. This life-giving energy flows through the middle of the street of the city, which symbolizes the central position of this energy or purpose to the existence of such an individual. Being the combined flow of the physical kundalini and the spiritual prana, this river supplies energy to both the physical and spiritual aspects of the glorified individual.

John also sees the **tree of life**, that symbol of creativity (see Appendix H), now growing on **either side of the river**. This implies that not only is the spiritual side of the individual infused with that eternal creativity, but the physical itself is constantly rejuvenated or recreated. The yielding **of twelve** kinds **of fruit** or results stemming from the tree of life (physical and spiritual creation) is a continuous process (each month) without any slowdown or period of inactivity. Even the **leaves of the tree** (the process of transformation of the energy to action) aid the bodily cells (**nations**), keeping them centered (cleansed) upon the purpose of being for others.[1]

The individual no longer has any selfish desire (**there shall be no more curse**) within any cell of the body. All thoughts, desires, etc., (**servants**) serve the will of God (**shall serve him**). Nothing separates them from the God given intentions within the spiritual energy (**shall see his face** and **his name shall be on their foreheads**). The seventh chakra, located in what mystics call the third eye area of the forehead, becomes that which directs God's will to be done throughout the physical body. All God's will is revealed at this time, so there is no hidden part of God-consciousness (**shall be no night there**). Moreover, no longer is there a need for a remnant of God's will to enlighten the different consciousnesses present within the body, now that all is one (**need no candle, neither light of the sun**). God himself is present within, and that presence serves to illuminate the whole person.

The angel in John's vision assures him that what he has seen (**these sayings**) are **faithful and true**. God is then identified as **the Lord God of the holy prophets**. John's vision is not simply a prophecy of what has happened or is going to happen in the physical world. The book of Revelation is not simply a story of the external, physical occurrences of God's action to save his saints in glory. It is certainly that, but it is also more. John was "in the spirit" for most of this vision, that is, he was in an altered state of consciousness. He was shown not just the external physical events and the spiritual foretelling of those events, which all true prophets experience, but John was also allowed to see the purposes behind even the spiritual foretelling. He saw the pure forces behind the will of God. What John has seen is not God as seen through the actions of the prophets, but the very spiritual force of God as it acts upon and within the prophets, before it is converted into a physical manifestation. In addition, since it is God's intentions which John is viewing, and since these intentions will soon find manifestation in the life of this purified individual, the angel states that he is showing **his servants the things which must shortly be done**. If God's energy is being transformed into physical action by a cleansed, spiritualized individual, then it will not be long before God's intended action takes place! In fact, the angel, being the messenger of God, speaks for God Himself in the phrase **and behold, I come quickly**. Whenever God's intentions for His spiritual energy are manifested completely, then God is wholly present at that moment.

Chapter 22:8-20

Scripture

Revelation 22:8

And I John saw these things, and heard them. And when I had heard and seen, I fell down to worship before the feet of the angel which shewed me these things.

Revelation 22:9

Then saith he unto me, See thou do it not: for I am thy fellow servant, and of thy brethren the prophets, and of them which keep the sayings of this book: worship God.

Revelation 22:10 And he saith unto me, Seal not the sayings of the prophecy of this book: for the time is at hand.

Revelation 22:11

He that is unjust, let him be unjust still: and he which is filthy, let him be filthy still: and he that is righteous, let him be righteous still: and he that is holy, let him be holy still.

Revelation 22:12

And, behold, I come quickly; and my reward is with me, to give every man according as his work shall be.

Revelation 22:13

I am Alpha and Omega, the beginning and the end, the first and the last.

Revelation 22:14

Blessed are they that do his commandments, that they may have right to the tree of life, and may enter in through the gates into the city.

Revelation 22:15

For without are dogs, and sorcerers, and whoremongers, and murderers, and idolaters, and whosoever loveth and maketh a lie.

Revelation 22:16

I Jesus have sent mine angel to testify unto you these things in the churches. I am the root and the offspring of David, and the bright and morning star.

Revelation 22:17

And the Spirit and the bride say, Come. And let him that heareth say, Come. And let him that is athirst come. And whosoever will, let him take the water of life freely.

Revelation 22:18

For I testify unto every man that heareth the words of the prophecy of this book, If any man shall add unto these things, God shall add unto him the plagues that are written in this book:

Revelation 22:19

And if any man shall take away from the words of the book of this prophecy, God shall take away his part out of the book of life, and out of the holy city, and from the things which are written in this book.

Revelation 22:20

He which testifieth these things saith, Surely I come quickly. Amen. Even so, come, Lord Jesus.!

Symbolism/Meaning

worship God - the desired process/result of following the path set forth throughout Revelation.

Seal not...-Do not close yourself to the flow of spiritual energy.

He that is unjust, let him be unjust still ...- do not impose the ego's will upon any thought, action, or desire. Allow God's intentions for the use of His energy to prevail.

I come quickly - the result of one's choices comes quickly.

reward - karma.

do his commandments follow these teachings.

tree of life - source of spiritual energy.

enter in through the gates - have all physical and spiritual centers cleansed and open to the flow of God's energy.

dogs ... sorcerers,... and idolaters ... - those still controlled by a deceiving, selfish ego.

the Spirit - the spiritual self.

the Bride - the physical self.

Come - follow.

let him that is athirst come - all the process of cleansing are to share their revelations.

athirst - those desiring to be One with God.

water of life- flow of spiritual energy.

freely - it is there for the taking.

God shall add unto him the plagues - the karma of actions not in accord with God's will.

God shall take away his part out of the book of life - there are no shortcuts.

Commentary

In verses 8 and 9 John repeats his performance of Chapter 19, again with the same result: the angel exhorts him to **Worship God** – the desired outcome of all actions resulting from manifesting God's intentions through the spiritual energy He provides. Some scholars view the final section of Revelation as an addendum added by those closest to John after his death. One reason for such a determination is the confusion regarding the speaker. John had listened to an angel in the earlier parts of this chapter, but the speaker in this section identifies with the title used by Jesus, "**the Alpha and the Omega.**" In verse 16, the speaker refers to himself as Jesus and uses other titles that are otherwise used for Jesus (**the root and the offspring of David, and the bright morning star**). Whether the speaker is an angel from God, or God's Son, Jesus, the words are spoken as if coming from God. Now that all are one in purpose, it does not matter who the speaker may be. My own opinion is that the angel is the one speaking through verse 11 and that either Jesus or the Christ Spirit begins speaking in verse 12. The reason for this opinion will be explained later in this section.

Verse 11 is a confusing statement. Why is there a desire for anyone who is **unjust** or **filthy** to continue to be **unjust** or **filthy**? Isn't Revelation a call for people to change? The answers to these questions go back to the concept o the energy flow through the body. As the individual either allows God's intentions to flow with the energy or adulterates this energy by imposing upon it the ego's selfish desires, the highest chakra manifests the energy into action either for self or for others, depending upon the intentions that arrive there with the energy. If this seventh chakra ever attempted to alter the energy once it has reached this level, then grave consequences would ensue for that individual. This verse is therefore an admonition to let the spiritual/ physical body reflect our faith (or lack thereof). If the energy God gives us is adulterated and altered into selfish channels, then our actions will reflect that fact. If we do what is right because of duty, then our actions will be those of the righteous. If we go beyond simple duty and allow God's intentions to shine clearly through our actions, then we have become holy.

The difference between being **righteous** and being **holy** is the difference between intentions. If we decide upon an action (which may be distasteful or difficult) because the law or duty says we must, then we have chosen to be righteous. Our intention in such a case is led by our desire to be righteous, and we therefore do the honorable thing. If, on the other hand, we decide upon an action (which also may be distasteful or difficult), because it is the action completely expressing God's will, then we have chosen to be holy. In this case, the intention for the action comes from God and was inherent within the energy given to us to accomplish that very action. This action then becomes a thing of honor – God's honor and not our own. It is in this latter case that we are "led by the Spirit" as we allow God's intentions to be made wholly manifest in the physical.

In verses 12 and 13, we encounter the statement **Behold, I come quickly**. Usually, this statement is attributed to Jesus, referring to his immanent return in the "Second Coming." Let me propose that these verses, coming from the Christ Spirit, are speaking of the "repayment" (**reward**) of the law of karma/grace within our lives. If we choose to impose our own will upon God's energy, then we receive the results of our own selfish choices. If we choose to do the right thing, then we reap the results of a righteous life. If we choose to accept the love of God and let His love flow unhindered through our actions, then we receive the holy, eternal life, here and now. This has been the case ever since God's creation of the individual entity and will continue as part of His unchanging faithfulness (**I am the Alpha and the Omega, the beginning and the end, the first and the last**). The reaping of the results from our actions is something that occurs constantly during our time here on earth, whether we are conscious of it or not. The Christ Spirit is always with us, and indeed, he does come **soon**!

The following two verses, 14 and 15, are again an admonition to cleanse the body of selfishness (**do his commandments**), so that the physical and the spiritual may unite as one in consciousness (**they may have the right to the tree of life)** and become one in the new, spiritualized humanity (**may enter in through the gates into the city**). If we do not totally cleanse ourselves, then we are controlled by the deceitful ego (**everyone who loveth and makes a lie**).

Jesus then enters the vision, speaking for himself, to assure John and those who read these words that He is fulfilling his promise to lead those who follow in his way. He is both the source (**root**) as well as the result (**offspring**) of an obedient life (**of David** – the Old Testament Jewish king).

In addition, the spiritual (**the Spirit**) and the physical (**the Bride**) aspects of our existence encourage us to unite them in the manner spoken of in Revelation (**Come**). If we hear the message of our true nature, we are to also share it with others (**let him that heareth say, Come**), so that anyone who desires to be one with God can drink freely from the flow of spiritual energy. We are warned (vv. 18 and 19), however, that, if we add our own intentions to God's energy, then we add to the karma we must experience (**if any man shall add unto these things, God shall add unto him the plagues**). Or, if we remove God's intentions, leaving only uncontrolled raw energy, we remove ourselves from the capability of uniting the spiritual and physical into one (**if any man shall take away from the words of the book of this prophecy, God shall take away his part out of the book of life ...**). This warning is to be taken seriously by all who seek to know God. If we do not choose to allow the spiritual energy to flow unhindered and to bring into physical manifestation the intentions of God, then we plunge further into the spiritual darkness. The warning begins with the phrase, **"I testify unto every man that heareth the words of the prophecy of this book."** The warning is directed toward the one who **hears** or understands the message within the book of Revelation: once you know what path to take back to God, and do not take it, that is sin. If you know what happens to you when you adulterate the spiritual energy flowing through you, and yet you choose to place your own intentions upon that energy, then the resulting karma will be worse than if you acted out of ignorance.

The book of Revelation ends with the restatement of the words of the Christ Spirit, **Surely I come quickly**. The resulting consequences of our actions will fall upon us as we either accept or reject responsibility for our choices. As the author of these final lines of Revelation expresses, when a life is lived in an attempt to be holy, then we welcome the coming of the Christ Spirit into our consciousness: **Amen. Even so, come, Lord Jesus!**

Epilogue

The Rainbow Promise

Revelation, as a book, is an enigma. So many attempts have been made at interpreting its images and prophecy that many modern day ministers refuse to preach from its pages. They are unsure of its meaning, and they are unable or unwilling to decide upon any one explanation above another. Many other individuals have read one or more explanations of the mystery behind Revelation and have chosen to believe portions or all of what they have read. Others have made their fortune by writing popular books espousing to be THE word behind God's word contained in this last book of the Bible.

Without discrediting any of the myriad explanations, we must acknowledge the usefulness of all descriptions of Revelation's mysteries for one important purpose: allowing us to understand ourselves and our relationship with our Creator. If an understanding of Revelation does not bring an individual into a closer relationship with God, then that individual has failed to truly understand what Revelation is all about. Each person stands at a unique location in the journey back to the Creator. Each of us must begin from his or her present position and either advance toward or retreat from our God. We must each use the tools and information that are around us or within us to assist us on this journey. Where we travel in our spiritual journey ultimately depends upon us. As envisioned within this commentary, the book of Revelation is a description of that journey, describing the difficulties and the path that has been taken before by Jesus. It is also the path which we must take if we are to receive the Christ Spirit within. This is the promise – the Rainbow Promise.

In Chapter 6, I wrote about how the Biblical Flood story can be understood in a symbolic sense. The story of Noah and the Flood is not only a story of a man and his family choosing to listen to the Spirit within – the still, small voice of God – but also a story about all of humankind and their relationship with the One who created them. Humankind was drowning in the flood of God's spiritual energy: They had access to the Spirit, but they were using it for selfish, ego-enhancing purposes. Realizing that our physical bodies would not be able to handle all of His spiritual energy until we had learned to be unselfish, God limited our access to it. One of the consequences of this limitation was that the life span of humanity dropped to 120 years from almost 1000 years; we dissipate our life energy through the process of giving life to our own, selfish creations. Just as we would not give a baby a loaded gun to play with, God would not give us an unlimited supply of energy until we are mature enough to handle it. That is why He made the covenant with humanity: "...never again shall all flesh be cut off by waters of a flood, and never again shall there be a flood to destroy all the earth" (Genesis 9:11). Never again would our physical, ego-led bodies be allowed to use a flood of God's energy to separate us from the presence of His Spirit, and never again would such unlimited spiritual energy be used to selfishly destroy all physical existence.

Revelation is the story of how the rainbow covenant functions and bears fruit in our lives as we go through the stages and progressions a person must endure in order to be allowed access to that river of spiritual energy once again. When we have chosen, of our own free will, to give up the ego and our will and to allow the Christ Consciousness to become our own, then we become worthy to open the seals and to gain access to unlimited spiritual power – power that is able to bring even the dead back to life!

I hope that this commentary presents a view of Revelation that might appeal to those who are searching for a path back to God that does not scare us into or out of a particular faith. Revelation reveals "what must soon take place" as we travel not just through this lifetime, but through many lifetimes. By examining Revelation as a book of symbols and relating those symbols to the psychology of the human mind, which we are only beginning to explore and understand, a description of Revelation emerges that seems to more fully encompass the goal of leading us back to the Creator. This description is also consistent with the beliefs of the time when Revelation was written and with the concept of God as One who loves us and gives us the opportunity to become aware of Him and His presence. In addition, this understanding of Revelation helps us to understand who we really are – spiritual/physical beings. Being neither wholly physical nor wholly spiritual, we are a developing hybrid whose realization will only appear with an emergence of consciousness as to our true nature. The first to achieve this consciousness was Jesus, the "first fruits" of humanity. We are to follow, for he has set the path, and has shown us the Way. Moreover, he has acted on our behalf in order to create the conditions to raise our consciousness. By showing us that death is not the end of life, he gave us assurance that there is more. We have not fully discovered what this "more" may be, yet we now know where to look: within ourselves, to the God who dwells within. Revelation reveals who we have been, who we are, and who we are to become. It was revealed to one long ago who was concerned with the issues of spiritual growth and becoming like the One who serves as an example for all of us. It is up to us to choose whether to follow the path that has been prepared for us or to travel some other direction. It is up to us whether we, along with the author of Revelation, can truthfully say, "Even so, come, Lord Jesus."

Chapter 21

The Rainbow Promise

Appendix A

An Outline of Revelation

I. Prologue 1:1-8
- A. Introduction 1:1-3
- B. Greetings 1:4-8

II. Vision One: Christ Instructs the Churches 1:9-3:22
- A. John's Introduction and Background Statement .... 1:9 - 1:20
- B. Letter to the Church in Ephesus 2:1-7
- C. Letter to the Church in Smyrna 2:8-11
- D. Letter to the Church in Pergamum 2:12-17
- E. Letter to the Church in Thyatira 2:18-29
- F. Letter to the Church in Sardis 3:1-6
- G. Letter to the Church in Philadelphia 3:7-13
- H. Letter to the Church in Laodicea 3:14-22

III. Vision Two: The Scroll in Heaven .... 4:1 - 16:21
- A. Introduction and Setting .... 4:1 - 5:14
  - 1. Prelude: Being in the Spirit in Heaven 4:1-2a
  - 2. Description of Heaven 4:2b-11
  - 3. Vision Background: The Scroll and the Lamb .... 5:1 - 5:14
- B. The Seven Seals and Two Interludes .... 6:1 - 8:1
  - 1. Opening the First Seal 6:1-2
  - 2. Opening the Second Seal 6:3-4
  - 3. Opening the Third Seal 6:5-6
  - 4. Opening the Fourth Seal 6:7-8
  - 5. Opening the Fifth Seal 6:9-11
  - 6. Opening the Sixth Seal 6:12-17
  - 7. The First Interlude: Sealing the 144,000 .... :1-8
  - 8. The Second Interlude: The Great Multitude in Heaven..... 7:9-17
  - 9. Opening the Seventh Seal: 8:1
- C The Seven Trumpets and Two Interludes .... 8:2 - 11:19
  - 1. The Angels of the Trumpets 8:2-6

Appendix B

Biblical Numerology

Alphabetic Assignment of Numbers

Although the symbolic use of numbers in the Bible is accepted by most scholars, there are some who would argue against such a use. For example, Casper Levias states: "In the Bible itself there is no reference to numerical gematria or the symbolic use of numbers, and their existence cannot be positively demonstrated."[1] Understanding that a disagreement among scholars exists, we must nevertheless look at the symbolic use of numbers up to the time of Revelation and temper any conclusions we may draw about its use in light of the information found.

According to John J. Davis, a professor of Old Testament and Hebrew at Grace Theological Seminary, there were at least three methods of writing out numbers used by the ancients living in the fertile crescent area:

A) Fully written words;
B) Symbols; and
C) the alphabetic method.[2]

The use of fully written words (e.g., "one," "two," " three") or symbols (e.g., "1," "2," "3") do not lend themselves to symbolic meanings for the numbers. Not until letters of the alphabet were associated with numbers did a way of assigning values to individual names or titles occur. Since, according to Davis, this practice originated with the Greeks, the Hebrews did not employ this method until after the time of Alexander's conquest in 333 B.C.[3] when Greek influence prevailed. By the time John wrote Revelation, therefore, a system of symbolic use of numbers could have been developed.

Once letters could be assigned numerical values, then a belief in the power of numbers behind certain words could also develop. When a word is used, the numerical value of that word is calculated, and the word's hidden meaning or significance could then be understood. On the following page are two tables, one for the Hebrew alphabet and one for the Greek. Following the charts is a listing of numbers and their possible significance in Revelation.

To understand the tables, the first column gives the name of the Hebrew or Greek letter as usually rendered into English. The second column gives the form of the Hebrew or Greek letter. The final column gives the numerological signification.

The Hebrew numbers in brackets refer to the "finals." The Greek letters in italics were added by Greek numerologists to complete the needed numbers.

Table 1 - The Hebrew Letters

NAME	LETTER	VALUE	NAME	LETTER	VALUE
Alef	א	1	Lamed	ל	30
Beit	ב	2	Mem	מ {ם}	40
Gimmel	ג	3	Nun	נ {ן}	{600}
Dalet	ד	4	Samech	ס	50
Hei	ה	5	Ayin	ע	{700}
Vav	ו	6	Pe	פ {ף}	60
Zayin	ז	7	Tzadik	צ {ץ}	70
Het	ח	8	Qof	ק	80
Tet	ט	9	Resh	ר	{800}
Yod	י	10	Shin	ש	90
Kaf	ך {כ}	20 {500}	Tav	ת	{900}

Table 2 - The Greek Letters

NAME	LETTER	VALUE	NAME	LETTER	VALUE
Alpha	Α or α	1	Xi	Ξ or ξ	60
Beta	Β or β	2	Omicron	Ο or ο	70
Gamma	Γ or γ	3	Pi	Π or π	80
Delta	Δ or δ	4	Koppa	ϙ	90
Epsilon	Ε or ε	5	Rho	Ρ or ρ	100
Stigma	Σ or ς	6	Sigma	Σ or σ	200
Zeta	Ζ or ζ	7	Tau	Τ or τ	300
Eta	Η or η	8	Upsilon	Υ or υ	400
Theta	Φ or ϕ	9	Phi	Φ or ϕ	500
Iota	Ι or ι	10	Chi	Χ or χ	600
Kappa	Κ or κ	20	Psi	Ψ or ψ	700
Lambda	Λ or λ	30	Omega	Ω or ω	800
Mu	Μ or μ	40	Sampsi	ϡ	900
Nu	Ν or ν	50			

Symbolic Use of Numbers

In addition to the assignment of numerical value to each letter of the alphabet, certain numbers also were given a symbolic or mystical meaning. During the inter-testamental period (400BC - 15 BC) "... the whole pseudo-science of mystical numbers received considerable treatment."[4] The following is a compilation of the symbolic significance of some of the numbers used in Revelation at that time.

[1] Although there are not many significant uses of the number one in Revelation, this number symbolizes God. Since the number one cannot be divided and is considered whole without any other number to be combined with it, it is a symbol of unity and primacy.

[2] Like many other numbers, the number two can symbolize opposites: When there are two people, for example, they can act and think as one, or there can be division and strife. Two is the number for adequate witness ... i.e., it takes two witnesses in court testifying to the same thing for it to be considered true. But when two disagree, then the truth is often absent. This number is an incomplete number because two straight lines cannot form any geometric figure. (Geometry was considered a mystical science that modeled God's world). The number two can also represent the Son, as the second person of the Trinity, but again, it is incomplete without all three members of the Trinity. It also represents the conscious and the subconscious, having been split apart at the time of creation.

[3] This number symbolizes completeness, since it forms the first geometric figure. It also denotes divine perfection,[5] as it refers to the completed Trinity. But one-third can mean incompleteness.

[4] The number four symbolizes anything concerning the earth. Since 4 = 3 + 1, it "marks that which follows the revelation of God in the Trinity, namely, His creative works."[6] By being the number of the earth, it can also symbolize that which

represents the weakness of humanity–our desire for the things of the earth.

[5] This number is used to represent a short time or anything concerning the state of creation. By following the number four (representing the earth or the worldly), the number five symbolizes the combination of God and the world (5 = 4 + 1) and is therefore sometimes seen as a symbol of God's Grace or of the redemption of humanity. It can also symbolize the five physical senses.

[6] Six represents sin because it is one short of the mark of perfection. (The Greek word translated as "sin" is "hamartia" ['μαρτια] which literally means "missing the mark.")

[7] Seven represents perfection or God. (Note: Three and one-half symbolizes physical perfection, because it is seven divided by two [or perfection split into two incomplete pieces].)

[8] There is no significant usage of the number eight in Revelation. In other Biblical passages, it refers to the superabundance of perfection (7 + 1, or more than God's perfection–used as a hyperbole).

[9] Nine is "The Number of Finality or Judgment."[7]

[10] Ten is another number of perfection. Since it represents the completion of the series of numbers one through nine, it symbolizes that all is complete or nothing is wanting.[8] Depending upon its context, it can also symbolize limitation (as in "there is nothing more...").

[12] This number represents perfection that deals with government or ruling. Some say it has to do with perfection in organization.[9] In Revelation, it often represents the Church–the perfect Church of God.

[24] In its simplest form, this number represents the totality of God's people: the two sets of twelve in the Bible (the Patriarchs or tribes of Israel [the Hebrew people] plus the twelve Apostles [the Gentile Church]).

[666] There has been much speculation concerning this number. In its simplest meaning, it represents complete sin (the number six [sin] three times [completeness]). By using the numbers assigned to letters (as in Chart #2), many names may be found whose numerical value equals 666.

[1000] This number signifies an intensification of fullness (10 x 10 x 10–i.e, three [completeness] times ten [completeness]).

[7000] An even greater intensification of God's perfection (1000 x 7 [perfection of God]).

[144,000] Being a combination of 12 x 12 x 1000, this number represents the fullness and perfection of God's people.

Appendix C

The Seven Spiritual Centers

In Eastern mystical thought, a comprehensive system had developed in order to explain how the spiritual arises and infuses with the physical. According to this system of thought, each physical individual has within them an energy force or fluid called the kundalini. The kundalini flows through the physical body and interacts with various energy vortices in the body called chakras, which are located along the spine.

Although these spiritual centers originally were associated with certain urges, emotions, desires, or characteristics of the human being, in the past two centuries their locations within the human body have been associated with specific organs and areas of the body. As the kundalini flows through the chakras, sounds, emotions, memories, and other phenomena arise. Movement of this kundalini energy occurs at different times within an individual's life. Since conscious movement of the kundalini is usually associated with an individual who is practicing some form of religious activity

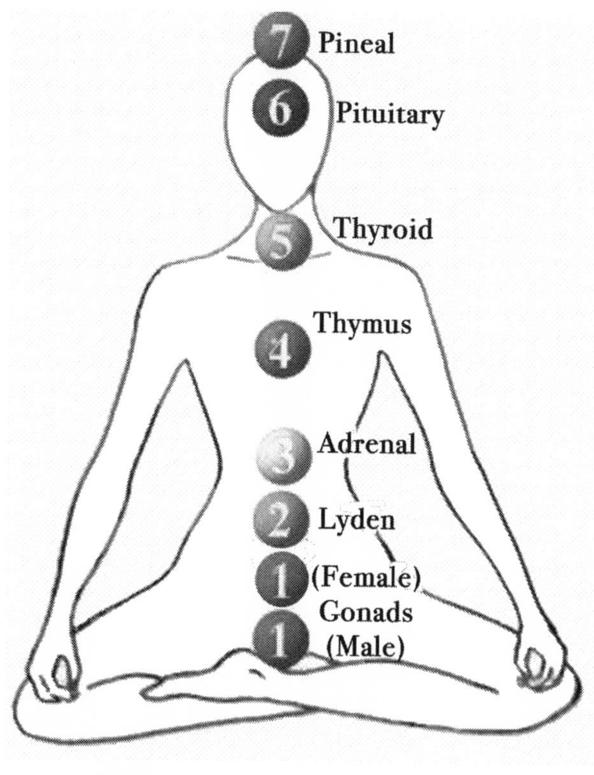

(such as deep meditation or prayer), it is important that the individual is also attempting to purify his or her motives and thoughts. Without this purification, the forces and images released as each chakra opens can become destructive to the individual.

Like all forms of power, the power of the open chakras is not to be taken lightly. Prayer, meditation, drugs and physical or emotional trauma may precipitate release of the kundalini.[1] Modern studies have correlated the chakras to the various parts of the human endocrine system.[2] The spiritual interacts with the physical through the endocrine glands – those "ductless" glands throughout the body which relate closely to the emotions.[3] When the individual is properly cleansed and becomes attuned to the Christ Spirit, these glands are fully opened to the spiritual, and then prana may then flow from the spiritual realm to the physical.

In addition to the kundalini, which is sometimes called the "earth force,"[4] there is also a spiritual energy which comes from God and can enter the body's system through the chakras. This spiritual force or energy is infused with the Will of God and is intended to be transformed from spiritual energy to physical actions or objects to be used in service for others. The chakras, if they are completely or partially blocked, are unable to correctly transform this energy. Instead, each partially or fully blocked chakra adds the individual's emotions, feelings, objectives, or intentions to the spiritual energy, altering it to suit the individual self.

It is this struggle of balancing the energies – of adding our kundalini to the prana – and of bringing harmony to both the spiritual and earthly energies that concerns the book of Revelation.

Appendix D

Emotional/Spiritual Relationships with the Spiritual Centers

One of the activities which have occupied individual spiritual-growth devotees over the years has been the process of associating various emotions or activities with each of the seven chakras or Spiritual centers. With the symbolism of the seven churches within the book of Revelation, this activity has expanded to associating various spiritual significances to the chakras. The table on the following page is one such attempt to analyze and categorize these spiritual characteristics which, admittedly, may not lend it self to an absolute system of categorization. Never-the-less, the attempt has been made, with the result as shown on the next page.

There are four columns of interest:

1) Actions and/or Emotions;
2) Spiritual Significance;
3) Highest Spiritual Expression; and
4) Related Phrase in Lord's Prayer.

The first column, *Actions and/or Emotions*, attempted to look at the listed characteristics of each church as expressed in Revelation, and to extract a significant generalization concerning the church. From the generalization, a relevant action or emotion was expressed. For example, in the first Spiritual center, the Church at Ephesus, Revelation spoke of making choices that are very basic to an individual's life. These choices are of one's desires and needs. This, along with the chakra being the root chakra and associated with the "root" or "being" of one's existence, may be generalized to the process of beginnings or birth. Thus the action of giving birth to one's desires or lusts – the creative processes, whether positive or negative, within our lives – becomes the associated action for this first Spiritual center. Spiritually, this process is related to creative energy. Further, the highest expression of the creative process, whether it is expressed in art, car mechanics, or the physical act of making love between the sexes, is dependent upon timing. Thus patience is the Highest Spiritual Expression of this spiritual center. The Lord's Prayer, which can be viewed as a prayer to strengthen all of the chakras, relates to this through the phrase , "Give us, *this day*, our *daily* bread." Notice the emphasis upon the timing of the request, as well as the relevance to the sustaining energy supplied by spiritual bread.

In this manner, all of the spiritual centers were examined and the relevant information gathered into the table which follows.

Emotional/Spiritual Relationships with the Spiritual Centers

Spiritual Center/ Church	Actions and/or Emotions	Spiritual Significance	Highest Spiritual Expression	Related Phrase in Lord's Prayer
1. Ephesus	Giving birth to or Creating one's desires – lusts.	Creative energy	Patience	Daily Bread
2. Smyrna	Bestowing value upon or accepting responsibility for one's creations	Suffering seen as a virtue when suffering the results of one's own actions	Faithfulness	Temptation
3. Pergamum	Flight (fear) – Fight (courage) instinct	Courage to accept responsibility for one's actions for others	Serving Others	Debts
4. Thyratira	Love of self or others– Instinct for self- gratification	A key spiritual center. When controlled by the first three centers, we tend to love the world and be bound by it. When controlled by the upper three centers, our love is giving and we are freed from worldly bounds	A Giving Love	Evil
5. Sardis	Attempting to discover who we are; Accepting God's will – Rebelling against outside authority	Free choice – the will	Obedience to God	Will
6. Philadelphia	Choosing to listen to that "still, small voice within"– Rationalizing our weaknesses and giving in to temptation	Maturity in Spirit	Being an example of faith for others to follow	Name
7. Laodicea	There is no response initiated by this level since it directs the physical responses to the creative energy arising through the other six levels	Making the choice for Christ (and thus for others) or for self	Christ-like behavior	Heaven

Appendix E

Divisions of the Physical Body

Taken from "A Commentary on the Book of The Revelation" based on a study of the twenty-four psychic Discourses of Edgar Cayce - Outline - (p. 94)

Function	Bodily Parts
Those of Construction	Bones–Muscles–Ligaments–Skin
Those that Keep Alive	Lungs–Heart–Blood–Liver
Those that influence that of the Physical, Mental and Spiritual	Central Nervous System, Cerebrospinal, Sympathetic Nervous System, Ductless Glands

Detail - p. 58 From a chart prepared by Helen Ellington and Gladys Davis

Spiritual (Hail - Water - Sea): 3 Attributes:

Light.......................... Zabulon............... Digestive

Soul (Love)................. Joseph .... Covering

Will .... Benjamin.............Bone Structure

Mental (Fire - Heat): 3 Attributes:

Desire........................ Simeon................Organs

Choice .... Levi .... Glands

Conscious..................Issachar..............Membranes

Heredity (Air - Blood): 3 Attributes:

Life (Sensation)........... Aser .... Lymph

Opportunity .... Nepthalim .... Nerves

Power .... Manasses .... Elimination

Environment (Earth - Physical): 3 Attributes:

Preservation .... Juda .... Assimilation (to Mental/ Material Spiritual)

Perpetuation............... Reuben .... Blood Circulation (Keeping Alive)

Attraction .... Gad ....Cells (Construction)

Appendix F

Colors

Have you ever attempted to describe color to someone who is blind? What would you say to them, "Uh, red is sorta warm and ... uh ... blue is cool, and ... uh ...yellow is exciting ... and..."? It is not an easy task, because color does not actually exist. It is always a quality of something else: a red rose, a blue sky, a green tree. What we perceive as color is simply a sensation within our consciousness. Light of specific frequencies or wavelengths appears as different colors to our eyes. The sensations we receive are caused by the stimulation of the rods and cones within our retina: The different wavelengths of light stimulate the different parts of our eyes to varying degrees, and we interpret this stimulation as color.

Even though colors do not physically exist by themselves,[1] we think of colors as separate entities that can provide specific energies to accomplish various tasks in our lives. Colors represent different energy levels (frequencies) of light. There is no doubt that different colors of light affect the human body as well as plant and animal life in various manners. For example, we know that the white light which comes from the sun can dispel the winter "blahs" or depression. There is even a "light therapy industry" which has developed because of this scientific finding. Many hospitals have discovered that different colors can affect the mood of patients. Green has always been a color that is associated with growth; while red light can detrimentally affect the growth rate of plants.

While we marvel at these relatively recent "scientific" revelations, the ancient people have known about the effects of colors for centuries. According to Edgar Cayce, the seven colors of the rainbow have been associated with the seven chakras of the human body, with each color symbolizing a different level or awareness or power within each particular chakra. On the following pages is a color summary, compiled from a booklet entitled "Color and the Edgar Cayce Readings." Written by Roger Lewis, this book presents an insightful view of the meaning of colors as related to the energies of each chakra and to the overall level of spiritual development within a person.

Chart of the Colors [2]

RED

* An outgoing vibration related to aggressiveness and conquest. It is an expression of vitality, of nervousness and glandular activity.
* Stimulates the autonomic nervous system by speeding up the rate of the heartbeat and the rise and fall of the respiratory organs, and by increasing the blood pressure.
* If seen in one's aura, according to Edgar Cayce, it 'indicates force,vigor and energy.'
* Is related to the gonad center or the first chakra.
* Symbolizes the Ephesus church in Revelation.
* Relates to the word bread in the Lord's Prayer.

ORANGE

* Indicates thoughtfulness and consideration of others.
* If seen in one's aura, indicates a tendency toward kidney trouble.
* Is related to the leyden center or the second chakra.
* Symbolizes the Smyrna church in Revelation.
* Relates to the word temptation in the Lord's Prayer.

YELLOW

* Golden yellow in the aura indicates health and well-being.
* Ruddy yellow in the aura indicates a timid individual.
* Is related to the adrenal center or the third chakra (the solar plexus).
* Symbolizes the Pergamos church in Revelation.
* Relates to the word debts in the Lord's Prayer.

GREEN

* The color of healing.
* Is helpful, strong, friendly.
* In the aura, when green tends toward blue is more helpful and trustworthy. When tending toward yellow it is weakened.
* Is related to the thymus center or fourth chakra.
* Symbolizes the Thyatira church in Revelation.
* Relates to the word evil in the Lord's prayer.

BLUE

* Is the color of the spirit.
* The symbol of contemplation, prayer, and heaven.
* Synonymous with the highest attainments of the soul.
* In the aura, deep blue indicates an immersion in one's life work, usually one dedicated to an unselfish cause.
* Is related to the thyroid center, or the fifth chakra.
* Symbolizes the Sardis church in Revelation.
* Relates to the word will in the Lord's Prayer.

INDIGO

* Indicates a seeker who has not yet attained the highest expression.
* In the aura, indicates a tendency toward heart trouble and stomach trouble.
* Is related to the pineal center or the sixth chakra.
* Symbolizes the Philadelphia church in Revelation.
* Relates to the word Name in the Lord's Prayer.

VIOLET

* Indicates strength of character and good judgment on the positive side, and self-centeredness and an overbearing nature on the negative side.
* Is the color of Royalty.
* Is related to the pituitary (the "master gland") or the seventh chakra. (Although, when this chakra is fully opened throug proper attunement, the color changes to golden.)
* Relates to the meaning of each section of the Lord's Prayer.

Appendix G

Gems of Revelation

The symbolic meaning of gems and gemstones in Revelation has always presented a problem to scholars: there is no definitive work explaining why certain stones were chosen. Many sources exist which will tell the healing use of stones, but these all vary in their conclusions.

Edgar Cayce, in a reading for an individual who had latent psychic ability made the following comments about stones:

> 10. (Q)You will examine the [lapis] stones which I hold, telling which is the most powerful for the various uses it may be used for. You will explain these various uses and recommend those that would be most helpful.
> (A) In giving that which may be helpful it is necessary, for this mind or body seeking same, that there be rather the analysis of the composition of the stones as related to their vibrations–as relate then to a human body, see? Either of these shows a variation of their composition; as to the elements of those influences that make for vibrations in the ether as related to that which may be effective in drawing to or disseminating from– through, of course, the vibrations being those that are of the positive and negative natures in the very stone itself–making for, then, the analysis; knowing same by what is called the constituents of it, through the mineralogy, the activity through those channels themselves. We would then find that the one that is the nearer in accord to the vibrations of the body that may use same would be the more effective with THAT particular body.

> Yet the very NATURE of the thing makes it effective with any - ANY–human body, you see; but the more effective with one that is more in accord, or whose positive and negative vibrations are according with the stone itself, see? For it throws off as well as draws in, you see, through the positive-negative vibration. This assists, then, in the unison as a relationship.
>
> This is as a comparison–don't confuse it and say that it is electricity; it is electrical, of course, in its vibration, but as the stone in its vibration, is then in sympathy with a body that is also sympathetic–or may be said to be SENSITIVE–it assists in "stepping up" the sensitiveness of the body as would the electrical vibration in an alternating force step up by the addition of influences or forces of electrical vibration being thrown off from other channels in making it more powerful. See? Towards what? Towards the effectiveness in its sensitiveness (that is, the body) as to what it may be seeking.
>
> Hence, as given of old, use such for the abilities to become more of all those influences called in the present psychic, clairaudient or any of those vibrations that build up or "step up" a body. Also effective, of course, in bringing to the body the abilities to become more effective in giving out of itself for activity in any of these various directions.
>
> READING 440-18

The stones, according to Cayce, aid the physical, mental or spiritual aspects of a person by increasing their sensitivity ("stepping up their vibrations") to whatever they may be seeking. In another reading, Cayce emphasized the importance of recognizing that the stones are only a tool and are not to be worshipped:

> 6. (Q) How can I use the astronomical, the numerical, the environs of the creations in the

vibrations from metal, from stones, which influence me, to advantage in my present life?
(A) As these are but lights, but signs in thine experience, they are as but a candle that one stumbles not in the dark. But worship NOT the light of the candle; rather that to which it may guide thee in thy service. So, whether from the vibrations of numbers, of metals, of stones, these are merely to become the necessary influences to make thee in attune, one with the Creative Forces; just as the pitch of a song of praise is not the song nor the message therein, but is a helpmeet for those that would find strength in the service of the Lord. So, use them to attune self. How, ye ask? As ye apply, ye are given the next step.

7. (Q) Should I carry these stones on my person? And how may I know thru meditation the message they would give me?
(A) If necessary. And how may ye know? These do not give the messages! They only attune self that the Christ Consciousness may give the message! Listen to no message of a stone, of a number, even of a star; for they are but servants of the Lord and Master of all–even as thou!

READING 707-2

Therefore it seems that the stones are symbolic only because they assist the human body in attuning to the higher vibrations of the mental and spiritual aspects of our existence. The degree to which they may assist any one human being will vary, depending upon that individual's talents, desires and abilities. For that reason, it is difficult to define, with conclusiveness, exactly what each stone does. The following charts are an attempt to summarize some of the general characteristics of the particular gemstones. The first chart is from material taken from Edgar Cayce's readings (not all gems were mentioned) while the second chart is a modern description of the uses of the stones.

Gemstones In the Cayce Material[1]

STONE NAME	SYMBOLISM OR USES
AGATE	Eighth stone in the Breastplate of the High Priest. Banishes fear, protect children against falling, hardens tender gums. Useful for attunement to receptiveness.
EMERALD	Antidote for poisons and a deterrent for possession by demons. Also used in the treatment of diseases of the eye.
ONYX	Symbolises the Love of Good and Light. Gives self-control, conjugal happiness and goof fortune. Useful for influencing the mental choices.
CHRYSOLITE	To exert its full power, it is required to be set in gold. Then it dispels the vague terrors of the night. Useful for attunement to healing.
BERYL	May be 10th stone in the breastplate of the High Priest. Banishes fear, quickens the intellect. Useful for attunement to receptiveness and for general protection.
TOPAZ	The Power of topaz increases as the moon increases. Strengthens the intellect, heightens psychic abilities. Useful for strengthen- ing the body.

Gemstone Chart[2]

Stone Name	Color(s)	Composition	Symbolism	Misc. Facts
Jasper	Red, brown, yellow, beige, purple, rose, green, black	Silicon Dioxide (SiO_2)	Balancing energies, especially those of the emotions	Many jasper carvings have been found in ancient Assyria
Sapphire	Blue, orange-, pink, golden, white, black, etc.	Variety of Corundum (Al_2O_3)	Clarity of inner vision, stimulates psychic experiences and spiritual awareness	Hardness: 9 - Second hardest natural mineral
Agate	Varied	Fine-grained Chalcedony (Si_20) with various colors arranged in stripes or bands or blended in clouds	Increases physical energy and guards against stress	Has luster of glass. Mainly occurs in basic and neutral lava beds
Emerald	Various shades of green	Variety of Beryl ($Be_3Al_2(SiO_3)_6$)	Improves intuition and clairvoyance	The color comes from Chromium
Onyx	Black, white, brown	Variety of Agate ($Si0_2$)	Enhances concentration, stimulates inspiration	Often heated to accentuate the intensity of its color
Carnelian	Clear, deep red or flesh red, reddish white	Variety of Quartz (SiO_2)	Gives protection and balances mental energy	Historically used to pull fever out from feet
Chrysolite	Green to yellow green	Variety of Olivine ($(Mg,Fe)_2SiO_4$)	Gives inspiration, stimulates prophecy	Also known as Peridot. Was favorite gemstone of Cleopatra

Gemstone Chart (Continued)

Stone Name	Color(s)	Composition	Symbolism	Misc. Facts
Beryl	Greenish-yellow (Heliodor), Pin, (Morganite), Colorless (Goshenite), Red (Red Beryl), Golden (Golden Beryl)	Beryllium Aluminum Silicate $(Be_3Al_2(SiO_3)_6)$	Helps restore physical health	Hardness: 7.5 - 8.0
Topaz	Clear, yellow, orange, red, blue and green	Aluminum Silicate Fluoride Hydroxide $(Al_2SiO_4(F,OH)_3)$	Excellent for mental clarity, focus, perceptivity, high level concepts, confidence, personal power, stamina	Hardness: 8 - Crystals can reach the size of several hundred pounds
Chrysoprasus	Apple-green	Variety of Chalcedony - Silicon Dioxide (SiO_2)	Provides protection	Most precious stone of the chalcedony group
Jacinth	Brown, red, yellow, green, blue, black and colorless	Zirconium Silicate $(ZrSiO_4)$	Aids steadiness, integrity and connection with "All That Is"	Also known as Zircon. Is sometimes fluorescent
Amethyst	Various shades of purple	Quartz $(Si0_2)$	Enhances psychic abilities, stimulates intuition	Name in Greek means "not drunken," referring to the almost wine color and beauty of some varieties

Appendix H

The Tree of Life

In the Cabbalistic view of the universe, all things begin with God – but it is a God consisting of an indefinable state of Consciousness (Kether). Within this concept of God are the two tools which define all else:

1) Energy without form, and
2) The capacity to take form or shape.

The energy without form is called Chokhmah (Wisdom), while the ability to take on form is known as Binah (Understanding or Intelligence). In the Big Bang theory of contemporary scientists, the energy is contained within the sub- atomic "bubble" that became our universe. Within that energy were the scientific "laws" of forces (gravity, the strong force, the weak force, motion, etc.) that gave form to the energy. The result was the physical universe (called Makluth [Kingdom]).

Yet this was not the only dynamic interaction occurring at this time. According to Cabbalistic thought, if we stopped at this point, the physical world would be void of life. It was the Biblical creation story at Genesis 2:5 where the earth was formed, but no living thing yet inhabited the earth. For life to exist there had to be consciousness: consciousness of God, of Form, of Energy. This consciousness of God (who is the primal Consciousness itself) is called Tipheret (Beauty), the consciousness of form is known as Hod (Splendor or Glory), and the consciousness of energy is Netzach (Victory or Firmness). This interaction of consciousness leads to a consciousness of the physical called Yesod (Foundation).

When all of these are put together, a diagram similar to the diagram on the next page emerges. Notice that the principles of consciousness have come between God (Kether) and the physical creation (Malkuth). This is similar to the "fall" in consciousness as recorded in Genesis. Also notice that there are several additions to the diagram. First, the principle of knowledge (Daath), coming between the primal Consciousness and a consciousness of God, is understood as a deficit or hole that was created when Malkuth fell from that position to its final position. Also, two modifying principles, Gevurah (Strength) and Chesed (Mercy or Love), have been inserted as limiting principles between understanding (Binah) and wisdom (Chokhmah) and their corresponding consciousnesses. In addition, the unknowable part of God (Ein Soph) is placed over all. The lines and arrows connecting the various sections represent the dynamics of the interactions.

The Tree of Life is simply an attempt to grasp the concept of One Creator from which emanates physical creation and the phenomenon of consciousness. The detail of this diagram has been greatly simplified for this discussion and does not represent the totality of the Cabbalistic concept of the Tree of Life. The most important idea is that the Tree of Life represents the dynamic connection between God as Spirit and the universe as a physical creation.

Cabbala Tree of Life Diagram[1]

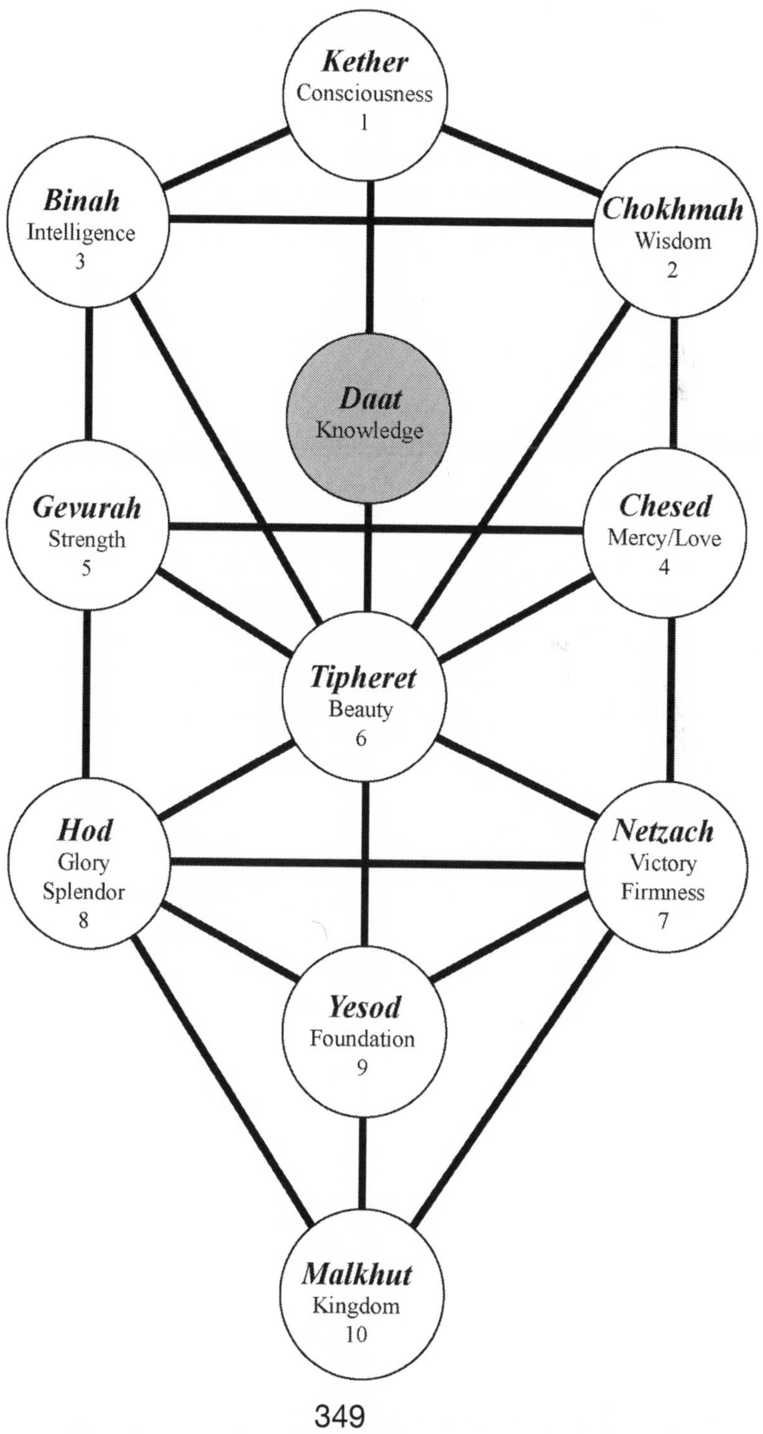

Appendix I

Glossary

Chakra – An opening, invisible to the physical senses, which allows spiritual energy to be transformed into physical energy and ultimately into physical action. Energy within the body can circulate through the chakras, allowing all memory of past actions, intentions and purposes to be cleansed. In addition, prana, or outside spiritual energy, can enter through the chakras, adding to our kundalini energy.

Christ Consciousness – The awareness of being one with the Christ Spirit. By putting into practice the behaviors and thoughts of the Christ Spirit, one takes on the Mind of Christ, and enters into Christ Consciousness. – Also, the acceptance or identification with being within God's perfected concept of humanity.

Christ Spirit – The original concept (Logos) within God's Mind of the perfected physical being. When we, as individual humans, take on the Christ Spirit, we put into practice (i.e., manifest in the physical) life as God conceives it to be. We become the Christ...e.g., we live the Christ-life while in the flesh.

Collective unconscious – A deeper level of the subconscious that includes the unconscious of the entire human race and thus contains wisdom and knowledge that is universal

Conscious mind – A limited facility utilized by the mind and the ego to organize and structure one's physical and mental life.

Ego – Each normal human being, as it grows and develops, constructs a protective mechanism, consisting of thoughts, reactions, and behaviors, whose purpose is to provide a safe environment for the individual. Since everyone's environment (both the external physical environment and the inner, mental environment) differs, all egos are different. The ego, because it is so central to one's existence, takes our identity. We come to believe "we" are the physical and mental attributes rather than the spirit within. It is central to accepting the Christ Spirit that the ego must give up its claim to the throne of our lives. The book of Revelation is the story of the reluctant ego.

God Consciousness – An awareness of being one with the Creator, of having the same mind as that of God (as much as this is possible).

God's will – The intention or purpose which God places upon the spiritual energy He provides us. God's will includes both an outcome and the methods of reaching that outcome.

Kundalini – The life energy or force. This is the energy which an individual has at birth and is often understood to be the energy with which one creates.

Mind of Christ – That totality of thoughts which originate from the perfected concept of humanity within the Mind of God. To have the Mind of Christ is to think the thoughts of God within the physical existence. This, in turn, leads to physical behaviors which totally reflect the will of God.

Prana – Energy from God. This is spiritual energy which comes from outside the individual. This energy includes God's intentions, but we have the ability to override God's intentions by placing our own intentions upon it.

Quabbala (also Cabala, Kabbalah) – The Jewish branch of mysticism and cosmological philosophy.

Soul-Mind – See Superconscious mind

Spiritual Center – See Chakra

Subconscious Mind – The unconscious mind; the part of the mind that the conscious mind is unaware of, containing personal forgotten memories, repressed desires and feelings, and subliminally absorbed events.

Superconscious Mind – The totality of one's Spiritual existence. Sometimes called the Higher Self or the Soul Mind.

Chapter Notes

Introduction

1 Bromiley, G. W., p. 172.
2 The Apostle John is believed to also be the author of the Gospel of John as well as I, II and III John.
3 Bromiley, G. W., p. 172
4 Some philosophers have denied the reality of the physical world while others hold that the spiritual, unseen world is more real than the physical world. For our purposes, we can accept this second philosophy, as long as we accept, in some way, the existence of both the physical and the non-physical realms.
5 This is very much like the philosophy of Socrates and Plato in their theories of the "Ideal." The non-physical world (or spiritual world) is more "real" than the everyday physical world in which we live. Just as my shadow seems to be alive because it moves around, it is but a "shadow" of the reality that is me. In a similar manner, the physical world seems to be "real," yet it is only a shadow of the higher reality called the spiritual world, or the "world of ideals."
6 The Interpreter's Bible, Vol. 12, p. 347.
7 This is not to say that they believed that everything repeated itself over and over again. The beginning of each new age simply meant that something was changed. For the Apocalyptic writings, this would mean that evil had been eliminated and goodness or fairness was again in control.
8 Efird, James M., p. 140.
9 Hall, Manly P., p. CXIII.
10 Theological Dictionary of the Old Testament, Editors: G. Johannes Botterweck and Helmer Ringgren, Vol 1, pages 75-87. This word generally has the meaning of a collective noun, thus "humankind." It is derived from a word meaning "red" or "ruddish" such as the red soil.
11 John Van Auken, Born Again and Again, p. 22.
12 Ibid, p. 27.
13 Manly Hall, p. LXXXVIII.

Chapter One

1 See the Forward for a detailed explanation of this position.

2 This was a title given to the early Christians before they were called "Christians"
(see Acts 9:2, 11:26)

3 Rev. 1:4

4 Caird, G.B., p. 15.

5 Lamsa, George M.

6 Fr. Gerarado Di Flumeri, editor, pp. 111 and following

Chapters Two And Three

1 Jung, Carl, Psychological Types or The Psychology of Individuation, 1923/1953, p. 585

2 Cayce, A Search for God, Books I and II, p. 5.

3 According to Edgar Cayce the term "physical" objects also encompasses what we normally think of as non-physical or intangible. In the famous Cayce phrase "thoughts are things," it is acknowledged that the only difference between a thought and what we normally consider to be a physical object is the higher vibrational quality or rate of thoughts as compared to tangible physical objects.

4 The story of Camelot and the triangular relationship between King Arthur, Guinevere and Lancelot is an example of a belief (or law) that became solidified until Arthur lost his kingdom while dealing with the conflict of worshipping his belief as opposed to being flexible enough to grow through a difficult situation.

5 Puryear, Herbert B, and Thurston, Mark S., Meditation and the Mind of Man, p. 33.

6 Karma is an ancient system of spiritual justice that was accepted in Biblical times. "You reap what you sow" is the Biblical quote. Essentially, it states that whatever we do unto others will be done, in a like manner, unto us. This is a corollary of the Golden Rule. Other equivalent statements are: "To have friends you must be a friend"; "What goes around, comes around"; "Cast your bread upon the waters.", etc. Sometimes karma is immediate, while at other times it may take years (or even lifetimes) to receive back what you have done. Karma also works at the level of institutions or nations. Thus one

generation may receive the karma of previous generations. "The sins of the Father are visited upon their children and their children's children."

7 Op Cit., Meditation and the Mind of Man, p. 32.

8 Op Cit., Meditation and the Mind of Man, p. 33.

9 David was described as "a Man after God's own Heart" even though David's life was full of troubles and sin. David possessed the ability to recognize and accept responsibility for his own sins (repent) and then choose never to repeat those sins. By studying the life and career of David in the Old Testament, you will be able to see evidence of the stages of spiritual growth described in Chapters 2 and 3 of Revelation.

10 Op Cit., Meditation and the Mind of Man, p. 33.

11 Irion, J. Everett, Interpreting the Revelation, pp. 116-117.

Chapter Four

1 In the author's own experience of beginning to meditate (by waking up at 2:00 a.m. and moving to the basement so as not to disturb anyone), both my wife and a house guest were awakened by a noise which they described as "a bunch of rocks in a tin can, which was spun around slowly at first, and then increased in speed." Since this happened for two or three consecutive nights, we concluded that as a beginning meditator, I was psychically producing the noise by "grinding my meditation gears!"

2 Irion, J. Everett, Interpreting the Revelation,. p. 136.

Chapter Six

1 Robertson, Robin, p. 31.

2 Ibid, page 55.

3 Cayce, Edgar, A Commentary on the Book of the Revelation, p. 91.

4 Irion, J. Everett, p. 166.

Chapter Seven

1 Cayce, Edgar, A Commentary on the Book of the Revelation, p. 173.
2 See Genesis 32:22-32 for the story of how Jacob's name was changed to "Israel" after he struggled with God.
3 Cayce, Edgar, A Commentary on the Book of the Revelation, p. 59.

Chapter Eight

1 At the risk of being offensive to some, I must relate a story that occurred early in my ministry. At a Revelation study group, we were somberly reading and discussing the symbolism of Chapter 7 when an older, white haired man, known for his wry humor spoke up and said "You know, I've been reading ahead a little, and I see where it says that there will not be any women in heaven!" The rest of us, looking a little puzzled, asked him what he meant. With a twinkle in his eye, he replied, "Well, right there in Chapter 8 it says there's going to be silence in Heaven for half and hour, and no woman could ever be quiet for that long!" – Needless to say, he was properly chastised by the group – other men as well as women – but we all enjoyed the relief of taking ourselves too seriously!
2 Cayce, Edgar, A Commentary on the Book of the Revelation, p. 175.

Chapter Nine

1 Isaiah 55: 11 - NCV.
2 Irion, J. Everett, p. 203.
3 1 Corinthians 15:44.
4 Cayce, Edgar, A Commentary on the Book of the Revelation, page 103.
5 Tanner, Wilda B., p. 262.

Chapter Ten

1 See appendix F for an explanation of the symbolism behind various colors.
2 Irion, J. Everett, p. 224.

Chapter 11

1 Such as the 40 days of the flood, the 40 years that the Hebrew people traveled in the wilderness and the 40 days that Jesus spent in the wilderness.

2 There are exceptions to this rule: Some numbers such as 11, 22, and 33 are considered "master Numbers" and are not always reduced any further. Other numbers (such as 26, 40 or 50) are special numbers that have specific emphasis.

3 Tanner, Wilda B., p. 212

4 Synchronicity is defined as those events that some see as "more than coincidence" in one's life.

5 Edgar Cayce was one who was acknowledged by many to possess such abilities. Gladys Davis, Cayce's secretary and stenographer, once remarked that on Monday mornings when she did not want Mr. Cayce to know what she had been doing on the weekend, she would sometimes sneak into her office through the back door just so that Edgar would not see her. Just by looking at someone, Edgar Cayce could tell what that person had been doing. " Sometimes," stated Gladys, "it was just none of his business!"

Chapter 12

1 Van Auken, John, The End Times, p. 12.

2 Psalm 103:5

3 Cayce, Edgar, reading #281-34.

4 Irion, J. Everett, p. 272

5 Some ancient scriptures sources translate the last phrase of verse 12:17 to read, "And I stood upon the sand of the sea," and they place this fragment at the beginning of verse 13:1.

Chapter 13

1 Hamblin, Collins, p. 20

2 Cayce, Edgar, Reading # 281-34

3 Irion, p. 289

4 Just as Elijah had to run away from Jezebel so that Elijah would not be beheaded, but later John the Baptist (whom Jesus claimed was Elijah-

see Matthew 11) met his karma by allowing himself to be beheaded at the request of Herod's wife (Jezebel reincarnate?)

5 Otto, Rudolf, p. 25ff.

6 In Mutant Message Down Under, the "real People" did not buy or sell except as needed to meet the minimal society standards. They trusted God to supply what they needed each day.

7 Some ancient manuscripts have 616 instead of 666 as the number of the beast.

Chapter 14

1 Compare 1st Corinthians 15: 35 ff.

2 Black, Matthew, pp. 27-35.

3 Cayce, Edgar, Reading # 281-36, question and answer 33.

4 Compare John 5: 19-47 and John 14:10 for instances when Jesus speaks of the Father who lives in him and works through him.

5 E.g., from one of Edgar Cayce's readings (T0479-001 M [Pg 3]): "14. Blessed is he whom the Lord chasteneth, for He loveth every one and will quicken those that call on His name and act in accordance with the directions that are given every soul to know to do good and to do it not becomes sin, but to know that He – the Christ – will stand within thy stead and will cleanse the soulbody every whit, that it may stand before the throne of grace every whit CLEAN!" (Emphasis added)

6 Romans 6:25. The book of Romans is Paul's way of explaining much of the same material as in Revelation.

7 See John 1:14

8 See Matthew 8:23-27.

Chapter 17

1 Irion, J. Everett, p. 353.

2 Stanford, Ray, p. 132, 133.

Chapter 19

1 Irion, J. Everett, p. 369 - 370.

2 Reading TO281-016 contains the following comment:

> "3 In making this worth while in the experience of individuals who are seeking for the light, for the revelation that may be theirs as promised in the promises of same, it would be well that there be considered first the conditions which surrounded the writer, the apostle, the beloved, the last of those chosen; writing to a persecuted people, many despairing, many fallen away, yet, many seeking to hold to that which had been delivered to them through the efforts and activities of those upon whom the spirit had fallen by the very indwelling and the manifestations that had become the common knowledge of all.
>
> 4 Remember, then, that Peter – chosen as the rock, chosen to open the doors of that known today as the church - had said to this companion, "I will endeavor to keep thee in remembrance; even after my demise I will return to you." [II Peter 1:15]
>
> 5 The beloved, then, was banished to the isle, and was in meditation, in prayer, in communion with those saints who were in that position to see, to comprehend the greater needs of those that would carry on.
>
> 6 And, as given in the beginning, "I was in the Spirit on the Lord's day, and beheld, and heard, and saw, and was told to WRITE."

3 Notice Peter's reaction immediately after the institution of the Lord's Supper when Jesus informs Peter of the prayers for Peter's strength of faith: Peter immediately boasts of his willingness to go to both prison and to death for Jesus. It is then that Jesus tells Peter of his upcoming denials before the rooster crows.

4 Cf. Hebrews 5:8

Chapter 20

1 This cry is a quote from Psalm 22:1 that essentially states that even though God's presence is not experienced, the actions and beliefs of the individual will continue to glorify God rather than fulfill some selfish desire and curse Him.

2 Irion, J. Everett, p. 384.

3 Compare John 12: 49-50.

Chapter 22

1 The tree of life as relates to the Cabbalah, is another attempt to understand how God (pure consciousness or Kether) uses His energy (Chokhmah) in forming all there is. See Colin Law, The Tree of Life <http://www.utu.if/~jounsmed/ asc/kab/>.

Appendix B

1 Singer, Isidore, ed., p. 589.

2 Davis, John J., p. 35

3 ibid, p. 45

4 ibid, p. 109

5 Bullinger, p. 107

6 ibid, p. 123

7 ibid, p. 235.

8 ibid, p. 243.

9 ibid, p. 253.

Appendix C

1 Paulson, Genevieve Lewis, p. 10 2 Puryear, Herbert B. and Thurston, Mark A., "Meditation and the Mind of Man", pp. 26-46

3 Ibid, p. 27.

4 Paulson, Genevieve Lewis, p. 191.

Appendix F

1 Although color does not exist by itself, I like to pretend that by placing your eye in the path of the rainbow colored light passing through a prism, you may see "pure color." In actuality this is simply radiated colored light rather than reflected colored light.

2 Compiled from pages 14 - 41 of Lewis, Roger, "Color and the Edgar Cayce Readings."

Appendix G

1 Taken from Scientific Properties and Occult Aspects of Twenty-two Gems, Stones and Metals.

2 Compiled from <http://www.scri.fsu.edu/~jeannie/crystals/crystals-magic. html>, <http://www.scri.fsu.edu/~jeannie/crystals/healing-stones.html>, <http://watarts.uwaterloo.ca/~ijrosens/070594.html>, and <http:// w w w.sun-angel.com/articles/stones/frames/>

Appendix H

1 The diagram and the concept of the Tree of Life have come from Colin Law, The Tree of Life, <http://www.utu.if/~jounsmed/asc/kab/>

Bibliography

Association for Research and Enlightenment. Scientific Properties and Occult Aspects of Twenty-Two Gems, Stones and Metals. Virginia Beach, VA: A.R.E. Press, 1972.

Black, Matthew. The Book of Enoch or 1 Enoch. Leiden, Netherlands: E. J. Brill, 1985.

Botterweck, G. Johannes and Helmer Ringgren (general eds.). Theological Dictionary of the Old Testament. Grand Rapids, MI: William B. Eerdmans Publishing Co., 1977.

Bromiley, G.W. (ed.). The International Standard Bible Encyclopedia, Vol. 4. Grand Rapids, MI: William B. Eerdmans Publishing Co., 1979.

Budge, E. A. Wallis. (translator). The Egyptian Book of the Dead. New York, NY: Dover Publications, Inc, 1987.

Bullinger, Ethelbert William. Number in Scripture: Its Supernatural Design and Spiritual Significance. London, England, 1894.

Caird, G. B. A Commentary on The Revelation of St. John the Divine. New York, NY: Harper & Row, 1966.

Cayce, Edgar. A Commentary on the book of The Revelation. Virginia Beach, VA: A. R. E. Press, 1969.

Cayce, Edgar. Auras. (Col. 10th printing 1970). Virginia Beach, VA: A.R.E. Press, 1945.

Cayce, Edgar. A Search for God Books I & II. Virginia Beach, VA: A. R. E. Press, 1992.

Davis, John J. Biblical Numerology. Grand Rapids, MI: Baker Book House, 1968.

Eliade, Mircea (ed.). The Encyclopedia of Religion, Vol. 15. New York, NY: Macmillan Publishing Company, 1987.

Di Flumeri, Fr. Gerarado (ed.). Padre Pio: His Early Years. Foggia, Italy, 1985. Efird, James M. Daniel and Revelation. Valley Forge, PA: Judson Press, 1978.

Hall, Manly P. The Secret Teachings of All Ages. Los Angeles, CA: The Philosophical Research Society, Inc., 1977.

Hamblin, Collins. Don't Worry ... Be Faithful. Berkley, CA: Lion and Lamb Publishers, 1994.

Harmon, Nolan B.(ed.). The Interpreter's Bible, Vol. 12. Nashville, TN: Abingdon Press, 1957.

Irion, J. Everett. Interpreting The Revelation With Edgar Cayce. Virginia Beach, VA: A.R.E. Press, 1982.

Johari, Harish. Chakras: Energy Centers of Transformation. Rochester, VT: Destiny Books, 1987.

Lamsa, George M. Idioms in the Bible Explained, 2nd ed. St. Petersburg Beach, FL: Aramaic Bible Society, Inc., 1971.

Lewis, Roger. Color and the Edgar Cayce Readings. Virginia Beach, VA: A. R. E. Press, 1973.

Morgan, Mario. Mutant Message Down Under. New York, NY: Harper Collins Publishing, 1995.

Otto, Rudolf. The Idea of the Holy. (Col. paperback reprint 1972). London, UK: Oxford University Press, 1923.

Paulson, Genevieve Lewis. Kundalini and the Chakras. St. Paul, MN: Llewellyn Publications, Inc., 1993.

Peterson, Richard. Creative Meditation. Virginia Beach, VA: A.R.E. Press, 1990.

Puryear, Herbert Bruce. Why Jesus Taught Reincarnation. Scottsdale, Arizona: New Paradigm Press, 1992.

Puryear, Herbert B., Mark A. Thurston. Meditation and the Mind of Man. Virginia Beach, VA: A.R. E. Press, 1978.

Robertson, Robin. After The End of Time. Virginia Beach, VA: Inner Vision Publishing Company, 1990.

Shepard, Leslie A. (ed.). Encyclopedia of Occultism and Parapsychology, 2nd ed. Detroit, MI: Gale Research Company, 1985.

Singer, Isidore (ed.). "Germatria," The Jewish Encyclopedia, vol. V. New York, NY: Funk and Wagnals, 1905.

Sparrow, Lynn Elwell. Edgar Cayce and the Born Again Christian. Virginia Beach, VA: Edgar Cayce Foundation, 1985.

Stanford, Ray. The Spirit Unto The Churches. Virginia Beach, VA: Inner Vision Publishing Company, 1987.

Tanner, Wilda B. The Mystical Magical Marvelous World of Dreams. Tahiequah, OK: Sparrow Hawk Press, 1988.

Van Auken, John. Ancient Egyptian Mysticism. Virginia Beach, VA: Inner Vision Publishing Company, 1994.

Van Auken, John, The End Times Virginia Beach, VA: , Inner Vision Publishing Company, 1994.

Van Auken, John. Born Again and Again. Virginia Beach, VA: Inner Vision Publishing Company, 1984.

Wilhelm, Richard, Translator. The Secret of the Golden Flower. New York, NY: Harvest / HBJ, 1931.

Wilson, David A. The Book of the Revelation Apocalypse! Vols. 1 and 2. Black Mountain, NC: Lorien House, 1973.

Made in the USA
Middletown, DE
27 January 2019